THE NEW YORK
LITTLE RENAISSANCE /

ICONOCLASM, MODERNISM,
AND NATIONALISM IN
AMERICAN CULTURE, 1908–1917

by
Arthur Frank Wertheim

New York: New York University Press 1976

The publication of this work has been aided by a
grant from the Andrew W. Mellon Foundation

Library of Congress Cataloging in Publication Data
Wertheim, Arthur Frank, 1935-
  The New York Little Renaissance.
  Bibliography: p.
  1. Arts–New York (City) 2. Arts, Modern–20th
century–New York (City) 3. History, U.S., Cultural and Intellectual I. Title.
NX511.N4W47   700′.9747′1   75-21805
ISBN 0-8147-9164-6

Manufactured in the United States of America

For Carol

CONTENTS

PART FOUR. WORLD WAR I AND AFTER:
THE DECLINE AND AFTERMATH OF THE LITTLE
RENAISSANCE

LIST OF ILLUSTRATIONS

PREFACE

This study focuses on the new literary and artistic renaissance in New York City between 1908 and 1917 led by a revolt of prominent artists and writers motivated by the ideas and spirit of iconoclasm, modernism, and nationalism. Chicago and New York were the two most important prewar urban centers where painters, writers, and critics formed communities sharing common aspirations. Like the Chicago writers, the participants in the New York movement rebelled against the past century's genteel artistic standards and wanted to replace the older culture with a new indigenous American art and literature more representative of their generation. This artistic ferment has been called The Confident Years, The Rebellion, The Liberation, The Joyous Season, The League of Youth, and The New Paganism, but the Little Renaissance seems the best term to apply to this important prewar flowering in the arts since it was a movement encompassing many areas of culture.

Although loosely connected, there were four important groups participating in the Little Renaissance. The first was the radical writers and artists affiliated with *The Masses* magazine and The Eight group of painters. Prominent among them were the literary rebels Max Eastman, John Reed, and Floyd Dell, while John Sloan, Art Young, and Robert Henri stood out among the social realist illustrators and painters. Their iconoclastic writing and drawings expressed a desire for social change in the areas of politics, feminism, and education. Many joined the Socialist, women's rights, and progressive education movements. They were also associated with Greenwich Village and involved with popularizing the new psychology. Behind their ideals lay the feeling that social change was conducive to artistic freedom.

A second group was the apolitical iconoclasts on *The Smart Set* staff, especially H. L. Mencken and Willard Huntington Wright. Compared to the Socialist writers, they were politically conservative and did not advocate the overthrow of capitalism. Their lack of radicalism did not prevent them from attacking commercialism and provincialism in order to improve the artistic climate at home. Like the other social critics, Mencken used convenient symbols to register his discontent with American society: the puritan, the Anglo-Saxon, and the businessman. His literary criticism supported writing that dealt realistically with American life, especially Theodore Dreiser's novels. Despite Mencken's and Wright's nihilism, the values of individual and artistic freedom underwrote their iconoclasm.

The third Little Renaissance coterie included the avid cultural nationalists associated with *The Seven Arts* and *The New Republic* magazines. Literary and social critics again dominated this group: Van Wyck Brooks, Randolph Bourne, Waldo Frank, James Oppenheim, Paul Rosenfeld, and Herbert Croly. Influenced by both European and American precedents, they rallied around the need to create a new indigenous culture. As a result the cultural nationalists also attacked the genteel tradition and shared with the apolitical iconoclasts and Socialists the belief that America's materialism and provincialism inhibited artistic growth. Inspired by the belief that a close community of artists could improve society and culture, *The Seven Arts* writers argued for collective spiritual regeneration through the creative instincts.

The modernists, the fourth Little Renaissance group, included the poets published in *Others* magazine, the Stieglitz circle of artists, and the members of various little theater movements. They also revolted against the genteel tradition, but their rebellion mainly took the form of developing new experimental forms in poetry, painting, and the theater. Modernism was as much an iconoclastic philosophy for them as socialism was for *The Masses* writers. Like *The Seven Arts* crowd, the artists affiliated with Stieglitz's Gallery 291 fought for a new culture expressive of the twentieth century. The little theater groups, especially the Provincetown Players, thought of themselves as a dedicated artistic company staging experimental modern plays that would revolutionize the American theater. Although there were aesthetic and political differences between these four groups, the spirit of rebellion against the genteel tradition and the need to create a new culture united them in a common cause.

Several major factors caused the prewar rebellion to begin in 1908. The writers and artists came of age in the progressive period, an atmosphere conducive to change, progress, and revolt. They were also simultaneously exposed to the newest European ideas in philosophy and art. With the breakdown of formal social and philosophical standards early in the twentieth century,

American behavior and thought was becoming less absolute and more relative. Old idols were being smashed in several areas so that it was only a matter of time that the arts would come under attack. Socialism, feminism, and progressive education were thriving movements during the prewar years and offered the participants a base from which to crusade for social and political change. The Little Renaissance was also touched off by a generational conflict between the older defenders of the genteel tradition and the younger Little Renaissance generation. According to the rebels, the established leaders of American culture prevented the development of experimental literature and painting by controlling publishing houses, magazines, and art institutions.

Another important reason behind their revolt was that New York City was a conducive place for such a movement. Boston had been America's leading cultural center during the nineteenth century, yet the migration of William Dean Howells to New York in 1889 suggested that Manhattan already rivaled the Massachusetts city in the arts and letters. At the turn of the century New York was already the headquarters of the nation's magazine and book publishing trade and an important art center. Around 1900 several of The Eight painters came to New York from Philadelphia, a pivotal event that increased Manhattan's predominance as a place of artistic ferment. New York's cosmopolitan atmosphere and architecture also offered appropriate subject matter for artists and writers. Because of its immigrant population and many universities, Manhattan was a stimulating intellectual environment where new European and American ideas circulated and the prewar radical, feminist, and progressive education movements thrived. In Greenwich Village the participants could freely practice their craft and their own life-style in an artistic community sharing similar ideas and aspirations. By the time the Little Renaissance ended in 1917, Manhattan could easily claim that it was the nation's leading cultural center.

I would especially like to thank Professor Paul R. Baker for his advice and encouragement in undertaking this study. A discussion of the Little Renaissance in his intellectual history course awakened my interest in the subject and set off the train of events leading to this book. I am also most grateful to Mrs. Helen Farr Sloan for granting me permission to see her husband's papers in the John Sloan Trust, Wilmington, Delaware. My thankfulness to my wife Carol is expressed in the dedication of this book.

PART ONE

Iconoclasm:
The Revolt Against the Genteel
Tradition

CHAPTER ONE

Puritans, Provincials, and Pioneers

As late as 1908 the genteel tradition still ruled American literature and art. Literary critics on "highbrow" magazines and English professors at Ivy League universities declared that fiction and poetry should reflect morality, truth, and beauty and espouse the values of idealism and the progress of civilization. The purpose of literature to them was to educate the reading public in proper behavior. The critics Paul Elmer More and Stuart Sherman of *The Nation*, Hamilton Wright Mabie of the *Outlook*, Bliss Perry of *The Atlantic Monthly*, and Robert Underwood Johnson of *The Century* staunchly defended these ideals in magazines catering to upper-class tastes. Professors who preached the genteel faith included Yale's William Lyon Phelps, Princeton's Henry Van Dyke, Columbia's George Edward Woodberry, and Harvard's Barrett Wendell and Irving Babbitt. As defenders of the moral order, political conservatism, and British culture, the critics and professors had little respect for literary realism, artistic experimentation, or social criticism attacking established standards in the arts and society.[1]

They had inherited the genteel tradition from a group of professional men of letters who had dominated American culture during the Gilded Age. Among them were the influential magazine editors George Curtis of *Harper's Weekly*, Richard Watson Gilder of *The Century*, and Thomas Bailey Aldrich of *The Atlantic Monthly*. These magazines had contained heavy doses of sentimental poetry and fiction on themes of love, marriage, and God by the leading genteel poets Richard Henry Stoddard and George Henry Boker. Their aesthetic creed, the doctrine that art must reflect beauty, was propounded by the writer Edmund

Clarence Stedman in several books. As friends and colleagues these literary gentlemen had formed a closed club controlling publishing standards and the nation's taste. Publicly they had been bedrock conservatives, defending poetic idealism, purity in literature, and elitism in culture and government. Privately the group had serious misgivings concerning the effect of America's post-Civil War industrial development on the arts. They had consequently staked their faith in culture as a means towards ameliorating the country's growing preoccupation with making money. Distrusting the new corporate wealth, foreign entanglements, and the hordes of new urban immigrants, they had actively supported civil service legislation, anti-imperialism, and immigration restriction. Despite their zeal for reform, the Little Renaissance participants accused them of stifling social change and artistic experimentation.

Literary taste in 1908 was also controlled by the demands of the marketplace. Large successful publishers such as Harper and Brothers and Charles Scribner's mainly issued commercially sound popular books. The typical best seller during the first two decades of the twentieth century was the romantic escape novel exploring the moral virtues of glamorous heroes and heroines. Saccharine novels such as Eleanor H. Porter's *Pollyanna* (1913) and Harold Bell Wright's *The Winning of Barbara Worth* (1911) appealed to women, while masculine readers thrived on Zane Grey's *Riders of the Purple Sage* (1912) and Edgar Rice Burroughs' *Tarzan of the Apes* (1914). H. L. Mencken called such best sellers "mush for the multitudes," whose "aim is to fill the breast with soothing and optimistic emotions—to make the fat woman forget she is fat—to purge the tired business man of his bile." The success of popular books convinced the Little Renaissance authors that commercialism dominated the book trade and that they would have difficulty finding an outlet for their iconoclastic writing.[2]

The situation in American painting was equally bleak. The art critics Royal Cortissoz, Frank Jewett Mather, and Kenyon Cox argued that a work of fine art had fixed standards which contemporary painters should follow. The powerful National Academy of Design regulated art shows and aesthetic taste by favoring pastoral landscapes and sentimental domestic scenes carrying a moral message. Paintings revealing the ugly aspects of American life, particularly the city, were excluded from their shows. Most art galleries, catering to the public taste, were reluctant to exhibit innovative works. Thus the Little Renaissance experimental painters faced extremely rigid conditions in 1908 and would have a difficult task overturning traditional artistic standards.

Leading the attack on the genteel tradition were the prewar little magazines, insurgent periodicals containing biting criticism of American society and the arts. They were basically a response to the slick commercial journal that closed its doors to avant-garde writing. Run on a limited budget, many magazines, like the now forgotten *Phoenix* and *The Bang,* folded after a few issues of limited circulation, but others such as *The Masses, The Smart Set, The Seven Arts,* and *The New Republic* became famous and influenced literary history. No target was out of bounds for the leading social critics on these four major magazines. "The broad purpose of *The Masses* is a social one," wrote John Reed, "to everlastingly attack old systems, old morals, old prejudices—the whole weight of outworn thought that dead men have saddled upon us." According to its editor, Max Eastman, the attack had no limits: "The state, the church, the press, marriage, organized charity, the liberals, the philanthropists, the Progressive Party—they were all game for our guns and always in season." [3]

Underlying the critics' revolt against conventionality was an abiding faith in progress, the feeling, according to Van Wyck Brooks, that we were "in the dawn of the great age of mankind." Although the writers despaired over the current state of the arts, they believed the situation for the artist could improve. The participants came of age during a tumultuous time of progressive reform, which served to underwrite their optimistic confidence. Thus Floyd Dell could write: "We have seen changes in machinery, and changes in institutions, and changes in men's minds—and we know that nothing is impossible. We can have any kind of bloody world we want." Not all the participants were as optimistic as Dell. Mencken believed that the average person rarely influenced events and that improvement in society could only be achieved by superior individuals or the iconoclast. If Mencken was somewhat less optimistic than the other critics, he joined them in believing that change could occur in society by criticizing outdated standards.[4]

The Little Renaissance writers and artists were a unique generation dominating American culture between the 1890s and 1920s. In many ways they continued the critical assault on Victorianism begun during the fin de siècle, but most participants felt that art had a social purpose and rejected the nihilistic dilettantism of the 1890s. The lost generation of the twenties later identified with the Little Renaissance critique of society yet found the participants' optimism naive and dated after 1917. The prewar belief in change was not based on an absolute theory of progress as in the nineteenth century but on an abiding faith in relativism that questioned the validity of immutable truths. "Instead of a world once and for all fixed, with a morality finished and sealed . . . ," proclaimed Walter Lippman, "we have a world bursting with new ideas, new plans, and new hopes. The world was never so young as it is today, so impatient of old and crusty things." [5]

The social critics' iconoclasm partly stemmed from European writing and philosophy, especially the work of George Bernard Shaw, Henrik Ibsen, Friedrich Nietzsche, and Henri Bergson. This cross-cultural influence worked several ways. New York City was crowded at this time with newly arrived immigrants, and among them were intellectuals who brought over the newest ideas in philosophy and literature. Many social critics and painters made frequent trips to the Continent where they met leading artists. Translations of European writers were also readily available in the United States. Mencken translated Ibsen's work, once wrote a praiseworthy study of Shaw, and in his own writing often used Shavian wit to ridicule society's foibles. Bourne also avidly read Ibsen and after hearing Shaw speak in England became an admirer of the dramatist. The critique of commercial greed and moral hypocrisy in Shaw's and Ibsen's plays especially appealed to the critics.

The philosophy of Friedrich Nietzsche also had a profound impact on the era. Nietzsche's attack on Christian morality and middle-class culture as well as his celebration of individualism and creativity perfectly matched the era's insurgent mood. His writing was then at the height of its popularity in America partly due to a translation of his complete works between 1909 and 1913. Several participants, particularly *The Smart Set* crowd and Bourne, admired Nietzsche's ideals. Both Willard Huntington Wright and Mencken wrote books analyzing his philosophy. In Nietzsche's works, Mencken found support for his own irreligious beliefs, aristocratic bias, and justification for his own assault on morality and conformity. Bourne, who was a fan of Nietzsche's iconoclasm for similar reasons, declared that the philosopher "stands for the splendid liberation from alien codes, the smashing of inequalities and cowardices." The liberation of the individual from society's restraints became a dominant theme in the prewar era.[6]

A belief in the emotions and senses as the source of artistic creation was also an important Little Renaissance value. Some participants had found the theories of Henri Bergson conducive to this belief. The French philosopher's ideas became extremely popular in Manhattan's intellectual circles after he delivered a series of well-attended lectures at Columbia University in 1913. Since Bergson viewed the universe as a place of evolutionary change where past ideas had little relevance for the present, his philosophy of relativity justified the critics' attempt to overturn traditional beliefs. Bourne once called Bergson's *Creative Evolution* "inspiring," while Lippmann referred to his philosophy as "a fountain of energy, brilliant, terrifying, and important." [7] According to Bergson, intuition could discover truth in those realms where reason was deficient. His belief in the intuitive creative act particularly appealed to the modern painters associated with Alfred Stieglitz's Gallery 291.

The rebellion also had American roots and can be traced back to the pragmatism of William James and John Dewey. Reed and Lippmann first encountered James while undergraduates at Harvard College. Reed quickly grew to like the philosopher, while Lippmann discovered that pragmatism permitted individuals to live life with an "open mind." Lippmann's two works, *A Preface to Politics* (1913) and *Drift and Mastery* (1914), which argue for government planning to meet social problems, reveal the influence of James's scientific relativism and Dewey's instrumentalism. Although James's ideas also influenced Bourne and Eastman, they were actually more disciples of Dewey since both had studied under the philosopher at Columbia University. Before quarreling with Dewey over America's intervention in World War I, Bourne had praised his attack on absolutism and belief in social engineering. Partly as a result of Dewey's influence Eastman also viewed science as a method to solve society's problems. Since pragmatic relativism undermined doctrinaire beliefs and values, the social critics used the ideas of Dewey and James in their writing to criticize standards in morality, education, politics, and culture. The work of the American pragmatists, in addition to Ibsen, Shaw, Nietzsche, and Bergson, helped prepare the critics to battle the genteel tradition.[8]

The Little Renaissance movement against outdated culture commenced auspiciously in 1908. During this year Brooks published *The Wine of the Puritans* and Mencken joined the staff of *The Smart Set*. The important Eight painting exhibition and the first modern art show at Gallery 291 also took place. These four pivotal events marked the beginning of the New York Little Renaissance.

Brooks's *The Wine of the Puritans* set the basic framework for the period's social criticism. In this seminal work, the author pointed to two inhibiting factors in America preventing the development of a new culture: materialism and morality. Brooks became the first Little Renaissance writer to use the term "puritan" in reference to the overly industrious and sanctimonious American. Avariciousness and a stern morality, he suggested, were derived from our earliest colonizers who viewed good works as evidence of God's favor. American culture was still dominated by the New England tradition, represented by contemporary Boston authors who shunned writing about the more unattractive aspects of American life. As a consequence our fiction and poetry was sentimental, escapist, and imitative of English literature. While writing *The Wine of the Puritans* in England, Brooks came to realize the paucity of American culture compared to the Continent. Our literature, he lamented, has "no bonds with a remote antiquity, no traditions of the soil old enough as yet to become instincts." [9]

As a student at Harvard College from 1904 to 1907, Brooks had earlier complained about the lack of a literary tradition: "What was there, we might have asked, in America to read. For the Harvard imagination the country was a void." [10] Professor Barrett Wendell lectured to Brooks on the English classics and treated American literature as a second-rate discipline. Another teacher, the humanist Irving Babbitt, disliked literary realism, but Brooks learned to enjoy reading French literature under his direction. Charles Eliot Norton, professor of Fine Arts, made a more profound impression on the young student. He taught him to revere the culture of the Middle Ages and the importance of the integral relationship between the arts and society, a concept that later dominated Brooks's work.

Another important early influence on the budding social critic was the philosopher George Santayana. At Harvard, Brooks heard Santayana elaborate in the classroom on the conflict between the American's professed altruism and pecuniary ambition. Several years after Brooks graduated, Santayana delivered his famous 1911 address at the University of California entitled "The Genteel Tradition in American Philosophy." His lecture criticized philosophical idealism and pictured our society as torn between crude aggressiveness and refined genteelism. This split in the American character, said Santayana, was partly caused by our Calvinistic heritage. Philosophy and the arts avoided the reality of life, preferring the never-never land of abstract sentimentality. Brooks was teaching at Stanford University during 1911 and may have attended the lecture. Nonetheless, the aspiring writer had been impressed by the philosopher's perceptive analysis since his Harvard days.

Santayana's influence is evident in the social critic's early work. The writer had first planned a book in 1907 called "Studies in American Culture," containing ten portraits of symbolic Americans.[11] Included in Brooks's outline were representative materialists (Benjamin Franklin and John D. Rockefeller), idealists (Whittier and Emerson), the alienated artist (Poe), and the expatriate (Whistler). Although never written, the proposed study was Brooks's initial attempt to analyze society in terms of conflicting ideas and it foreshadowed his important essay, *America's Coming-of-Age* (1915).

In this major Little Renaissance manifesto the author again followed Santayana's analysis by depicting his countrymen as torn between monetary pursuits and unrealistic cultural and religious ideals. He coined the famous terms the "lowbrow" and the "highbrow" to symbolize the conflict between materialism and idealism. As in his first published work Brooks blamed the Puritans for originating this split in values. The piety of puritanism had led to the sanctimonious idealism of Jonathan Edwards, the Transcendentalists, and the Boston Brahmins, while their work ethic had influenced Franklin's utilitarianism and the commercial greed of the Gilded Age. In Brooks's hands the Puritans had now become a metaphor for everything that was wrong in American life.

The term "Puritan" began to lose its original historical connotation when other Little Renaissance critics started to follow Brooks's interpretation. The word was still used to ridicule New England colonial society, but now it was stretched to cover a whole range of contemporary aversions, including censorship, bigotry, and prudery. During the prewar period poets, painters, and art critics applied the term freely to almost anything inhibiting the artist. The most notorious Puritan baiter was Mencken. As a series of important prewar *Smart Set* articles on the American character suggests, he had already developed the boisterous iconoclasm that would bring him more fame in the next decade. In these groundbreaking essays Mencken depicted the middle class citizen as a sanctimonious fool who masqueraded as a moral individual while simultaneously living a life of fraudulent deceit. Crass and tasteless, he lacked aesthetic values and was unappreciative of the arts. Puritanism, he insisted, was still a powerful moral force in America causing conformity, hypocrisy, and sentimentality. Mencken's portrait of the American character was dripped in acid. In 1916 he wrote his friend Theodore Dreiser that "my whole life . . . will be devoted to combatting Puritanism. . . . The only attack that will ever get anywhere will be directed not at the Puritan heroes but at the laws they hide behind. In this attack I am full of hope that shrapnel will play a part." Well before 1920 Mencken had discovered a successful formula to satirize his countrymen.[12]

If Mencken's ideas complemented those of Brooks's, his critical method and style were entirely different. The latter's prose was graceful, melodious, and erudite, while Mencken's style was biting and emotional, relying on a turn of phrase or quip to assault his opponent. Through wit, irony, and sarcasm Mencken popularized what Brooks calmly perceived, and his social criticism derived from different influences. As mentioned earlier, Nietzsche was one of his favorite writers as well as Poe. Furthermore, Poe's tragic life proved to him that America was inhospitable to the arts and the artist's role was one of constant frustration. He also was influenced by the fin de siècle criticism of Percival Pollard and James Huneker and their admiration of German literature. Like the 1890s iconoclasts, Mencken aimed to tear down the shrines of genteel culture.

At the same time Mencken was criticizing puritanism, Bourne was writing an equally scathing attack on bourgeois conventionality. "To the modern young person who tries to live well there is no type so devastating and harassing as the puritan," he declared in an article. By 1917 this statement was hardly unique; nonetheless, Bourne gave the argument against puritanism a new twist by using terminology borrowed from Freud and Nietzsche. He accused religious leaders and censors of using the mask of self-righteousness to control the nation's morals and repressing natural creative instincts. Much like Nietzsche's superman, the contemporary puritan had a tyrannical drive to rule society. As a way of countering this repressive atmosphere he urged his followers to live a pagan life, "cultivating the warmth of the sun, the deliciousness of love-experience, the high moods of art." The celebration of the senses, artistic creativity, and ancient Greek civilization became a dominant motif in the Little Renaissance.[13]

The most stifling environment to the prewar writer was the American small town. Typical of the critics' skeptical attitude was Bourne's opinion of his birthplace, Bloomfield, New Jersey. Analyzing its class structure, he found an elite group of ministers, educators, and other professionals ruling the town by enforcing strict moral codes. For Bourne and his colleagues the small town was the home of middle-class provincialism and an inhospitable place for the arts to flourish. The social critics' attitude towards the small town was nonetheless ambivalent. Those born and raised in the Middle West often remained tied to the rural values of an older America and preferred residing close to nature.

Bourne acknowledged that the small country town once represented something fine in the American heritage but through urban growth and industrialization its charm had disappeared. Born in Plainfield, New Jersey, Brooks also regretted the transition of his quaint village home into a colorless suburb because of urbanization. Floyd Dell nostalgically remembered his childhood in rural Illinois as a time when he could freely roam the countryside but as he grew older he began to feel the restraints of the small town. During the 1920s Dell became a prominent writer of the "revolt from the village school," and in his *Bildungsroman Moon-Calf* criticized the country town for its provincialism.[14]

Many artists and writers left their homes in the Middle West and Northeast to settle in New York City. Most resided in intimate Greenwich Village where through a sense of community and informality they recaptured the values of country living. Some participants found uptown New York impersonal and unattractive but stayed out of necessity because of the availability of work and mutual stimulation. One compromise was to spend the hot summer months in such seaside resorts as Provincetown, Massachusetts. When the Little Renaissance ended many participants left Manhattan for art colonies in New Mexico, Connecticut, and upstate New York. Basically the artists were torn between a nostalgic yearning for an older rural America and the recognition that the small town was a stupefying environment.

The social critics blamed the pioneer for the destruction of pastoral America. The two terms, the puritan and the pioneer, were often used interchangeably in their writing. They viewed the pioneer as a migrant New Englander who had conquered the soil for profit and who had brought to the frontier strict morals. The harshest critique of the pioneer was presented in Waldo Frank's *Our America* (1919). Although published after the Little Renaissance, this scathing attack on materialism stemmed directly from the earlier writings of Brooks, Bourne, and Herbert Croly. In Frank's hands the enterprising pioneer became a synonym for everything that was wrong in America. According to the author, the pioneer-commercial drive had determined historical developments from the Constitutional Convention to the Gilded Age and stifled artistic development. The virgin West, suggested Frank, had been destroyed by lumberjacks and real estate agents.[15]

Besides attacking the puritan, the small-town provincial, and the pioneer, the critics also opposed organized religion. Eastman made *The Masses* the most outspoken journal against the church. Although his parents were Protestant ministers, a reading of Herbert Spencer and an interest in science had made him an agnostic early in his life. The church, he once wrote, was "doomed to dismantle herself and dissolve away before a more sincere, and more free, and more humane, and more scientific idealism." Articles and drawings in a special Christmas number of *The Masses* pointed out that the church was a capitalist institution defending the rich and well-born.[16]

The staff's views on religion were nonetheless ambiguous. In a Christmas cover Art Young depicted Jesus as a workingman of Nazareth sympathetic to the rights of labor. This drawing suggests that the social critics were not ready to denounce the basic Christian morals guiding behavior but only the disregard of Christ's original teachings by the church. The arrest of the young radical Frank Tanenbaum for leading a group of hungry and cold unemployed workers into St. Alphonsus Church proved their point. When the church refused to admit them and called the police, Eastman labeled their action a crime. John Sloan's drawing, *Calling the Christian Bluff,* implied that religion ignored the needs of the poor. According to the contributors, the church had violated the social justice precepts of its original founder. If the social critics sounded sacrilegious, few were willing to deny basic morals.[17]

In Little Renaissance writing the word Anglo-Saxon was also used in a derogatory sense as much as the terms puritan, provincial, or pioneer. According to the critics, the worship and imitation of British literature by the genteel novelists, poets, and critics prevented the development of our own literary tradition. Bourne's ardent Anglophobia best exemplified their bias against the English. During a trip through Europe he wrote home that England "made me just about ready to renounce the whole of Anglo-Saxon civilization. Henceforth the Irish, the Welsh, the French for me, no Anglo-Saxons." [18] Bourne might be an admirer of Wells and Shaw, but he found Great Britain a dreary uninspiring place. Returning home, he became an ardent champion of a new indigenous American arts and letters free from foreign influence.

Other critics, especially *The Smart Set* crowd, joined Bourne in criticizing our literary ties to Great Britain. Mencken, who was a devotee of German culture, referred to the Anglo-Saxon as uncivilized and materialistic. The crusade against England's intellectual colonization of America reached its peak in Willard Huntington Wright's *Misinforming a Nation* (1917), a scurrilous muckraking attack on the *Encyclopaedia Britannica*'s influence in the United States. Not only was the encyclopedia a symbol of England's control over our culture, stated Wright, but its articles were prejudicial. Too much space was devoted to obscure British authors while other important European and American writers were excluded. "No more fatal intellectual danger to America can be readily conceived than this distorted, insular, incomplete, and aggressively British reference work," concluded the angry author. Wright, Mencken, and the others wanted to draw attention to the writing of neglected Europeans, especially French and German authors, in order to widen America's cultural horizons.[19]

Literary critics who defended the genteel British tradition were ruthlessly attacked by the participants. By judging literature according to moral content and generally disfavoring realism these traditionalists were opposed to the aesthetic values of the Little Renaissance. Mencken's vitriolic essay, "Puritanism as a Literary Force," in *A Book of Prefaces* (1917) attacked critics who supported "a literature almost wholly detached from life." Where could a reader discover novels dealing realistically with life and human problems, Mencken asked. The moral scruples of the genteel literati had forced writers to turn out sentimental escapist trash. As a result "books are still judged among us . . . by their conformity to the national prejudices, their accordance with set standards of niceness and propriety." The literary battle between the two groups often turned into mud slinging. Mencken called Stuart Sherman an amateurish ineffectual critic mainly because the latter had criticized Dreiser's naturalism. Sherman, in turn, had little respect for Mencken's criticism and accused him of pro-German prejudices during World War I.[20]

The literary battle between the writers and the genteel defenders came to a head over the issue of censorship. The social critics were particularly sensitive to the question of purity in literature since it effected them directly when moral crusaders suppressed artistic freedom. The censor seemed to embody the most iniquitous characteristics of the puritan and the provincial. Eastman once accused the Associated Press of suppressing information of a strike and Young drew a cartoon depicting the AP as a capitalist monopoly poisoning the news by lies and distortions. The news bureau consequently sued Young and Eastman for criminal libel. The battle between the little magazine, run on a shoe string, and the AP, a news monopoly, had all the overtones of a fight between David and Goliath. *The Masses* seemed to have little chance of winning until the AP suddenly dropped the indictments because of insufficient evidence. The Socialist artist and writers celebrated their tussle with the AP as a moral victory.[21]

A second major court case occurred when the notorious John Sumner, head
of the New York Society for the Suppression of Vice, confiscated Dreiser's novel
The "Genius" (1915). After learning that the book had been banned in
Cincinnati, Sumner read the novel and concluded that many passages were lurid
and capable of offending women readers. He immediately ordered John Lane,
Dreiser's publisher, either to delete the profane passages or to cease marketing
the book. Since Dreiser refused to revise the novel, J. Jefferson Jones, Lane's
representative in New York, succumbed to Sumner's pressure and withdrew *The
"Genius"* from circulation. Desiring to test the Vice Commissioner's authority,
Dreiser promptly sued his publisher.[22]

Since the novelist had earlier experienced the suppression of *Sister Carrie* by
the firm of Doubleday and Company, this second censorship of his work deeply
angered him. In a vehement article in *The Seven Arts* he called America a "dull,
conventionalized, routine, material world" because it stifled artistic freedom.
Censorship proved that puritanism was still a powerful repressive force in the
country. "When will we lay aside our swaddling clothes, enforced on us by
ignorant, impossible puritans and their uneducated followers, and stand up, free
thinking men and women?" he asked. Suppression of his novel caused Dreiser to
write one of the most vitriolic attacks on morality published during the era.[23]

Mencken and other Little Renaissance writers quickly came to Dreiser's
defense. As an outspoken critic of vice commissions and censorship, Mencken
plunged into the foray with gusto. He got the Author's League of America to
back Dreiser, and he personally supervised the circulation of a petition
protesting the censorship. Approximately 500 writers signed the document,
including Eastman, Dell, and Reed. When Dreiser's suit reached the Appelate
Court in 1918, the judge ruled that he was not empowered to render advisory
opinions on the censorship of novels and ordered the case dropped. *The "Genius"*
was finally reissued in 1923.

In their social criticism the writers had used several synonyms representing
wrongs in American society: the puritan, the small-town provincial, the pioneer,
and the Anglo-Saxon. Eager to overturn tradition, their analysis was at times too
glib, prone to stereotypes and historical inaccuracy. Their opponent, the genteel
critic, was no doubt formidable, but hardly the bête noire they feared. They were
also guilty of oversimplification. Their view of puritanism was distorted and
their attack on England came close to xenophobia. Despite these faults their

attack on the older established culture created a body of high quality nonfiction writing that formed a major part of the new Little Renaissance literature that influenced the next decade. Mencken's forays against puritanism and Babbitry became famous during the 1920s, but the roots of his iconoclasm lay in the prewar period. The twenties assault on business and provincialism was not a new departure but originated during the Little Renaissance.

NOTES

1. On the genteel tradition see Henry F. May, *The End of American Innocence, A Study of the First Years of Our Time, 1912-1917* (Chicago: Quadrangle Books, 1964), pp. 30-79; Malcolm Cowley, "The Revolt Against Gentility," *After the Genteel Tradition, American Writers 1910-1930,* ed. Malcolm Cowley (Carbondale, Ill.: Southern Illinois University Press, 1969), pp. 89-90; William Van O'Connor, *An Age of Criticism, 1900-1950* (New York: Gateway Editions, 1966), pp. 3-18; Howard Mumford Jones, "The Genteel Tradition," *The Age of Energy, Varieties of American Experience, 1865-1915* (New York: The Viking Press, Inc., 1971), pp. 216-58; John Tomsich, *A Genteel Endeavor, American Culture and Politics in the Gilded Age* (Stanford, Calif.: Stanford University Press, 1971).

2. James D. Hart, *The Popular Book, A History of America's Literary Taste* (Berkeley: University of California Press, 1963), pp. 201-23; H. L. Mencken, "Mush for the Multitudes," *H. L. Mencken's Smart Set Criticism,* ed. William H. Nolte (Ithaca, N.Y.: Cornell University Press, 1968), p. 167 (first published *Smart Set,* December 1914).

3. John Reed, "The Masses Statement," unpublished MS., Reed Collection, Houghton Library, Harvard University, Cambridge, Massachusetts; Max Eastman, *Enjoyment of Living* (New York: Harper & Brothers, 1948), p. 475.

4. Van Wyck Brooks, *Scenes and Portraits, Memories of Childhood and Youth* (New York: E. P. Dutton & Co., Inc., 1954), p. 215; Floyd Dell, "Mr. Dreiser and the Dodo," *The Masses,* V (February 1915), 17.

5. Walter Lippmann, "The Most Dangerous Man in the World," *Everybody's Magazine,* XXVII (July 1912), 100.

6. Willard Huntington Wright, *What Nietzsche Taught* (New York: B. W. Huebsch, 1915); H. L. Mencken, *The Philosophy of Nietzsche* (Boston: John W. Luce, 1908); *The Gist of Nietzsche* (Boston: John W. Luce, 1910), and his translation of *The Antichrist* (New York: Alfred A. Knopf, Inc., 1920). Letter of Randolph Bourne to Alyse Gregory, March 18, 1914; printed in *Twice-a-Year,* no. 5-6 (Fall-Winter 1940 and Spring-Summer 1941), 84.

7. Letter of Randolph Bourne to Prudence Winterrowd, January 16, 1913; printed in "Randolph Bourne: Letters (1913-1916)," *Twice-a-Year,* no. 7 (Fall-Winter 1941), 79; Walter Lippmann, "The Most Dangerous Man in the World," 100.

8. Walter Lippmann, "An Open Mind: William James," *Everybody's Magazine,* XXVII (July 1912), 100-101; Randolph Bourne, "John Dewey's Philosophy," *New Republic,* II (March 6, 1915), 154-56.

9. Van Wyck Brooks, *The Wine of the Puritans* in *Van Wyck Brooks: The Early Years. A Selection from his Works, 1908-1921,* ed. Claire Sprague (New York: Harper Torchbooks, 1968), p. 11.

10. Van Wyck Brooks, *An Autobiography* (New York: E. P. Dutton & Co., Inc., 1965), p. 115; see also pp. 101-26.

11. From an unpublished 1907 autograph notebook entitled "A Book of Limitations" in the Brooks Collection, University of Pennsylvania Library, Philadelphia, Pennsylvania.

12. The *Smart Set* articles were "The American," XL (June 1913), 87-94; "The American: His Morals," XL (July 1913), 83-91; "The American: His Language," XL (August 1913), 89-96; "The American: His Ideas of Beauty," XLI (September 1913), 91-98; "The American: His Freedom," XLI (October 1913), 81-88; "The American: His New Puritanism," XLII (February 1914), 87-94. Letter of Mencken to Dreiser, July 28, 1916, in *Letters of H. L. Mencken,* ed. Guy J. Forgue (New York: Alfred A. Knopf, Inc., 1961), p. 87.

13. Randolph Bourne, "The Puritan's Will to Power," *War and the Intellectuals, Essays by Randolph Bourne, 1915-1919,* ed. Carl Resek (New York: Harper Torchbooks, 1963), pp. 156, 161 (first published *Seven Arts,* April 1917).

14. Randolph Bourne, "The Social Order in an American Town," *Atlantic Monthly,* CXI (February 1913), 227-36; Van Wyck, Brooks, *An Autobiography,* p. 7; Floyd Dell, *Homecoming* (New York: Farrar & Rinehart, Inc., 1933), passim.

15. Waldo Frank, "The Land of the Pioneer," *Our America* (New York: Boni and Liveright, 1919), pp. 13-58.

16. Eastman, *Enjoyment of Living,* pp. 197-98, 220, 237, 346-47. For the special Christmas number see *The Masses,* V (December 1913); especially Eastman, "Knowledge and Revolution," 6.

17. On the Tanenbaum incident see "The Church and the Unemployed," *The Masses,* V (April 1914), 10-11; Max Eastman, "The Tanenbaum Crime," *The Masses,* V (May 1914), 6-8. Sloan's drawing appeared in the April 1914 issue.

18. Letter of Randolph Bourne to Carl Zigrosser, December 13, 1913, Bourne Collection, Columbia University. See also Randolph Bourne, "Impressions of Europe, 1913-14," *Columbia University Quarterly,* XVII (March 1915), 109-26.

19. H. L. Mencken, "The Anglo-Saxon," *A Mencken Chrestomathy* (New York: Alfred A. Knopf, Inc., 1949), pp. 169-77 (first published in *Prejudices: Fourth Series,* 1924). Willard Huntington Wright, *Misinforming a Nation* (New York: B. W. Huebsch, 1917), p. 127; see also Wright's, "England's Intellectual Colonization of America," *The Seven Arts,* I (February 1917), 395-401.

20. H. L. Mencken, "Puritanism as a Literary Force," *A Book of Prefaces* (New York: Garden City Publishing Company, 1927), pp. 274, 225 (first published 1917).

21. Art Young, *Art Young, His Life and Times,* ed. John N. Beffel (New York: Sheridan House, 1939), pp. 295-301; Max Eastman, *Enjoyment of Living,* pp. 464-67.

22. Paul S. Boyer, *Purity in Print, The Vice-Society Movement and Book Censorship in America* (New York: Charles Scribner's Sons, 1968), pp. 36-40; Robert H. Elias, *Theodore Dreiser: Apostle of Nature* (New York: Alfred A. Knopf, Inc., 1949), pp. 193-207; W. A. Swanberg, *Dreiser* (New York: Bantam Books, 1967), pp. 244-74; Theodore Dreiser, *Letters of Theodore Dreiser,* ed. Robert H. Elias (Philadelphia: University of Pennsylvania Press, 1959), pp. 220-46; Edgar Kemler, *The Irreverent Mr. Mencken* (Boston: Little, Brown and Company, 1950), pp. 78-84; Charles Shapiro, *Theodore Dreiser, Our Bitter Patriot* (Carbondale: Southern Illinois University Press, 1962), p. 54.

23. Theodore Dreiser, "Life, Art, and America," *The Seven Arts,* I (February 1917), 379, 389.

CHAPTER TWO

Youth and Education

The Little Renaissance can be interpreted as a revolt of youth against outdated values. This "league of youth" was not an official body but a spirit of rebellion shared by the participants who idealized the prime of life in contrast to what they called the staid conservatism of middle and old age. Most artists and writers were in their twenties and thirties when they participated in the movement. Born at the end of the nineteenth century, they came of age in a new century that called for new customs and art forms. Generational conflict is particularly intense in America where society places great emphasis on being young as a necessary element for success. This factor serves, as it did for the New Yorkers, to make new generations overly conscious of group self-identity and to rebel against parental standards in morality and the arts. The participants revolted against their parents not only by attacking their values but also by creating a new life-style. Many escaped their family's stern morality by living in Greenwich Village and distinguished themselves from the culture of the older generation by creating new art forms, a development typical of cultural movements led by young people. American literary history is highlighted by movements of new writers revolting against established tradition: the Young America Movement of the 1840s and 1850s, the fin de siècle poets, and the Beat Generation. The band of young artists that emerged in 1908 called for a renaissance expressive of their own aesthetic standards. Like other youth-cultural revolts, the New York movement was partly motivated by a generational need to forge a new culture.

This feeling of youth consciousness became accented while the participants were undergraduates at Columbia and Harvard Universities. Among the writers and artists attending Harvard during the prewar years were Lippmann, Brooks, Reed, Alan Seeger, Harold Stearns, Lee Simonson, Robert Edmond Jones, and Willard Huntington Wright. Simonson, who later became a famous theatrical set designer, initiated what Reed called The Harvard Renaissance. In the *Harvard Advocate* he accused the students of being too conventional and called on his classmates to be more socially conscious and active in college affairs. Several campus clubs were taken over by the radicals, while other new organizations were formed around the need for change in culture and politics. When feminism became a cause célèbre on campus, the male feminists organized the Harvard Men's League for Women's Suffrage. The Socialist Club was the most militant organization; and, according to Stearns, "practically the only place at Harvard where contemporary politics was discussed seriously." The club was active in Massachusetts politics, petitioned the university for a course in socialism, and attacked the college for underpaying its employees.[1]

As with the New York movement, the various campus political, dramatic, and literary groups were interrelated. The new clubs were partly formed as a reaction against the older established groups that admitted members according to social standing and family legacy. Most student radicals with a wide variety of interests joined several of them. Lippmann, the unofficial leader of the rebels, was editor of the *Harvard Monthly,* founder of the Socialist Club, and a member of the Dramatic Club. He was also active in social work in Boston and wrote articles supporting women's suffrage and attacking governmental leadership.[2] Reed's involvement with the Dramatic and Cosmopolitan Clubs equally sharpened his awareness of social inequality. Before they came to New York, Reed and Lippmann had already developed interests in various reform causes. Their Cambridge years had made them conscious of the relationship between politics and literature, and a circle of friends had been established which would continue over the next few years. As a preliminary stage of the era's youth rebellion, The Harvard Renaissance was a crucial development leading to the New York movement.

At Columbia University the student unrest was more motivated by new ideas taught by progressive instructors. Among a generally conservative faculty were stimulating professors who taught the undergraduates the latest interpretations in the social sciences and humanities. They included Franz Boas in anthropology, John Dewey and Fredrick Woodbridge in philosophy, and James

Harvey Robinson and Charles Beard in political science and history. "Ideas were sprouting up through the bricks at Columbia," wrote Eastman who attended the graduate school. As an undergraduate Bourne encountered several professors whose "philosophy and science are not mere games, but real aids in understanding the world and living a worthy part in it." Campus clubs also played an important role in the ferment. Bourne joined several organizations expressing student dissent, including literary societies favoring modern literature and the Intercollegiate Socialist Society.[3]

As editor of the *Columbia Monthly,* Bourne made the journal a sounding board for the radical students' views. Stirred by the ideas of progressive education, the young student began criticizing the university. He belittled the atmosphere at Columbia where extracurricular activities such as sports and fraternities seemed more important than course work. The average student got by with a minimum of studying and sought a degree only to qualify for a job. Bourne criticized the traditional curriculum, especially what he called the boring and uninspiring lecture system. What was needed were more courses stressing interpretations rather than factual data. The purpose of education was not to memorize but to stimulate the mind and develop self-awareness. By the time he graduated Bourne had become an avid educational reformer committed to the current crusade for progressive education.[4]

While at Columbia he wrote an angry rebuttal to an article in *The Atlantic Monthly* criticizing the younger generation for their lack of respect towards their elders. Bourne stated that the conservative hypocritical beliefs of older people have little to offer the young. After this article Bourne continued to write vitriolic essays defending his generation and soon became the unofficial leader of the prewar league of youth. "You felt that in him the New America had suddenly found itself and was all astir with the excitement of its first maturity," commented Brooks.[5]

In his important book, *Youth and Life* (1913), Bourne urged young people to fight for social justice and cultural change. Idealism and rebelliousness were the beneficial qualities of youth, he suggested, conducive to rejecting conformity and fighting for social change: "It is the glory of the present age that in it one can be young. Our times gives no check to the radical tendencies of youth." Now was the time to ask questions, experiment with life, and to be open to new ideas and interests. Elderly people, by contrast, were creatures of habit: "The ideas of the young are the living, the potential ideas; those of the old, the dying, or the already dead." He warned his peers to avoid going into business where they would be "swallowed up in the routine of a big corporation. It is even doubtful," he noted, "whether business or professional success . . . can be attained without a certain betrayal of soul." Through the deadening influence of the press, pulpit, and university the older generation had perpetuated false values. Written in fiery prose, *Youth and Life* was an ardent call to rebellion and a poignant expression of the values of the Little Renaissance generation.[6]

Like Bourne, Floyd Dell also characterized the time of youth as one of revolt, adventure, and searching. Dell's interest in this area was best expressed in his novels, which, although published after 1917, often take place during the prewar period and reflect the idealistic aspirations of his time. The autobiographical *Moon-Calf* (1920) chronicles the adventures of Felix Fay from adolescence to maturity. An idealistic Socialist poet, Fay represents the young prewar intellectual who questions the values of his elders and commits himself to writing and social change. Like Dell, he rejects his small-town midwestern environment and departs for Chicago at the book's end. He has grown during the story from a rebellious dreamer to a mature young man who accepts the reality of life. His growth corresponds to the author's view that rebellion is useless without ideals based on realistic expectations. Dell's young protagonists are different than the disenchanted youth of F. Scott Fitzgerald. Although Dell has often been represented as a spokesman of the 1920s, he was nine years older than Fitzgerald and a member of an earlier literary generation. Fitzgerald's novels reflect the alienation of young people during the 1920s, while Dell's work mainly chronicles the experiences of the Little Renaissance participants.

Dell was also a proponent of the progressive education movement and wanted education to be based more on life's experiences than abstract principles. Schools, he insisted, should reflect society while teachers should be keenly aware of the world they live in. Instead of leading sheltered lives, instructors ought to become well-rounded individuals and have a larger voice in running the schools. The control of school boards by business interests rather than educators was putting power into the hands of groups that failed to understand the educational process. Teachers should instead elect their own principals and administrators, and form trade unions to voice their demands.[7]

In the treatise *Were You Ever a Child* (1919) Dell summarized his views on education. Arguing for a more democratic educational system, he accused schools of following outdated principles by teaching classical languages and modeling the curriculum on finishing schools. Too many irrelevant facts, useless for adulthood, were taught in the classroom. Laboratories, workshops, and playgrounds were equally important as textbooks in preparing the child for everyday life. He called on the school to develop creative instincts at an early age through painting and drama courses. Behind Dell's opinion was the idea that the school should stimulate the child's artistic creativity in the hope that the teaching and practice of the arts would lead to more appreciation of culture. Written in a light humorous conversational form, Dell's book was a readable progressive education tract for the layman. It further revealed how the writers popularized reform causes originally conceived by professional scholars.

After graduating from Columbia Bourne also continued to promote Dewey's educational theories, and was sent by *The New Republic* to report on the Gary school system in Indiana. He found the progressive education experiment an ideal work, study, and play system emphasizing educating the whole child through intellectual, vocational, and artistic studies. As a perfect model of progressive reform, the curriculum stressed relating subjects to everyday life. The school's buildings were used for adult education, while the city's parks, museums, and libraries served the needs of students and teachers. His book on the Gary system revealed his avid enthusiasm for the educational reforms in the Indiana city.[8]

A more caustic critique of contemporary pedagogy was Bourne's *Education and Living,* which attacked the antiquated curriculum of American education. His own high school education, he wrote, "had been practically valueless in giving me the background of the intellectual world in which I was henceforth to live." The teaching of classical languages was outdated "class-education" that had "no place in a society which is trying to become democratic." The author called for an educational system reflecting everyday experience and preparing the child for adulthood. "The whole school must be loosened up," he asserted, "the stiff forms made flexible, children thought of as individuals and not as 'classes.' " [9]

In another section of the book Bourne renewed his attack on the university. Colleges, he suggested, were unfortunately not controlled by professors and students but by trustees and business corporations who misunderstood the purposes of higher education. As a result trustees could dismiss professors for dissenting opinions and thereby curtail free thought on campus. Under such

a system the professor was merely an employee of a commercial enterprise. Bourne recommended that the faculty be given more control over
administering the university. As for the undergraduate, he was mostly
interested in fraternities and sports while degrees were sought merely as a means
for acceptance into society. The college should not be an "undergraduate
country club . . . but more of an intellectual workshop where men and women
in the fire of their youth, with conflicts and idealisms, questions and ambitions
and desire for expression, come to serve an apprenticeship under the masters of
the time." [10]

Bourne and Dell were the leading spokesmen for educational reform among
the participants, but there were others who identified the university with the
genteel tradition and political conservatism. These critics were especially
troubled by the lack of academic freedom on campus. George Cram Cook's
experience as an English instructor at Stanford and Iowa proved that the
university was a debilitating environment for the creative artist. Cook, who
later was to direct the Provincetown Players, found the undergraduates
uninterested in learning and the teachers conventional and uninspiring. The
control of colleges by trustees and business interests, he wrote, was responsible
"for the fact that America is intellectually second rate." In a short story Cook
portrayed a conservative university president who prevents the organization of a
teachers' union on campus. Like Bourne, Cook urged the faculty to choose the
administrative officials; otherwise, he thought the university would remain an
institution with little freedom of thought.[11]

The failure of colleges and schools to train creative thinkers became a
familiar theme in prewar writing. Another educational critic was Harold
Stearns, who was a *New Republic* contributor during the Little Renaissance. His
student years at Harvard had convinced him that college was mostly a waste of
time. He found his fellow students lacking a "vigorous intellectual discipline"
and more concerned with extracurricular activities than scholarly work. The
university was partly to blame, Stearns suggested, for it "fails to stimulate the
majority of its students to take advantage of this rich opportunity. It furnishes
a totally inadequate intellectual discipline. And instead of teaching man good
habits of work and steady concentration, it encourages lazy and vicious habits."
He found most students still uneducated at commencement time: "I distinctly
remember the feeling of despair which came over me as I stood in my cap and
gown in the Commencement procession, suddenly realizing how so many of us

were hopelessly uneducated—we who, ten minutes later, were to be welcomed into the fellowship of educated men!" [12]

The participants' ideas on educational reform were also voiced in the magazine *Slate,* published during 1917 and edited by Jess Perlman, a New York City elementary school teacher. As a voice of progressive education and the new art and literature, the Greenwich Village periodical contained articles on education as well as short stories, poetry, and drawings. In format and content the magazine resembled *The Masses;* indeed, it drew on talented contributors from the more famous periodical. Dell published articles on education, while two *Masses* artists, Maurice Becker and Stuart Davis, drew illustrations. *Slate* carried the work of young poets such as Louis Untermeyer, Kenneth Burke, Malcom Cowley, and Witter Bynner. The journal was no doubt a minor little magazine with a brief existence, yet it successfully brought together two major features of the Little Renaissance: artistic creativity and educational reform.

The social critics were also involved in several radical educational experiments, including the Rand School of Social Science and the Modern School. Founded in 1906, the Rand School was established mainly for the purpose of offering courses in socialism, but it also offered adult evening and correspondence courses. Evening lectures on socialism and feminism were well attended by the Greenwich Village artists and writers. The Rand School became an important Little Renaissance center and its restaurant a favorite meeting place to discuss art and politics. The manager of the school's cafeteria, Piet Vlag, founded the original *Masses* in 1911 and made the journal an official mouthpiece of the Rand School cooperative socialism.

The Modern School of the Ferrer Center, founded in 1910 by several radical intellectuals, including Emma Goldman and Alexander Berkman, was first located in Greenwich Village before moving uptown in 1912 to Morningside Heights. Since philosophical anarchism lay behind the founders' beliefs, the school aimed to create an educative environment conducive to freedom of expression and artistic creation. The school's emphasis on creativity and individualism appealed to the participants who often attended the Saturday night discussion group led by prominent radicals. Emma Goldman persuaded her friend Robert Henri to teach an art class two nights a week at the Modern School. Among his pupils were Man Ray, Niles Spencer, and Ben Benn.

At the Ferrer Center and at his own art school Henri formulated a philosophy of art education, which made him one of the country's most stimulating painting instructors. He offered a radical approach to teaching that challenged academic principles by urging his students to paint the city, everyday life, and the underprivileged. The leader of The Eight broke with tradition by using experimental instructional methods. Inside the classroom he would often talk more about literature, philosophy, and music rather than art. He permitted his pupils to commence painting without first doing line drawing exercises and allowed them to draw from a nude model. After finishing their work at home, the students would bring their compositions to class where Henri would criticize them. Creative self-expression, artistic freedom, and cultural nationalism were the Little Renaissance values Henri expounded in the classroom.[13]

Belief in the sanctity of youth inclined the writers and artists to feel that the school must develop a young person's artistic sensibility. They staked great faith in the idea that a young generation dedicated to the arts and social change could improve society. An educational system encouraging children to be uninhibited and creative was the first step towards a new society. Several schools that specialized in a cultural approach to teaching children drew their support. Mabel Dodge Luhan helped organize and finance a dancing school for children under the direction of Elizabeth Duncan, sister of the famous dancer. Mary Heaton Vorse, a *Masses* contributor and labor writer, aided in the formation of a Montessori school in Provincetown, Massachusetts.

The Greenwich Villagers were particularly involved in two local elementary schools stressing the free development of the child's personality. Influenced by new pedagogical methods, the instructors at the Play School gave their pupils toy blocks, clay, and paints in order to recreate experience. The sculptor William Zorach, an innovative teacher at the school, presented his youngsters with large pieces of paper and colors and told them to draw whatever they desired. Because of its unusual curriculum many Villagers sent their children to the Play School. According to its founder, Caroline Pratt, the artists and writers were among the first "to recognize and value an approach to children which would cherish the child's innate creativeness instead of stifling it." [14]

Another experimental school related to the prewar artistic ferment was the Greenwich Village Children's School (later called the Walden School), founded by Margaret Naumburg in 1915. A disciple of Freud and Jung, Naumburg aimed to apply the principles of psychology to progressive education because she believed that artistic expression could relieve a child's emotional problems. Several writers and artists supported her school because it stressed creativity at an early age and offered courses in the arts. She and her husband Waldo Frank, who she married in 1916, shared a deep belief in artistic creativity as a source of self-expression and cultural nationalism.[15]

The social critics' interest in educational reform and the cause of youth reflected their desire to change American culture. Bourne and Dell declared that young people could no longer accept the elder generation's outdated aesthetic and moral values preventing artistic and social change. The educational system from grade school to the university seemed a bastion of genteel culture to the writers and artists. They felt instead that the values of individuality, spontaneity, and creativity should be taught in the schools. Such changes would hopefully result in a new creative generation and a society more conducive to the arts.

NOTES

1. John Reed, "The Harvard Renaissance" and "Harvard's Coming-of-Age," unpublished MSS., Reed Collection, Houghton Library, Harvard University, Cambridge, Massachusetts; Harold Stearns, "The Confessions of a Harvard Man," *Forum* LI (January 1914), 76.

2. Walter Lippmann, "In Defense of the Suffragettes," *Harvard Monthly*, XLIX (November 1908), 64-67; and "Harvard in Politics: A Problem in Imperceptibles," *Harvard Monthly*, XLIX (December 1909), 95-98.

3. Max Eastman, *Great Companions; Critical Memoirs of Some Famous Friends* (New York: Farrar, Straus, & Cudahy, 1959), p. 281; letter of Randolph Bourne to Dorothy Teall, October 23 [1913], Bourne Collection, Columbia University, New York City.

4. Randolph Bourne, "The College: An Undergraduate Review," *Atlantic Monthly*, CVIII (November 1911), 667-74; "College Life Today," *North American Review*, CXCVI (September 12, 1912), 365-72; "The College Lecture Course As the Student Sees It," *Educational Review*, XLIX (June 1913), 66-70; "Individuality and Education," *Columbia Monthly*, IX (January 1912), 88-90.

5. Randolph Bourne, "The Two Generations," *Atlantic Monthly*, CVIII (April 1911), 591-98; Van Wyck Brooks, *Emerson and Others* (New York: E. P. Dutton & Co., Inc., 1927), p. 127.

6. Randolph Bourne, *Youth and Life* (New York: Houghton Mifflin Company, 1913), pp. 3, 25, 41, 274-75.

7. Floyd Dell, "Our Village School Board," *The Masses*, VI (March 1915), 11; "The Sacred Sisterhood," *Slate*, I (January 1917), 8-9.

8. Randolph Bourne, *The Gary Schools* (Boston: Houghton Mifflin Company, 1916).

9. Randolph Bourne, *Education and Living* (New York: Century Company, 1917), pp. vi, 9, 36, 165.

10. Ibid, pp. 228-29.

11. George Cram Cook, "The Third American Sex," *Forum,* L (October 1913), 445; George Cram Cook, "The C.T.U.," *Forum,* LII (October 1914), 543-61.

12. Harold Stearns, "The Confessions of a Harvard Man," *Forum,* L (December 1913), 819; *Forum,* LI (January 1914), 69-81.

13. William Innes Homer, *Robert Henri and His Circle* (Ithaca, N.Y.: Cornell University Press, 1969), pp. 173-74; Man Ray, *Self Portrait* (Boston: Little, Brown and Company, 1963), pp. 21-30. Henri's aesthetics are best presented in his book *The Art Spirit* (New York: Keystone Books, 1960, first published 1923). See also his articles: "My People," *The Craftsman,* XXVII (February 1915), 459-69; "An Ideal Exhibition Scheme, the Official One a Failure," *Arts and Decoration,* V (December 1914), 49-52, 76; "What About Art in America?," *Arts and Decoration,* XXIV (November 1925), 35-37, 75.

14. Caroline Pratt, *I Learn from Children* (New York: Simon & Schuster, 1948), p. 40. William Zorach, *Art Is My Life* (New York: World Publishing Co., 1967), p. 73.

15. Margaret Naumburg, *The Child and the World, Dialogues in Modern Education* (New York: Harcourt, Brace and Company, Inc., 1928), passim; Robert H. Beck, "Progressive Education and American Progressivism: Margaret Naumburg," *Teachers College Record,* LX (January 1959), 198-209.

CHAPTER THREE

Culture and Politics

The Little Renaissance occurred when radicalism was at its height in the United States and the I.W.W. and the Socialist party attracted a considerable following. In 1912 many Socialists were elected to political office, including mayors and congressmen. New York City, with its large immigrant population, was a major Socialist center with twelve radical newspapers and magazines, some like *The Masses* directly related to the Little Renaissance. "Every writer I came to know called himself a radical committed to some programme for changing and improving the world," recalled Brooks.[1] As this comment suggests, many participants were dedicated to social change and supported several radical ideologies, including pragmatic socialism, utopianism, philosophical anarchism, and syndicalism. Radicalism attracted the more socially conscious artists and writers who were generally practitioners of realism in the arts and letters, while the more modern poets and painters, experimenting with form rather than content, remained mostly apolitical. Some Little Renaissance figures, particularly *The Smart Set* writers, were skeptical of socialism. As a staunch believer in individuality and a society led by a talented aristocracy, Mencken was a traditional conservative who feared that socialism would lead to conformity and the rule of the masses. Even if quarrels sometimes broke out between the Little Renaissance liberal progressives and Socialists, radicalism united the participants around a common cause.

In the minds of the radicals, especially *The Seven Arts* staff, politics was directly related to culture and the free enterprise system viewed as antithetical to artistic creation. "We were all sworn foes of capitalism," declared Frank, "not because we knew it would not work, but because we judged it, even in success, to be lethal to the human spirit." Socialism seemed a means towards creating a better society in which the profit motive was minimized and the arts flourished. It was also viewed as a panacea towards more freedom of expression and sexual equality. For James Oppenheim, editor of *The Seven Arts,* radicalism stood for liberation in various aspects of American life, culture, politics, and social relations. Oppenheim was a utopian Socialist who fervently believed in the coming of a New America where economic equality and a cultural renaissance flourished side by side. As a social settlement worker the young idealist had earlier been concerned with eradicating immigrant poverty; later, in 1911, he wrote a radical novel arguing for a world community of united nations tied together by common political and social beliefs.[2]

Frank and Oppenheim were not the only utopian Socialists on *The Seven Arts* who believed that political change was conducive to artistic development. By reading Whitman and Ruskin early in his career, Brooks had become aware that materialism was antithetical to creativity. While teaching in California he joined a Socialist party local of immigrant intellectuals, and a subsequent teaching assignment at the Workers' Educational Association in England further awakened him to the needs of the working class and brought him under the influence of the Fabians. Brooks's politics became integrally related to his social criticism. Socialism, he hoped, would ameliorate commercialism and thus create a better atmosphere for the arts. An indigenous culture expressive of the American scene and linked to a Socialist utopia was Brooks's ideal.

Bourne's association with *The Seven Arts* caused his politics to become more idealistic and related to his aspirations for American culture. He called his beliefs "intellectual radicalism," a combination of pragmatic thinking and idealism. At Columbia Bourne became a dedicated Socialist and wrote a letter to the college newspaper protesting the low pay of the university's scrubwomen and the use of child labor. Although the social critic probably never joined the Socialist party, his early political views urging a practical reform socialism reflected the influence of pragmatism. As the years past, Bourne became more radical and increasingly analyzed American society in terms of class conflict, but he was never a pure Marxist and felt that Marxism was too dogmatic as an ideology. Practicing a socialism based on science and idealism, his experience proved that the ideas of pragmatism and utopian socialism could be merged into a viable radical philosophy.[3]

Fig. 1. Above left: Walter Lippmann. Above right: Robert Hallowell, *Portrait of John Silas Reed.* Reproduced by permission of the Harvard College Library. Below left: Max Eastman. Below right: Floyd Dell. Courtesy, The Newberry Library, Chicago.

Lippmann's early career also illustrates the appeal of a pragmatic type of socialism. Attracted to Fabianism while at Harvard, he advocated state planning based on workable rational solutions to economic and social problems. After graduation from college the energetic young man joined Branch One of the New York Socialist party, which had a reputation as one of the most radical groups in Manhattan. In 1912 he was appointed executive secretary to the Reverend George R. Lunn, the newly elected Socialist party mayor of Schenectady, New York. Excited by the· opportunity to put socialism into action, he called "Schenectady . . . a laboratory in which we can hope to develop a certain amount of experience." [4] When Lunn entered into intraparty squabbles with the city's Socialist party local and failed to initiate social change, Lippmann became disillusioned with the mayor and his lack of planning. After four months he left the post dubious about whether socialism was a practical political program.

Lippmann's books written shortly after his Schenectady experience reflect a growing disenchantment with radicalism. In *A Preface to Politics* (1913), Lippmann viewed socialism as an important philosophy, but he noted its failure to appeal to the majority of Americans. He also accused the Socialist party of concentrating too much energy in vote getting. A year later in *Drift and Mastery* he attacked the violent methods of the Industrial Workers of the World. As these two books suggest Lippmann had practically abandoned his Socialist beliefs by 1914 and had become a liberal progressive.[5]

Since the journalist's socialism had been motivated by a strong social conscience and a commitment to workable reform, his change to progressivism was not an abrupt departure from his former views. His moderate liberalism and connection with the progressive *New Republic* seemed an about-face to his Socialist friends. Reed accused him of now advocating a dreary practical politics. Lippmann, he wrote, was a person

> Who builds a world, and leaves out all the fun,–
> Who dreams a pageant, gorgeous, infinite,
> And then leaves all the color out of it,–
> Who wants to make the human race, and me,
> March to a geometric Q. E. D.

Upset by this criticism, the journalist called Reed a playboy rebel superficially committed to socialism:

Revolution, literature, poetry, they are only things which hold him at times, incidents merely of his living. Those who have tried to bank on some phase of him, to regard him as a writer, a correspondent, a poet, a revolutionist, or a lover, lose him. There is no line between the play of his fancy and his responsibility to fact; he is for the time the person he imagines himself to be.

The two had been close friends at Harvard but Lippmann's scientific liberalism now clashed with Reed's visionary socialism, proving that politics could become a divisive issue in the Little Renaissance community.[6]

The conflict between Lippmann and Reed represented a larger disagreement between the political positions of *The New Republic* and *The Masses.* At first *The Masses* welcomed the founding of *The New Republic* as another magazine dedicated to social change, but after a time it became clear that the latter's progressivism and the former's radical bohemianism differed over certain issues. *The Masses* often denounced the piecemeal reforms of the progressives. Eastman accused the liberals of accomplishing their reforms through the "enlightened self-interest of the privileged, combined with a little altruism and a great deal of altruistic oratory. Essentially they represent the *enlightened* self-interest of capitalists. We represent the enlightened self-interest of the workers and the fight goes on." [7]

When Lippmann once criticized *The Masses* staff for their impractical idealism, Eastman became outraged and directly attacked *The New Republic.* The real utopians, Eastman declared, were the editors of *The New Republic.* "They have never any of them faced the hard and biting fact that economic self-interest is a dominating force in all history." Although Eastman shared Lippmann's admiration for pragmatism, the two men and the magazines they edited differed over the issue of the class struggle. *The Masses,* the editor stated,

rests its great hope of democracy in agitation and organization of the lower classes, rather than in telling the upper classes, who do not want democracy, how they might get it, if they would only be entirely practical and consent to go very slowly step-by-step. We of *The Masses would like to assemble the power that will do something;* they of the *New Republic* are satisfied to instruct the power that won't. That is the big difference between these two groups of editors.[8]

When Piet Vlag started *The Masses* in 1911 he had no idea that it would later become one of the most famous little magazines in America. Nor did its first year look very auspicious when Vlag and the editors made *The Masses* a doctrinaire voice of cooperative socialism by filling the magazine with dull articles promoting share-the-wealth schemes. Several contributors, including Art Young, John Sloan, Louis Untermeyer, and Mary Heaton Vorse prevented the magazine from folding in 1912 due to financial problems. They decided to continue publication rather than have *The Masses* merge with a Chicago Socialist women's magazine. The problem now was to find a new editor. At a staff meeting Young suggested they hire Eastman and read an article by the then unknown writer. When the group approved, Young promptly dispatched a note to Eastman informing him that "you are elected editor of the *Masses,* no pay." [9]

The new *Masses* soon took on a more humorous undogmatic tone. The art editors modeled the journal's satirical bite on *Jugend* and *Simplicissimus,* two famous German iconoclastic journals, and other flippant European magazines such as *Gil Blas, Le Rire,* and *Punch.* Eastman avoided the doctrinaire quality of the earlier *Masses* by gathering a staff representing various types of radical philosophies. Although the contributors' political viewpoints verged from moderate to militant, the staff rallied behind the common cause of supporting individual and artistic freedom. Even if the magazine was rarely read by the "masses" or working class because of its specialized intellectual and literary content, all the writers and artists avidly backed the working-class struggle.

Eastman preached a doctrine called scientific socialism, a political philosophy stressing applied logic and experimentalism, which was a radical version of Dewey's program of social engineering. At Columbia he had taken Dewey's course in logical theory and modern philosophy, and had taught logic under his supervision. Eastman admired pragmatism, he wrote, "because it gave a biological foundation to my instinctive scepticism," and could be applied to solving social problems. My socialism, "was not a mystical cure-all, but merely a plan which I considered practical for solving the one specific problem of making freedom more general and democracy more democratic." [10]

Because of his background and interests Eastman was capable of arguing for social change in both moral and Marxist terms. His social conscience can be traced back to the influence of his parents, who were Congregational ministers in upstate New York. Tolerant and liberal, they had created an environment at home, "where kindness and fair-dealing and sound logic prevailed to such a degree that, when I got out into the public world, it looked excessively unjust, irrational, a subject for indignation and extreme action." [11] Although he later rejected his mother's orthodox religious views, her Christian moralism brushed off on her son who grew up with a zeal to amend injustice.

The philosophy of Karl Marx later reinforced Eastman's faith in social change. After reading Marx through the urging of his wife, he immediately accepted the idea of the class struggle as necessary for revolution. "It was this clash of impetuosities," he confessed, "the thirst of extreme ideals and the argumentative clinging to facts, which led me to sieze so joyfully upon Marx's idea of progress through class struggle." He viewed Marx's ideas, however, as a working hypothesis to be altered and adapted to existing situations. Thus Eastman's political views derived from several sources and was flexible enough to enable him "to take an independent position on concrete questions: feminism, population-control, peace and war." [12]

In the pages of *The Masses* the editor defended the poor, the disadvantaged, and the unemployed. His editorials angrily attacked the capitalist system and championed the underdog, including striking iron workers, lumberjacks, and miners. His support for the wage earner was illustrated by articles he wrote on the 1914 Ludlow mine workers' strike. The writer's dramatic account of the burning of the workers' homes and the shooting of their families was sensitively written, revealing the author's genuine sympathy for the working class.[13]

Like Eastman, Floyd Dell's politics derived partly from early experiences. Because of his parents' strong religious convictions, Dell had developed a tenacious social conscience early in life. He had been raised during the turbulent 1890s in small towns in Illinois and Iowa where he heard Populist and Socialist orators speak of inequality in American society. His adolescent years had been spent in Davenport, Iowa, a town that had a stimulating intellectual climate in the early 1900s. After hearing a Socialist street sweeper in Davenport speak glowingly of radical change, Dell joined the Socialist party at the age of sixteen. In the Iowa town he met George Cram Cook and Susan Glaspell, who would later play prominent roles in the theater movement. Dell converted the older Cook from Nietzschian individualism to socialism and together the two became involved in local politics.[14]

Before coming to New York, Dell had been a leading member of the Chicago Renaissance. As editor of the insurgent *Friday Literary Review,* a weekly supplement of the *Chicago Evening Post,* he had established a reputation as a progressive literary critic favoring social realism in literature. Because of personal problems and the fact that New York offered more opportunity for the aspiring writer, Dell decided to move to Manhattan in 1913. Since he was one of several Chicago Renaissance figures who settled in New York, his early career signified the close relationship between the two leading centers of prewar artistic ferment.

Dell's socialism had little chance to develop in Chicago, so it was not until his affiliation with *The Masses* as associate editor that he became an activist. As a symbol of his newfound militancy he often wore a blue flannel worker's shirt to show his commitment to radicalism during his Greenwich Village days. "I was an enemy of the established order, Church and State both, out to destroy it," the young idealist declared. Dell's radicalism was based less on intellectual theories than on the emotions involved in fighting injustice and identifying with the dispossessed. In short stories and articles he crusaded for women's rights, birth control, and the rights of workers. His monthly book review column praised literature realistically portraying society's problems and the need for change, especially the fiction of Dreiser, Anderson, and Upton Sinclair. The critic practiced what he called social revolutionary criticism, "the genuine aesthetic response of those who feel themselves to be living in a changing world lighted by the hope of revolutionary improvement." [15] Politics and culture were integrally related in Dell's writing during the prewar period.

Dell and the other editors' literary preferences limited *The Masses'* effectiveness in publishing experimental literature. Except for a few short stories by Dell, Reed, and Anderson (whose contributions were incorporated into *Winesburg, Ohio)* most of the fiction was overly sentimental and didactic. Poets such as Harry Kemp, Clement Wood, and Arturo Giovannitti celebrated utopian bliss or bohemian individualism, while others wrote poems inspired by strikes or paeans to romantic love. An occasional imagist poem by Amy Lowell, William Carlos Williams, and Carl Sandburg was published, but the majority of the poetry lacked significance from a literary standpoint. One reason for this was that the editors' taste in poetry was traditional. Dell, Eastman, and Untermeyer wrote conventional verse early in their careers and had little admiration for experimentation. Eastman insisted that meter and rhyme were necessary for a poem's structure and that free verse was "lazy" formless poetry.[16] Because they believed in orthodox poetic concepts, the editors missed publishing the early work of leading modern poets.

If the periodical's poetry lacked importance, its illustrations and covers were noteworthy achievements. *The Masses* represented a new departure in magazine format with advertising separated from reading matter and illustrations often laid out on two pages. The pen, charcoal, and crayon drawings were reproduced by line cuts rather than by the more expensive process of half tones. The general use of long captions and stale he-she jokes beneath an illustration was scrapped in favor of one or two-line satirical sentences. The art editor, John Sloan, was mainly responsible for the new pictorial innovations. "Sometimes we drew on thin paper laid over canvas or pebbly surface, combined with pen work," Sloan recalled. "This technical factor is one reason for the strength and textural interest of the *Masses* drawings." [17]

The use of radical subject matter also represented a break with commercial magazine art. Drawings of half-nude ladies, bloated capitalists, striking workers, and the poor contrasted sharply with the prudish illustrations and stereotype Gibson Girl covers found in large circulating slick magazines. Political caricature and social realism mixed with a spice of humor were the dominant motifs in the drawings. Art Young best typified *The Masses* artist who enjoyed poking fun at bourgeois conventionality, the smugness of the wealthy, and the insensitivity of capitalists. The illustrator had been a staunch Republican early in his life, but after reading and listening to Eugene Debs he was converted to the ideal of the cooperative commonwealth. He eventually became active in politics by drawing posters for the New York Socialist party and running unsuccessfully as a Socialist candidate for the State Assembly. Although the artist also drew for commercial publications it was in *The Masses* that he was given complete artistic freedom. "I could draw cartoons striking openly at those who took the best years of the worker and then threw him on the scrap-heap," he wrote. "I didn't have to think about whether a picture of mine might offend an advertiser and thus violate a business office policy." [18]

Young angrily attacked established institutions identified with outdated tradition and social inequality, especially large corporations, the church, and the press. His drawings depicted a society riddled with class conflict: rich against poor, pacifists versus imperialists, the laborer battling the employer, and the censor against the artist. A favorite device was picturing capitalism as a fat giant

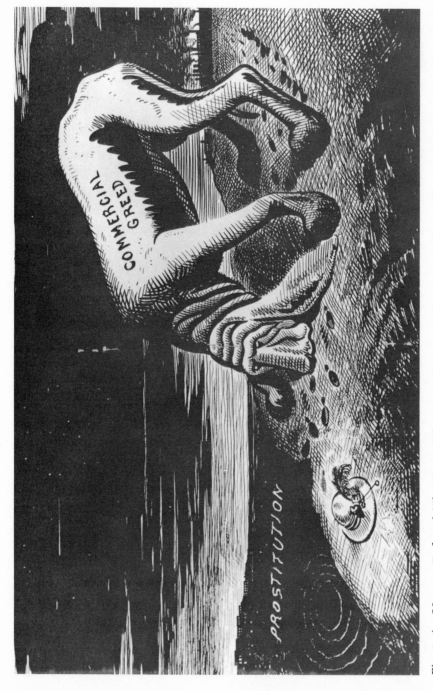

Fig. 2. Art Young, *Defeated*, *The Masses* (May 1913). Courtesy, Tamiment Library, New York University, New York City.

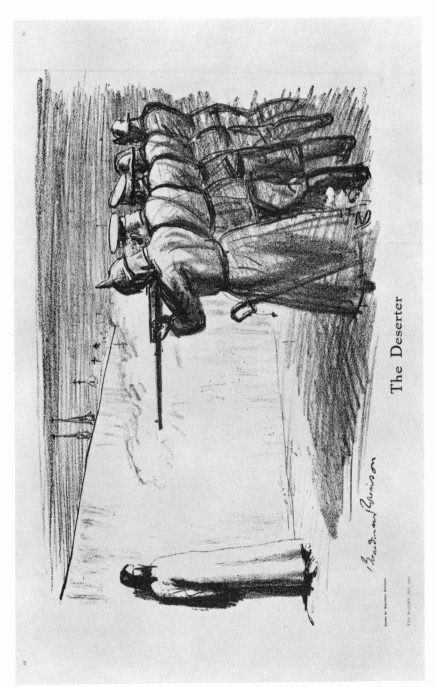

The Deserter

Fig. 3. Boardman Robinson, *The Deserter*, *The Masses* (July 1916). Reproduced by permission of The Huntington Library, San Marino, California.

PITTSBURGH

Fig. 4. Robert Minor, *Pittsburgh*, *The Masses* (August 1916). Reproduced by permission of The Huntington Library, San Marino, California.

or hideous animal overpowering the worker. His use of allegory, fantasy, and distorted figures stemmed from the illustrations of Gustave Doré and Thomas Nast and the graphic art of Hogarth and Daumier. Young's satirical drawings were finely executed works in the best tradition of political cartooning. (See Fig. 2.)

Two of the most militant artists on *The Masses* were Boardman Robinson and Robert Minor. While employed as a social worker in 1905, Robinson had become deeply committed to eradicating poverty. As a cartoonist for New York newspapers, he developed a realistic style based on the work of Daumier and Michelangelo. He joined *The Masses* staff in 1916 and quickly became one of its leading illustrators. In contrast to Young, there was little humor in Robinson's work which revealed a serious compassion for human suffering. His drawings were religious moral lessons, conveying the feeling that society had betrayed Christian ethics. One powerful antiwar cartoon, for example, showed Christ being executed by a firing squad (Fig. 3). Motivated by a strong moral conscience and Socialist beliefs, Robinson created poignant dramatic illustrations that cried out to his viewers to rectify social inequities. Minor's work on *The Masses* was also a powerful form of commentary in which figures were drawn to a huge scale, and the technique sometimes sacrificed to the message (Fig. 4). Revolution was serious business to the left-wing artist who flayed away at the capitalist structure and inequality.[19]

Another major radical artist responsible for the magazine's artistic success was John Sloan. As a young man he had become a free thinker and agnostic by reading the works of Voltaire, Rousseau, Darwin, and Ingersoll. Sloan joined the Socialist party in 1908 convinced that only socialism could bring about change in society. "I feel that if 5,000 people in this city [New York] are wealthy and content and two million unhappy, something is wrong," he commented.[20] The artist was a member of Branch One of the Socialist party, a chapter whose membership included Lippmann, Ernest Poole, William English Walling, and Sinclair Lewis. Like Young, he drew campaign posters, and twice ran unsuccessfully on the Socialist ticket for municipal judge and the State Assembly. Sloan avoided outright political propaganda in his paintings and reserved his attack on social injustice for *The Masses*. Sketches of the Lawrence and Ludlow strikes (Fig. 5) blamed ruthless employers for discriminating against the workingman while other illustrations showed concern for the poor.

Fig. 5. John Sloan, *Ludlow, Colorado, 1914, The Masses* (June 1914). Courtesy, Tamiment Library, New York University, New York City.

Skillfully executed and ironic in tone, his drawings called for more equality in American society.

Sloan eventually broke with the editors because he felt that the journal was becoming too propagandistic. He criticized Eastman and the other literary editors for putting lines "under our human interest drawings to give them a propaganda slant which we never intended." Glenn Coleman, H. J. Glintenkamp, and Stuart Davis, the apolitical artists on the magazine, also charged the editors with prevention of artistic freedom. According to Sloan, the quarrel was "between those who wanted social propaganda and those who wanted social satire. . . . I was on the side that felt satire and good observation that had social import was more useful to the cause of Socialism." The artist also accused Eastman of having too much control over editorial policy, and destroying the journal's independence by borrowing money from wealthy people to finance the magazine. In an editorial board meeting he submitted a long resolution separating the functions of the literary and art editors. When his motion was defeated, Dell moved that Sloan, Davis, Coleman, and Maurice Becker be dropped from the staff. Young, siding with the literary editors, seconded Dell's proposal, stating that *The Masses* exists for the Socialist cause and that anyone who does not believe in radicalism should resign. Although Dell's motion lost, the meeting created irrevocable dissension among the staff.[21]

The squabble attracted much attention in the daily press. When asked by a reporter about the argument, Eastman replied that "it was just our semi-annual scrap. We live on scraps. Twenty fellows can't get together to paste up a magazine without scrapping about it." Sloan lamented that "it just proves that real democracy doesn't work. . . . I don't think you'll see my name in the *Masses* for a long time." In another interview Young became the first person to apply the words "ash can" to Sloan's work when he accused the dissenting artists of wanting to "run pictures of ash cans and girls hitching up their skirts in Horatio Street—regardless of idea—and without title." As a consequence of the conflict, Sloan, Davis, Becker, and Coleman resigned from the journal. Sloan wrote a bitter regretful letter of resignation to Eastman:

> Dear Max: 'If thy right hand offend thee, cut it off.' This afternoon I played the part of one of the five fingers in the above-suggested tragedy, and foolishly resisted amputation. Now, alone at night, I have decided to submit to the operation. I hereby tender my resignation as Contributing

Editor of the Masses and as Vice President of The Masses Publishing Company.

May the Masses live long and prosper is the sincere wish of yours truly, John Sloan.

Replying to Sloan's letter, Eastman wrote: "Dear Sloan—I shall regret the loss of your wit and artistic genius as much as I shall enjoy the absence of your co-operation." With the departure of its most outstanding illustrators in 1916 the best years of *The Masses* were over.[22]

Despite the editorial dispute, most radicals, whether pragmatic Socialists or utopians, were basically united during the Little Renaissance. Socialists of all stripes contributed to *The Masses* and this made the journal a dynamic periodical. The scientific radicalism of Eastman, Lippmann, and Bourne and the idealistic utopianism of Dell, Frank, and Brooks had different roots but *The Masses'* and *Seven Arts'* contributors joined in the fight to overturn the established order in culture and politics. They viewed materialism as antithetical to artistic creativity and believed that socialism would usher in a society more conducive to the arts and individual freedom. The alliance of culture and politics also caused other writers and artists to support the I.W.W. and philosophical anarchism.

NOTES

1. Van Wyck Brooks, *Days of the Phoenix, The Nineteen-Twenties I Remember* (New York: E. P. Dutton & Co., Inc., 1957), p. 20.

2. Waldo Frank, "Symposium on Little Magazines *(Seven Arts),*" series 3, no. 1, *The Golden Goose* (1951), 20. James Oppenheim, *The Nine-Tenths: A Novel* (New York: Harper & Brothers, 1911).

3. Letter of Randolph Bourne to Prudence Winterrowd, March 2, 1913, Bourne Collection, Columbia University, New York City; Randolph Bourne, "The Price of Radicalism," *New Republic,* VI (March 17, 1916), 161; "For Radicals," in *Youth and Life* (New York: Houghton Mifflin Company, 1913), pp. 291-310.

4. Walter Lippmann, "Two Months in Schenectady," *The Masses,* III (April 1912), 13.

5. Walter Lippmann, *A Preface to Politics* (Ann Arbor: University of Michigan Press, Ann Arbor Paperbacks, 1962), pp. 139, 182-83, 210-11; *Drift and Mastery* (Englewood, N.J.: Prentice-Hall, Inc., 1961), pp. 62-63.

6. John Reed, *The Day in Bohemia* (New York: privately printed, 1913), p. 42; Walter Lippmann, "Legendary John Reed," *New Republic* I (December 26, 1914), pp. 15-16.

7. Max Eastman, "Knowledge and Revolution," *The Masses,* IV (January 1913), 6.

8. Max Eastman, "Utopian Reality," *The Masses,* IX (December 1916), 12.

9. Art Young, *Art Young, His Life and Times,* ed. John N. Beffel (New York: Sheridan House, 1939), pp. 296-97.

10. Max Eastman, *Enjoyment of Living* (New York: Harper & Brothers, 1948), p. 285; *Reflections on the Failure of Socialism* (New York: Devin-Adair Co., 1955), p. 9.

11. Max Eastman, *Love and Revolution: My Journey Through an Epoch* (New York: Random House, Inc., 1964), p. 12.

12. Ibid., pp. 14-15; *Reflections on the Failure of Socialism,* p. 8.

13. Max Eastman, "Class War in Colorado," *The Masses,* V (June 1914), 5-8; "The Nice People of Trinidad," *The Masses,* V (July 1914), 5-9.

14. Floyd Dell, *Homecoming* (New York: Farrar & Rinehart, Inc., 1933), pp. 90-91, 140-41, 149-57, 170.

15. Ibid., p. 73; Joseph Freeman, *An American Testament: A Narrative of Rebels and Romantics* (New York: Farrar & Rinehart, Inc., 1936), p. 371.

16. Max Eastman, "Lazy Verse," *New Republic,* VIII (September 9, 1916), 138-40; "Science and Free Verse," *The Seven Arts,* I (February 1917), 426-29.

17. Sloan, "1950 Notes," p. 21; unpublished MS. in the John Sloan Trust, Delaware Art Center, Wilmington, Delaware.

18. *Art Young, His Life and Times,* p. 277.

19. Albert Christ-Janer, *Boardman Robinson,* (Chicago: University of Chicago Press, 1946), passim. Robinson's antiwar cartoon appeared in *The Masses* (July 1916); Robert Minor, "How I Became a Rebel," *Labor Herald,* I (July 1922), 25-26; Theodore Draper, *The Roots of American Communism* (New York: The Viking Press Inc., 1957), pp. 122-26.

20. Bruce St. John, ed., *John Sloan's New York Scene; from the Diaries, Notes, and Correspondence, 1906-1913* (New York: Harper & Row, 1965), p. 315.

21. Sloan, "1950 Notes," pp. 16, 194. "Copy of Sloan's Handwritten Notes Taken to the 1916 Meeting of *The Masses,*" in the John Sloan Trust.

22. "Editorial Split Mars Harmony on the Masses," *New York World,* April 7, 1916; "Clash of Classes Stirs 'The Masses,' " *New York Sun,* April 8, 1916; untitled article, New York *Morning Telegraph,* April 8, 1916; clippings in the John Sloan Scrapbook, Museum of Modern Art.

CHAPTER FOUR

Anarchists and Wobblies

The most interesting prewar Anarchist journal was Emma Goldman's *Mother Earth,* a "Monthly Magazine Devoted to Social Science and Literature." Started in 1906, the periodical aimed to be a mouthpiece for libertarianism as well as a voice of radicalism in the arts. According to Goldman, its purpose was to "combine my social ideas with the young strivings in the various art forms in America, to voice without fear every unpopular progressive cause, and to aim for unity between revolutionary effort and artistic expression." [1] Goldman's expectations never materialized. Repetitious doctrinaire essays on anarchism dominated the journal and its literary content was not very notable. Several Little Renaissance artists and writers contributed to *Mother Earth;* however, their contributions lacked originality. Although lively articles on feminism and birth control were published, its book reviews and drama criticism were prejudiced in favor of social realism. The editors published Socialist poetry and illustrations, including some fine social protest drawings by Robert Minor, but illustrations were kept to a minimum and often a bland table of contents appeared on the cover.

There were several reasons why *Mother Earth* lacked the flair of *The Masses.* Alexander Berkman, the journal's editor from 1908 to 1915, was mainly responsible for its polemical tone. A militant Anarchist who had shot Henry Clay Frick during the 1892 Homestead Strike, Berkman was more interested in revolution than art. He consequently made the journal a dogmatic mouthpiece for his political views while literature and illustrations were used as embellishments. One problem the staff faced was that anarchism lacked a sustaining literary tradition in the United States and was mostly limited to political tracts. *Mother Earth*'s editorial policy was too dogmatic for most Little Renaissance social critics. The writers and painters viewed anarchism as a personal philosophy articulating individual freedom and never as a doctrine to be preached in their work.

Because of her charisma Goldman converted a few participants to her philosophy. Writers and artists flocked to her lectures on the theater, birth control, and feminism and heard her defend artistic freedom, educational reform, and sexual equality. She also was interested in the social implications of literature and wrote a book suggesting plays should reflect contemporary problems and the tragedy of poverty. Her most enthusiastic admirer was the journalist Hutchins Hapgood, who was attracted to philosophical anarchism because it espoused individual freedom. Practical-minded Socialists like Eastman and Sloan found her beliefs too utopian and doctrinaire but others such as the romantic individualist Robert Henri were inclined to be drawn to philosophical anarchism. Henri became friendly with Goldman, often attended her lectures, and invited her to talk at his Thursday evening discussion group. He called her "one of the world's greatest fighters for the freedom and growth of the human spirit." [2]

The leader of The Eight was never interested in militant tactics nor did he ever officially join an Anarchist organization. For Henri, anarchism was a philosophy justifying his own ideals concerning individualism and artistic freedom. "We only ask for each person the freedom which we accord to Nature," Henri wrote. "Each in his own way must develop according to Nature's purpose. . . . Everywhere freedom must be the sign of reason." [3] Sloan once attempted to convince his colleague to join the Socialist party but the individualist Henri feared the collectivism of their program. Henri's picturesque rural landscapes and city scenes are pleasant "snapshots" of the American scene rather than documents of social protest. His portraits, including a study of Emma Goldman, capture the unique personality of each subject. They reveal the artist's belief in the dignity of the individual and the ideals implied in his Anarchist beliefs. His oils thus can be taken as philosophical statements about life rather than political propaganda.

George Bellows, Henri's pupil, was also a philosophical Anarchist. As a boy Bellows had rebelled against his strict middle-class upbringing and had developed an instinctive sympathy for the poor. By reading Nietzsche the young artist had acquired an admiration for individualism. Bellows's virtuoso portraits reveal his interest in the individual while his poignant studies of boxers suggest the artist's worship of Nietzschean strength. His *Masses* drawings also reflect a sympathy for the underdog and support of various reform causes.[4]

In the fall of 1908, Eugene O'Neill roomed briefly with Bellows in the Lincoln Arcade Building at Sixty-sixth Street and Broadway. The two had much in common because O'Neill was also enthusiastic about anarchism. The budding playwright, who would soon play a major role in the prewar little theater movement, had become friendly with Benjamin R. Tucker, a former Boston journalist and libertarian Anarchist. O'Neill often visited Tucker's Unique Book Shop on Sixth Avenue, where he read Anarchist books and magazines and was introduced to Nietzsche's and Goldman's work.[5]

O'Neill's apprentice writing reveals an attraction to philosophical anarchism. As a student in George Pierce Baker's drama workshop at Harvard he wrote a play about a young Anarchist's involvement in a violent dock strike. O'Neill's radical views were also evident in the early poem "Submarine" published in *The Masses.* Inspired by the events of World War I, the poem expresses the author's dislike of commerce and suggests the destructive militant side of anarchism. Another poem, "Fratricide," printed in the Socialist *New York Call,* deals with the Mexican revolution and urges farmers to "rise up in your might" and "awaken to new birth." Despite his early Anarchist leanings, O'Neill's commitment to radicalism was short-lived. Utopianism became antithetical to his growing pessimistic view of human nature and a feeling that a playwright should avoid outright political propaganda in his writing.[6]

O'Neill was friendly with the colorful bohemian Anarchist Hippolyte Havel and once used him for the model of a character in *The Iceman Cometh.* (See Fig. 20.) Havel was the cook and waiter at Polly Holliday's restaurant, a popular Greenwich Village rendezvous for writers such as O'Neill. With his foreign accent, goatee, and long hair, he looked the picture of a typical nonconformist revolutionary. While visiting a *Masses* editorial meeting, Havel ridiculed the editors for voting on poetry submissions: "Bourgeois pigs!" he exclaimed. "Voting! Voting on poetry! Poetry is something for the soul! You can't vote on poetry!"[7] The Greenwich Villagers liked him because of his unorthodox opinions and hatred of middle-class culture.

Havel had lived an adventurous life before coming to New York. A

Hungarian by birth, he had been arrested for anarchism in Austria and committed to an insane asylum. Upon examination by the psychiatrist Krafft-Ebing he was pronounced sane and transferred to a regular prison. After serving his sentence Havel went to London where he met Emma Goldman, who brought him to the United States. The revolutionist then settled in Chicago where he edited the Anarchist newspaper *Arbeiter Zeitung.* During 1916 he began another Anarchist magazine in New York entitled *Revolt,* which vehemently denounced the capitalist system by calling for imminent revolution. After a few issues the magazine was suspended by the Post Office because of its ultraradicalism.

Other writers and artists became affiliated with left-wing socialism through their support of the Industrial Workers of the World. Formed in 1905 as a syndicalist labor organization, the I.W.W. attempted to organize the worker into one large union, and to precipitate a revolution through the call of a national general strike. The I.W.W.'s effectiveness as a strong union reached its peak during the prewar years when it successfully organized many unskilled immigrant factory workers on the East Coast, miners in the Rocky Mountain states, and lumberjacks in the Pacific Northwest. The union's program appealed to certain participants because its message was colorful, dynamic, and revolutionary. Like anarchism, the Wobbly cause attracted the more romantically inclined Village writer who found right-wing socialism too moderate. After witnessing the Wobbly-led Paterson strike in New Jersey, Reed wrote that "I like their understanding of the workers, their revolutionary thought, the boldness of their dreams. . . . Here was a drama, change, democracy on the march made visible–a war of the people." [8] The theme of rebellion in colorful I.W.W. songs and poetry also appealed to the literary partisans, who, like the Wobbly poets, tended to romanticize the underdog and hobo in their writing.

Two violent I.W.W. strikes on the East Coast were mainly responsible for rallying the rebels to the Wobbly cause. The first was the 1912 textile strike in Lawrence, Massachusetts, where mill workers had walked off their job because of a wage cut. Considerable violence and several arrests occurred, and one woman was killed when the police broke up a picket line. An Italian striker was accused of the crime, while two strike leaders, Joseph Ettor and Arturo Giovannitti, three miles away at the time of the slaying, were arrested as accessories to the murder. All three were kept in jail for eight months without trial.

Radicals in New York rallied behind Giovannitti and the mill workers by organizing mass meetings and a parade. Besides being a strike organizer and a radical journalist, Giovannitti was an important Wobbly poet who wrote Whitman-like rhapsodic free verse attacking social injustice. He was friendly with *The Masses* group and contributed poems to this magazine. Consequently, articles and drawings condemning the labor violence appeared in *The Masses*. Others donated money to the strike fund and formed a committee to take care of the striking workers' children in New York City. Even if the strike eventually failed and Giovannitti was acquitted, the rebels were now solidly behind the Wobbly cause.[9]

Big Bill Haywood, who was a colorful personality to the radicals, further increased their enthusiasm. As a chief organizer of the 1913 Paterson silk workers' strike, the charismatic founder and leader of the I.W.W. was often in New York. When Haywood was expelled in 1913 from the Socialist party's National Executive Committee for violating the party's plank against the use of direct action and sabotage, several writers rallied to his defense. *The Masses* magazine spoke out against his expulsion while a resolution supporting Haywood was signed by Eastman and Lippmann. Big Bill met several participants at Mabel Dodge Luhan's Greenwich Village salon, an important meeting place for the Little Renaissance community. One night a large crowd gathered at Luhan's to hear Haywood defend syndicalism in a debate with the Anarchists Goldman and Berkman and the right-wing Socialist William English Walling. Discussions like these were important for introducing the artists and writers to radical ideas. On another evening Haywood spoke on the subject of proletarian art, stating that the worker was too busy fighting for decent wages to be interested in culture.[10]

The presence of a union leader at the elegant Luhan salon created a sensation in the daily newspapers. One account was headlined "I.W.W. Men Starve as Leaders Eat," while another read "Fifth Avenue Society Entertain I.W.W. Army." While attending Frank Tanenbaum's trial, Luhan was asked by a reporter about her relationship to the I.W.W. and her reasons for going to court. "I have come merely as a matter of pursuing my education along sociological lines," she replied. "I am interested only in that justice be done."

Was she an Anarchist, the reporter inquired. No, she answered, she could not condone violence, but she insisted "that the unemployed are justified in doing anything to call attention to their condition." Years later she still described her attitude toward anarchism as one of "wonder, horror, and admiration," and reiterated her dislike of militant tactics. She confessed that Berkman once tried to kiss her in a taxi. "This scared me more than murder would have done," she admitted. Although she was captivated by the emotions revolution inspired, she was never a dedicated Socialist but a wealthy art patroness who attached herself to social causes.[11]

Luhan was also instrumental in calling for a pageant in support of the striking Paterson silk workers. One night at a gathering in Haywood's apartment she and others discussed the need to raise money to help the strikers. Low salaries, a wage cut, and an increase in the number of looms operated per worker had caused approximately 25,000 textile mill laborers to leave their jobs. The I.W.W.-led strikers demanded an eight-hour day, higher wages, and the abolition of the multiple loom system. As the strike dragged on during the cold winter months, tension increased between the unemployed, the mill owners, and the police. About 3,000 pickets were arrested and two strikers were killed by detectives. The immigrant workers were unable to feed and clothe their large families. Because of these circumstances the Paterson strike quickly became a cause célèbre in the Little Renaissance community. When Luhan suggested a pageant to popularize the strikers' demands and raise money, her idea was accepted with enthusiasm.[12]

Reed, who attended the discussion in Haywood's apartment, offered to produce the spectacle. As a romantic idealist with inexhaustible energy, Reed was temperamentally suited for the task. At Harvard he had been a cheer leader, an experience that proved helpful in directing the 1,000 participants in the pageant. He had also written plays and songs for the Dramatic and Hasty Pudding Clubs and for New York's Dutch Treat Club, an organization of writers and artists.

A major influence on Reed's radicalism was his contact with the muckraking movement in New York and acquaintance with Lincoln Steffens. A family friend, Steffens acted as Reed's counselor, obtained a position for the aspiring writer on the *American Magazine*, and for a short time lived in the same rooming house at 42 Washington Square South. He also introduced him to other reformers and told him to walk the city's streets in search of subject matter. Inspired by his investigations, Reed wrote two early articles on immigrant life and the corrupt ethics of big business. The muckraking movement showed signs of decline by 1910, but it still served as a training ground for Reed and Lippmann. The social critics came to share the muckrakers' disdain for corrupt American institutions; however, the era's writers eventually found muckraking a limited movement led by middle-of-the-road liberal reformers who lacked a Socialist perspective.[13]

Reed's social consciousness was further shaped by New York's cosmopolitan atmosphere. "There I got my first perceptions of the life of my time," he observed, and "within a block of my house was all the adventure of the world; within a mile was every foreign country." In Manhattan, Reed found ample subject matter for his writing:

> I wandered about the streets, from the soaring imperial towers of down-town, along the East River docks, smelling of spices and the clipper ships of the past, through the swarming East Side—alien towns within towns—where the smoky flare of miles of clamorous pushcarts made a splendor of shabby streets; coming upon sudden shrill markets, dripping blood and fish-scales in the light of torches, the big Jewish women bawling their wares under the roaring great bridges; thrilling to the ebb and flow of human tides sweeping to work and back, west and east, south and north. I knew Chinatown, and little Italy, and the quarter of the Syrians; the marionette theatre, Sharkey's and McSorley's saloons, the Bowery lodging houses and the places where the tramps gathered in winter; the Haymarket, the German Village, and all the dives of the Tenderloin.

At Harvard he had been intellectually attracted to socialism but now conversations with many radicals further confirmed his growing class consciousness, while New York's poverty awakened his eyes to social inequalities:

> In my rambles about the city I couldn't help but observe the ugliness of poverty and all its train of evil, the cruel inequality between rich people who had too many motor cars and poor people who didn't have enough to eat. It didn't come to me from books that the workers produced all the wealth of the world, which went to those who did not earn it.[14]

Reed's involvement with the Paterson strike further roused his dedication to radicalism. While investigating the walkout, he was arrested for loitering and sentenced to twenty days in the county jail where he became acquainted with Haywood and other I.W.W. leaders. It was an important turning point in his life. In prison, "I talked with exultant men who had blithely defied the lawless brutality of the city government and gone to prison laughing and singing. There were horrors in that jail too; men and boys shut up for months without trial, men going mad and dying, bestial cruelty and disease and filth—and all for the poor." Bailed out after four days, *The Masses* writer wrote an inflammatory article defending the strikers' cause and proclaiming class warfare in Paterson.

> There's war in Paterson! But it's a curious kind of war. All the violence is the work of one side—the Mill Owners. Their servants, the Police, club unresisting men and women and ride down law-abiding crowds on horseback. Their paid mercenaries, the armed Detectives, shoot and kill innocent people. Their newspapers, the Paterson *Press* and the Paterson *Call,* publish incendiary and crime-inciting appeals to mob-violence against the strike leaders. . . .
>
> Opposing them are about twenty-five thousand striking silk workers. . . .[15]

Determined to rectify the injustices, Reed began to organize the pageant by enlisting the talents of various participants. Luhan volunteered to aid in the arrangements, and her friend, the stage designer Robert Edmond Jones, drew the show's poster and program cover (Fig. 6). Sloan helped paint Jones's scenery—a 200-foot-wide backdrop of a large silk mill surrounded by other factories on a cold winter's morning. Reed went to work drafting a scenario of eight scenes but it was later cut to six. He selected approximately 1,000 striking workers and their families in order to realistically recreate the most dramatic strike episodes. He next taught them how to sing Harvard songs with new revolutionary lyrics he especially composed for the occasion.[16]

On the night of June 7, nearly 15,000 spectators filled the old Madison Square Garden on Twenty-sixth Street. Hundreds of police were hired to keep the crowd orderly, while outside a sign of glowing red lights on the auditorium's tower spelled out "I.W.W." The crowd cheered to a reenaction of the strikers' wretched working conditions, a raucous strike meeting, a colorful May Day

Fig. 6. The Paterson Pageant. Above: Program cover. Below: The scene, "Picketing the Mills." Courtesy, Tamiment Library, New York University, New York City.

parade, and the picketing of the mills (Fig. 6). The audience was particularly touched by the portrayed murder and funeral of an innocent bystander and the speeches of Haywood and Elizabeth Gurley Flynn. Despite the attempt of local police officials to prohibit foreign revolutionary songs, the strikers' singing of the Marseillaise and Internationale stirred the crowd's emotions. If some conservative newspapers attacked the show because of its revolutionary message, most journalists agreed that this was one of the most moving stage presentations they had ever seen. Participants such as Bourne interpreted it as an exciting form of new proletarian theater:

> Who that saw the Paterson Strike Pageant in 1913 can ever forget that thrilling evening when an entire labor community dramatized its wrongs in one supreme outburst of group-emotion? Crude and rather terrifying, it stamped into one's mind the idea that a new social art was in the American world, something genuinely and excitingly new.[17]

The pageant was certainly a climactic event of the prewar rebellion in the radical arts.

The I.W.W. leaders, however, viewed the pageant as a financial disaster contributing to the strike's eventual failure. The show lost approximately $2,000 and failed to financially aid the unemployed workers. Admission prices ranged from 10 cents to $20, but hundreds of unsold expensive seats were given away free or at reduced rates before curtain time. The financial loss disappointed Wobbly organizers such as Flynn, who felt that the spectacle had diverted workers from the pressing activities of the picket line. A month after the pageant the strike collapsed due to lack of morale and continued mass arrests of strikers. The defeat seriously undermined the union's influence in the East. Even John Reed felt exhausted from his work and went to Europe with Mabel Luhan to recover his nerves.

Reed's involvement with the I.W.W. nonetheless made him a lifelong revolutionary, and after his return to America he again engaged in radical activities. The *Metropolitan Magazine* sent him to Mexico in 1914 as its correspondent to cover the Mexican revolution. He spent four grueling months with the Constitutionalist armies, experiencing battle and witnessing death. Reed's dispatches formed the basis of *Insurgent Mexico* (1914), an excellent piece of reporting that brought to life the tragedy of the civil war. As the Little

Renaissance progressed, Reed continued to gain fame as a radical journalist and became more outspoken in his denunciation of economic inequality. His iconoclastic journalism contributed greatly to the number of nonfiction works the social critics were creating in reaction to outdated standards. In 1917, he turned to communism while reporting on the Bolshevik revolution for *The Masses,* and two years later published his famous *Ten Days That Shook the World.* During the Little Renaissance Reed had thus moved from being a Greenwich Village rebel poet and muckraker to a Communist sympathizer. Although he went through various stages of radicalism and even began to question communism before his death, he was basically a dedicated revolutionary whose political convictions lay between nineteenth-century utopian idealism and the doctrinaire Marxism of the 1930s. More of a serious Socialist than legend leads us to believe, Reed based his beliefs more on instincts than theories. Also important, the rebellious atmosphere of the Little Renaissance had a lasting influence on his political views because Reed's dedication to the I.W.W. derived from a need to overturn nineteenth-century culture and politics.

The attraction of Reed and the other participants to the Wobblies and Anarchists had significant results. No doubt the literature in *Mother Earth* suffered from didacticism, yet anarchism was an inspiring philosophy for artists such as Henri and Bellows. Philosophical anarchism underwrote the Little Renaissance values of liberation in the arts and society. The revolutionary program of the I.W.W. also inspired the drama of the Paterson Pageant. Anarchism and syndicalism were two more iconoclastic ideologies the rebels used to overturn nineteenth-century standards. The participants' attraction to bohemianism and Freudianism had motives similar to their commitment to socialism.

NOTES

1. Emma Goldman, *Living My Life,* vol. 1 (New York: Alfred A. Knopf, Inc., 1931), pp. 377-78, 352.

2. Emma Goldman, *The Social Significance of the Modern Drama* (Boston: Richard G. Badger, 1914); Hutchins Hapgood, *A Victorian in the Modern World* (New York: Harcourt, Brace and Company, Inc., 1939), p. 277; Robert Henri, "An Appreciation by an Artist," *Mother Earth,* X (March 1915), 415.

3. Robert Henri, "My People," *The Craftsman,* XXVII (February 1915), 460-61.

4. Charles Hill Morgan, *George Bellows, Painter of America* (New York: Reynal & Company, Inc., 1965), pp. 149-50; Milton W. Brown, *American Painting from the Armory Show to the Depression* (Princeton: Princeton University Press, 1955), pp. 35-36; Art Young, *On My Way: Being the Book of Art Young in Text and Picture* (New York: Liveright Publishing, 1928), p. 282; Art Young, *Art Young, His Life and Times,* ed. John N. Beffel (New York: Sheridan House, 1939), p. 388.

5. Louis Sheaffer, *O'Neill, Son and Playwright* (Boston: Little, Brown and Company, 1968), pp. 105-6.

6. "Submarine," *The Masses* (February 1917), p. 43; "Fratricide," *New York Call,* May 17, 1914.

7. Albert Parry, *Garrets and Pretenders: A History of Bohemianism in America* (New York: Dover Publications, Inc., 1960), p. 289.

8. John Reed, "Almost Thirty," *The New Republic Anthology,* ed. Graff Conklin (New York: Dodge Publishing Company, 1936), p. 70.

9. On Giovannitti see Stanley Kunitz and Howard Haycroft, eds., *Twentieth Century Authors* (New York: H. W. Wilson Company, 1942), p. 537; Anonymous, "Poet of the I.W.W.," *Outlook,* CIV (July 5, 1913), 504-6; Kenneth McGowan, "Giovannitti: Poet of the Wop," *Forum,* LII (October 1914), 609-11; "Social Significance of Arturo Giovannitti," *Current Opinion,* LIV (January 1913), 24-26. Margaret Sanger, *An Autobiography* (New York: N. W. Norton & Company, 1938), pp. 80-85. See also various newspaper articles on the strike in the John Sloan Scrapbooks, Library of the Museum of Modern Art, New York City, N.Y.

10. *International Socialist Review* (February 1913), 623; Theodore Draper, *The Roots of American Communism* (New York: Compass Books, 1963), pp. 45-48; Mabel Dodge Luhan, *Movers and Shakers* (New York: Harcourt, Brace & Company, Inc., 1936), pp. 59, 90; Max Eastman, *The Enjoyment of Living* (New York: Harper & Brothers, 1948), p. 523.

11. From newspaper clippings in "Many Inventions" (1914), scrapbook owned by Mabel Luhan in the Mabel Dodge Luhan Collection, Beinecke Library, Yale University; Luhan, *Movers and Shakers,* p. 58.

12. *A Victorian in the Modern World,* p. 350; Elizabeth Gurley Flynn, *I Speak My Own Piece* (New York: Masses and Mainstream, 1955), pp. 144-48.

13. Lincoln Steffens, *The Autobiography of Lincoln Steffens,* vol. 2 (New York: Harvest Books, 1969), pp. 653-54; see also Steffens's letter to Reed, October 27, 1912, in *The Letters of Lincoln Steffens,* vol. 1 (New York: Harcourt, Brace, and Company, Inc., 1938), p. 311; Lincoln Steffens, *John Reed Under the Kremlin Wall* (Chicago: Will Ransom, 1922); John Reed, *Sangar to Lincoln Steffens* (Riverside, Conn.: Hillacre, 1913); John Reed, "Immigrants," *Collier's* (May 20, 1911); and "The Involuntary Ethics of Big Business, a Fable for Pessimists," *Trend* (June 1911). Steffens had appointed Lippmann as his secretarial assistant on *Everybody's Magazine;* see Charles Wellborn, *Twentieth Century Pilgrimage* (Baton Rouge: Louisiana State University Press, 1969), p. 19.

14. Reed, "Almost Thirty," *The New Republic Anthology,* pp. 68-70.

15. Ibid., pp. 70-71; John Reed, "War in Paterson," *Echoes of Revolt: The Masses 1911-1917,* ed. William L. O'Neill (Chicago: Quadrangle Books, 1966), p. 143; originally published in *The Masses,* V (June 1913).

16. See Mabel Luhan's scrapbook entitled "Paterson Strike" in the Mabel Luhan Collection, Yale University; Philip S. Foner, *A History of the Labor Movement in the United States,* vol. 4: *The Industrial Workers of the World, 1905-1917* (New York: International Publishers, 1965), pp. 366-72; William D. Haywood, *Bill Haywood's Book: The Autobiography of William D. Haywood* (New York: New World Paperbacks, 1966), pp. 261-77. Reed's scenario entitled "Pageant" is in the Reed Collection, Houghton Library, Harvard University, Cambridge, Massachusetts. The most authentic document is the Program of the Paterson Strike Pageant, which shows six episodes; copy in the Tamiment Library, New York University, New York City, N.Y.

17. Randolph Bourne, "Pageantry and Social Art," unpublished MS., p. 6, Bourne Collection, Columbia University, New York City, N.Y.

CHAPTER FIVE

Bohemianism and Freudianism

Artists and writers had resided in Greenwich Village well before the Little Renaissance. The area had originally been a tobacco plantation under the Dutch West India Company, and after the capture of New Amsterdam by the British most of the land was purchased by Sir Peter Warren, an English naval officer, who built a large country home on his estate called Greenwich. The district had remained a rural adjunct of the city until the early 1800s when a series of smallpox and yellow fever epidemics forced many New Yorkers to move to the more healthy environs of the Village. By the middle of the nineteenth century wealthy aristocratic families had built elegant Greek Revival houses along Washington Square and lower Fifth Avenue. Thomas Paine and Edgar Allan Poe had been among the first American writers to live in the Village before the Civil War. Towards the century's end, as the center of the city moved further northward, Greenwich Village became less fashionable and these handsome residences were abandoned by their owners. The town houses were converted into rooming houses and the stables transformed into art studios. Around this time many artists had moved into the Washington Square area, including such famous late nineteenth-century writers as Frank Norris, Stephen Crane, and Henry James.

The Village attracted the participants for a variety of reasons. The area had an intimate charm with its handsome brownstones and quaint quiet side streets such as Milligan Place, Patchin Place, and Minetta Lane. Its small-town atmosphere contrasted sharply with the impersonal skyscrapers of uptown. Dell recognized the congeniality of the prewar settlement when he wrote:

Where now the tide of traffic beats,
There was a maze of crooked streets;
The noisy waves of enterprise,
Swift-hurrying to their destinies,
Swept past this island paradise:
Here life went to a gentler pace,
And dreams and dreamers found a place.

He also suggested that artists resided in the Village because they were "need-ful of a place to sleep" and "the rents were cheap." Inexpensive living was a necessity for the noncommercial artist. A needy individual could rent a room from eight to twelve dollars a month; for thirty dollars a floor-through apartment in a brownstone could be leased. Louis Untermeyer interpreted the Village not as an "exotic escape" or an "erotic utopia" but as "a casual, a commercial, convenience." [1]

The writers and artists felt less constrained living among the Italian immigrants in the district. The area actually contained three major social groups: the older Village families who had lived there for years, the newer residents (the participants, young professional people, and single women), and the ethnic community composed mainly of Italian-Americans. The im-migrants' customs were a source of colorful romantic subject matter for the painters and writers. The participants had little or no contact with these local people due to their different social, economic, and educational backgrounds. The immigrants sometimes criticized the loose morals of the Village rebels and viewed their favorite restaurants and bars as dens of iniquity. If there was some animosity between the two groups, it was not strong enough to overcome the conviction that living among these immigrants was conducive to freedom and spontaneity.[2]

Through its many clubs, restaurants, and salons the Village gave its artists and writers a sense of identity and comraderie. These meeting places tended to relieve the lonely impersonality of the large city, to break down the isolation of the Little Renaissance artist, and to aid in the dissemination of the era's important ideas. Several restaurants and bars catered particularly to the literary crowd. Among the most popular dining places were Polly's, Mother Bertol-otti's, the Pepper Pot, and the Dutch Oven. A customer could find convivial companionship at these restaurants and an inexpensive meal from sixty cents to a dollar. Intimate tea rooms such as the Mad Hatter with its wooden tables and candlelight atmosphere were also popular. More elaborate expensive eating places were the Lafayette and the Hotel Brevoort café, which was popular because of its cosmopolitan atmosphere. Less fancy was the earthy Golden Swan saloon on Sixth Avenue and Fourth Street, better known as the "Hell Hole" to its patrons. Among its clientele were gangsters, Irish longshoremen, prostitutes, and gamblers. O'Neill, who frequented the "Hell Hole," found material for his plays here, while Sloan drew a famous illustration of the saloon.[3]

The largest and most famous Village salon was run by Mabel Dodge Luhan. Before organizing her evenings in 1913, she had established a reputation as an elegant hostess of leading European and American intellectuals at her villa in Florence, Italy. Returning to New York in 1912, Luhan soon became the chief "promoter of spirit" in the prewar artistic ferment. Besides her involvement in the Paterson Strike Pageant, she also aided in preparations for the Armory Show and was instrumental in getting Gertrude Stein's early work published in America. Her lavishly decorated Greenwich Village apartment on Fifth Avenue and Ninth Street was ideally suited for social occasions. Because of her natural flair as a hostess, Lincoln Steffens suggested to her that she hold evening discussion groups.[4]

Luhan's plan was to give writers and artists a "meeting place for the [free] exchange of ideas and talk." Evenings were set aside to debate particular issues such as socialism, anarchism, free speech, psychoanalysis, modern art and poetry, birth control, and feminism. The attractive hostess described her salon as a conglomeration of "Socialists, Trade-Unionists, Anarchists, Suffragists, Poets, Relations, Lawyers, Murderers, Old Friends, Psychoanalysts, I.W.W.'s, Single Taxers, Birth Controlists, Newspapermen, Artists, Modern-Artists, Club-women, Women's-place-is-in-the-home Women, [and] Clergymen." Reed, Eastman, Lippmann, and Marsden Hartley were among the most prominent Little Renaissance figures attending her salon. Other frequent visitors included her friends Carl Van Vechten, Hutchins Hapgood, Lincoln Steffens, Jo Davidson, and Robert Edmond Jones. Luhan's salon tended to bring together individuals pursuing different careers in the arts and to expose them to important prewar ideas and movements.[5]

Besides Luhan's salon, there were other smaller equally stimulating meeting places. An important center for heated conversations and parties was William and Marguerite Zorach's apartment on Tenth Street and Sixth Avenue. Their flat was wildly decorated in stark colors and the walls covered with murals. The writer Alyse Gregory's flat on Milligan Place became another important Village salon. Bourne brought his *Seven Arts* colleagues to her home, where discussions ranged from feminism to anarchism.[6]

Many artists and writers belonged to the Liberal Club, an important Greenwich Village social organization. Founded by the Reverend Percy Stickney Grant and other liberal reformers, the club was originally a political reform association and lecture society located on Nineteenth Street. Genteel progressives and wealthy philanthropists controlled the organization until certain radicals began to challenge their leadership, particularly the militant feminist Henrietta Rodman. Her views on free love were too unconventional for the conservatives who were disturbed when she married a club member and consented to live together with him and his first wife. The radicals were also angered when the club turned down Emma Goldman's application for membership and refused to admit black people.[7]

Rodman and her friends consequently bolted the organization in 1913 and established their own branch of the club in a brownstone at 137 MacDougal Street. The rooms were colorfully decorated with modern paintings and posters, bizarre furniture, and an old electric piano. As "a social center for those interested in new views," the club soon became a favorite meeting place for writers, artists, school teachers, social workers, journalists, feminists, and theater people. The dramatist Lawrence Langner described the club "as a focal point where all young men and women who were interested in what was new and modern in the arts and economics mixed and mutually stimulated one another." Among the many writers and artists participating in its activities were Reed, Dell, Susan Glaspell, Art Young, Alfred Kreymborg, Mary Heaten Vorse, and Hutchins Hapgood. Illustrious visitors often lectured at the club and took part in evening discussions on such subjects as the tango, eugenics, the slit skirt, free verse, and birth control. Some women members noted for their feminist activity cut their hair short and wore short skirts and rolled down stockings. One night Horace Traubel reminisced about Walt Whitman, while on two other occasions William Haywood talked on socialism and Vachel Lindsay recited *The Congo*. The club also sponsored modern art exhibitions, poetry readings, and protest rallies supporting radical causes.[8]

Connected to the club via a passageway was the Washington Square Bookshop run by the brothers Albert and Charles Boni. The bookstore, containing a fireplace and large comfortable armchairs, resembled a cozy home where writers congregated and engaged in stimulating conversation. Lectures on literature and painting and experimental plays by the Liberal Club members took place in the bookshop. The store later changed owners and moved to Eighth Street where it eventually became known as the Eighth Street Bookshop.

The Liberal Club was one of several organizations staging dances and parties. At their annual fund-raising balls, called "Pagan Routs," partygoers came dressed as Greek and Roman figures. Other colorful affairs were staged by the Kit Kat Club, an artists' organization, and the little magazines such as *Rogue, Mother Earth,* and *The Masses.* When *Rogue* magazine folded because of financial reasons, the staff put on a gala party called the "Rogue's Funeral Ball," to which guests were transported in a hearse. The *Mother Earth* balls were especially noted for their lavish food, Russian samovar, and joviality. On the magazine's tenth anniversary the journal staged the "Red Revel," in which Emma Goldman came dressed as a nun and waltzed to a tune called the "Anarchist's Slide." These lively affairs revealed the participants sense of fun and humor and their desire for self-expression.[9]

The most notorious masquerade balls were given by *The Masses* magazine at Webster Hall on East Eleventh Street. At one noisy romp on Christmas Eve, 1914, Bellows wore a bullfighter's costume, Eastman dressed as a classical Greek figure, and Glenn Coleman came as a ballerina. A reporter for the *New York World* called the affair a "Wild Arty Cut Up Night for the Insurgent Devil-May-Cares!" Shocked at their actions, the journalist criticized their behavior as "ultra-indifferent and violent . . . and gentle custom nowhere in sight." "We may never see another eve like this," concluded the reporter after the ball lasted until seven in the morning.[10]

Being a Villager gave one an identity, a particular state of mind, and a defiant attitude towards society. One major event especially represented this feeling. On the evening of January 23, 1917, six people climbed to the roof of the Washington Arch for a midnight picnic of food and drink in order to proclaim the independent republic of Greenwich Village. The party included the painters John Sloan, Marcel Duchamp, Gertrude Drick, a pupil of Sloan's, and three people from the theater, Forrest Mann, Charles Ellis, and Betty Turner. They decorated their austere surroundings with Chinese lanterns and red balloons and made themselves comfortable by sitting on hot-water bottles. (See Fig. 7.) Accompanied by the firing of toy pistols, Drick read from a document declaring

Fig. 7. John Sloan, *The Arch Conspirators* (1917). Courtesy, Kraushaar Galleries, New York City. Geoffrey Clements, Photographer. Sloan appears at the far right.

the secession of Greenwich Village from the United States. The celebration of the area's independence lasted until morning. Though few participated in the incident, it symbolized the feeling that the Village was a special place with a different life-style and values.[11]

This spirit of independency was voiced in several minor little magazines published in Greenwich Village. *The Masses* and *The Seven Arts* had their offices in the area, but the tone, contents, and editorializing of these major journals went well beyond articulating Village artiness. Among the periodicals more exclusively identified with the prewar settlement were the publications edited by Guido Bruno, who had a penchant for publishing one-man little magazines popularizing the Village as well as his name. Along with Hippolyte Havel and Harry Kemp, the Village vagabond poet, he was one of the era's most colorful bohemians. His Greenwich Village apartment served as a boarding house, newspaper office, lecture hall, art gallery, and tourist trap. Not only were his journals responsible for commercializing the Village, but he charged uptowners admission to visit his garret to see how a typical bohemian lived. Although Bruno's eclectic literary taste and dilettantism dated back to the fin de siècle, his many periodicals reflected the area's prewar spirit. Bruno's *Greenwich Village,* a fortnightly published during 1915, contained many articles celebrating the locale. The editor often used its pages to glowingly describe the Village as a paradise for dedicated idealists. One typical article by Hippolyte Havel called the Village a "rallying point for new ideas" and "a spiritual zone of mind." Havel and Bruno were essentially voicing the ideals of the Arch Conspirators, the idea that bohemianism represented liberation and artistic freedom.[12]

Bruno was not the only booster of Greenwich Village during the prewar days. Another ardent admirer was Reed, who fell in love with the neighborhood when he was living in the Washington Square area. In his long poem, *The Day in Bohemia* (1913), he glorified the area's intimate charm and comraderie. Reed thought that Greenwich Village was the best locale in the city because of its restaurants, art galleries, picturesque streets, and colorful immigrant life. He described the neighborhood as a place of personal and artistic freedom where the inhabitants defied conventionality and uptown genteel society. One particular stanza cogently summed up the meaning the Village had for the participants:

> Yet we are free who live in Washington Square
> We dare to think as Uptown wouldn't dare,
> Blazing our nights with arguments uproarious;

What care we for a dull old world censorious
When each is sure he'll fashion something glorious?
Blessed art thou, Anarchic Liberty
Who asketh nought but joy of such as we! [13]

Dell's affiliation with *The Masses,* the Provincetown Players, and the feminist movement also made him a good representative of the prewar Village intellectual. Like his colleagues, he viewed the district as a "refuge from mother's morality" and "a moral health resort." In a collection of short stories and essays, entitled *Love in Greenwich Village* (1926), Dell wrote of lonely people who reside in the area in order to be free from the restraints of conventional society. One essay nostalgically described the prewar Village as conducive to spontaneity, creativity, and comraderie. Dell clearly favored the Little Renaissance settlement, for in another article he lamented that the Village of the 1920s had become commercialized as a tourist attraction.[14]

Despite his writings and reputation as a Greenwich Village rebel, Dell was never a wild bohemian. Although he was noted for his many amours, he never acted promiscuously and desired mainly to sustain one stable sexual relationship. Dell named the Liberal Club balls "Pagan Routs," yet he did not like to dance or drink to excess. He believed that drinking was a form of escape and once wrote that "in a world where action is still to be initiated a second-rate idea or even a third-rate desire is better than a first-rate drink." In his autobiography Dell revealed the true nature of his Village life:

I never cared for or could abide disorderly, pig-sty, lunatic Bohemianism. The Bohemia I learned to like was, moreover, a quiet and seclusive place, not a show-off place; and a place with some outdoors in it—trees, flowers, streams, a sky; and all these remained a part of my notion of Bohemia.[15]

A strong moral conscience tempered Dell's bohemian activities and the other Villagers. The same righteous indignation that motivated the participants to rectify injustice in American society constrained their social behavior. Despite their noisy parties and balls, the Villagers worked diligently at writing and painting. The many little magazines, theaters, and art galleries in the area reveal that the prewar Village was a neighborhood of dedicated artists. No doubt there were a few pseudo-intellectuals indulging more in bohemianism than serious creative work, but they were not the important members of the Renaissance. Although Eastman could write that the Village "meant being alive" and a "free and easy mode of life," he personally disliked self-conscious bohemianism and dilettantism.[16] The writers might celebrate the personal freedom of the Village, but they were never promiscuous "improper" bohemians.

Bourne's experience suggests that the growing commercial atmosphere of the Village disturbed the Little Renaissance social critic. Although he enjoyed living in the area, he basically had an ambivalent attitude towards the Village. He once called the neighborhood "a poisonous place which destroys the souls even of super Villagers." [17] Bourne probably felt this way because he was once hurt personally by an ultra-Village feminist. Like Dell, he was well aware that Village bohemianism was quickly becoming a commercialized cult by 1917.

Not every participant lived in the Village or looked favorably upon bohemianism. Mencken and the other *Smart Set* critics tended to disassociate themselves from the area. Although the social critic felt the neighborhood served a useful function by challenging conventional society, Mencken believed that the district lacked serious artists and contributed little to the country's literary development. "Greenwich Village, for all its noisy pretensions, is quite sterile," he commented. "It has never produced a first-rate poet, or a first-rate novelist, or a critic worth a hoot." [18] According to him, culture derived more from an aristocratic elite than bohemian groups. Despite Mencken's reservations, Greenwich Village was *the* major area in the city where the prewar revolt against the genteel tradition occurred. Other participants resided in popular neighborhoods such as Chelsea, Gramercy Park, and Morningside Heights, but even Chelsea residents like Sloan would eventually move to the Village or would frequent its many restaurants. The Village was hard to resist because it embodied two essential values of the Little Renaissance generation: individual liberty and artistic freedom.

Freud and his writings were a frequent topic of conversation at Village restaurants since the social critics also used the ideology of the new psychology to battle the genteel tradition. During the prewar years Freud's ideas were popularized and widely disseminated by lecturers and magazines. Crucial to the development of the country's psychoanalytic movement was Freud's visit to America in 1909, when he delivered a lecture series at Clark University in Worcester, Massachusetts. His presence in the United States and the publication of his lectures in the *American Journal of Psychology* created an avid interest among psychiatrists. Other scientific journals immediately began publishing articles discussing his ideas, including the theory of dreams. Freud's beliefs became popular in the Little Renaissance community, especially Greenwich Village where they were used to attack restrictions in the arts and society.[19]

Dr. A. A. Brill, a leading American disciple of Freud, was mainly responsible for creating an interest in psychoanalysis among the participants. He was one of several psychoanalysts in New York City, an important center of the early psychoanalytic movement. As early as 1908, Dr. Brill had begun translating Freud's work into English and his translations were important not only for introducing the American reader to psychoanalysis but also for directly informing the social critics about the new science. Several participants first heard about Freud when Lippmann invited the eminent doctor to give a lecture on psychoanalysis at Luhan's salon. "My talk," declared Brill, "aroused a very interesting and lively discussion." [20] Other writers came to Brill curious to know more about Freud's ideas. Among Brill's patients during these years were Eastman and Luhan; indeed, being psychoanalyzed became a craze in the Village community.

The social critics generally interpreted psychoanalysis as a positive science that could be applied to solving social problems. Rarely did they view it as a pessimistic philosophy stressing irrational abnormal behavior. Freudianism instead became a useful tool to battle conventionality, outdated morality, and censorship. The idea that social inhibitions were unhealthy underwrote the writers' call for artistic freedom and new sexual relationships based on equality and freedom of choice. They never used his theories to condone sexual permissiveness as was later done by Villagers in the 1920s. Freud was thus viewed as a liberator whose ideas could be put to work to undermine the genteel tradition.

Eastman was one of several social critics attracted to Freud's theories. He had first become interested in mental healing during his stay in a health sanitarium in upstate New York in 1906. His mother, who underwent therapy under Brill, also admired psychology. Eastman's enthusiasm continued to grow through his own psychoanalysis in 1914 and his reading of Freud's writings. Reminiscing later about his early admiration for the new science, Eastman wrote: "Freud was not only in many things my teacher, but by proxy at least, my Father Confessor." [21]

During the prewar years Eastman helped introduce psychoanalysis to the general reading public. The editor wrote an article in *The Masses* praising the publication of the new journal *Psycho-Analytic Review* and urging the magazine's readers to subscribe to the periodical which "heralds the advent of a new method of healing. One might almost say it heralds a new science–the science of applied psychology." The next year he wrote two important articles in a slightly humorous tone explaining the meaning of dreams, the unconscious, and repressions. Behind his lightheartedness lay Eastman's view that psychoanalysis was a science that aided the mentally sick and explained abnormal behavior. For Eastman, Freudianism was a newfound faith that could change bourgeois social conventions by liberating the emotions.[22]

Dell was attracted to the new psychology for similar reasons. He had read several books on the science in Chicago where psychoanalysis was a frequent topic of conversation among writers. As an amateur authority on the subject, Dell had introduced Sherwood Anderson to Freud's theories. In Chicago, "all the young intellectuals were busy analyzing each other and everyone they met," Anderson recalled.[23] Arriving in Greenwich Village in 1913, Dell found psychoanalysis already a craze. At parties he joined the Villagers in games of free association and interpreting one another's dreams.

An article Dell wrote for *Vanity Fair* illustrates his attitude towards the new psychology. Like Eastman, Dell spiced his essay with a good deal of humor, but the author was seriously committed to his subject. "Psychoanalysis," he wrote, "is at once a science and a philosophy, and it has in it the making of a religion." Dell noted that the science had become a cause célèbre in the Village:

> Psycho-analysis is the greatest discovery made by intellectual conver-
> sationalists since Bergson and the I.W.W. Nothing quite so provoc-
> ative of argument has happened since Nietzsche. As a science it has
> been going on quietly this score of years or more. But as a topic of polite
> conversation, it first saw the light of day a short while ago in the throbbing
> studios of Washington Square, where it immediately implanted Cubism,
> Imagism, and Havelock Ellis.

Like his colleagues, the writer interpreted psychoanalysis as a science that could be freely applied to ameliorating social and personal problems.[24]

Dell's interest in psychoanalysis eventually tempered his rebellious instincts. During 1917-18 he went to the Freudian disciple Dr. Samuel A. Tannenbaum because he thought it might help him in his personal life and career. His treatment gave him stability, self-awareness, and confidence in his writing and had an overall conservative effect on Dell's personality. As a result he became less of a rebel after 1918 and urged in his work the benefits of adjusting to adult responsibilities such as marriage. He had once interpreted psychoanalysis as a liberating science for radical change, but during the 1920s and 1930s he viewed it as an aid to adjusting to society. Despite this ironic change, he continued to use Freud's ideas in his novels and nonfiction.[25]

Since ideas were infectious in Greenwich Village the new psychology soon became a popular subject for other artists and writers. In a *Masses* drawing Cornelia Barnes depicted a young girl jokingly informing her boy friend: "I dreamt you were drafted! Wish–dream–or nightmare?" George Cram Cook's and Susan Glaspell's one-act comedy *Suppressed Desires* made fun of Village amateur psychologists. The story concerns Henrietta Brewster, who analyzes her husband's and sister's dreams and becomes convinced that they have repressed desires. She sends them to a psychoanalyst who informs them that they have "suppressed desires" for one another. Discovering this embarrassing fact, Henrietta renounces her pretense as an amateur psychoanalyst. Spoofing the Village fad for psychoanalysis became a familiar subject in Little Renaissance writing.[26]

A more serious approach to Freud's ideas was taken by Lippmann. He interpreted the new psychology as an aid to scientific reform and specifically urged the application of psychoanalysis to governmental problems. In *A Preface to Politics,* Lippmann called for a new political structure based partly on Freud's discovery of the irrational. Using the concept of sublimation, the author wrote that malevolent impulses could be channeled into a beneficial direction: "Instead of tabooing our impulses we must redirect them. Instead of trying to crush badness we must turn the powers behind it to good account. The assumption is that every lust is capable of some civilized expression." Politics, he insisted, must be responsive to human instincts but more time was needed to fully understand the implications of Freud's ideas: "The impetus of Freud is perhaps the greatest advance ever made towards the understanding and control of human character. But for the complexities of politics it is not yet ready. It will take time and endless labor for a detailed study of social problems in the light of this growing knowledge." [27]

A major influence behind *A Preface to Politics* was Alfred Booth Kuttner, another important popularizer of psychoanalysis avidly interested in Freud's theories. During 1912, he and Lippmann shared a cabin in Maine where the latter wrote *A Preface to Politics* and Kuttner translated Freud's *Traumdeutung*. Kuttner's enthusiasm for Freud's work brushed off on the young journalist. During the era Kuttner also wrote several articles on the science for *The New Republic* and *The Seven Arts*. His essays in the latter journal discussed the importance of the unconscious in the creative process and pointed out how neurosis was often the source of artistic creativity. These groundbreaking articles made Kuttner a leading interpreter of Freudian thought during the Little Renaissance.[28]

The new psychology was also used by social critics to attack outdated morality and provincialism. Although Mencken's enthusiasm for the subject never matched *The Masses* staff, he once wrote that psychoanalysis gives "us a new understanding of the forces which move us in the world, and shows us the true genesis of our ideas, and enormously strengthens our grip upon reality." In his writing he often used Freudian terminology to lambast middle-class culture and inhibitions. Freud's ideas were one more piece of shrapnel in his attack on genteel society.[29]

The new psychology was also used by *The Seven Arts* group, especially by Bourne who viewed Freud's and Jung's work as an aid to understanding personal and social problems. Words such as repression appear frequently in his essays attacking puritanism. Bourne was also partly responsible for introducing Brooks to psychology, yet the effect of Freud on the latter's writing really did not materialize until after 1917. Another *Seven Arts* writer influenced by Freud was the novelist Waldo Frank, who first discovered psychoanalysis about 1913 and was particularly drawn to the subject because it explained the secrets of human behavior. His first novel, *The Unwelcome Man* (1917), and *Our America* (1919) use Freudian terms to attack provincialism and show the effect of psychoanalytic theory. As in the case of Brooks, Freud's and Jung's work continued to be an important influence on his later writing.[30]

Jung had attended the 1909 Clark University symposium and made a second visit to the United States in 1912 when he delivered a series of lectures at Fordham University. Jung's presence in the city at this time stimulated interest in his ideas. Some participants must have met him when he also spoke at the Liberal Club. Because many social critics were dedicated to forging a new national arts and letters expressive of American society, Jung's research into the psychic origins of creative instincts and the mythological roots of indigenous culture carried great appeal. Untermeyer called Jung's *Psychology of the Unconscious* "the greatest contribution to the history of thought that our generation has produced," while Dell praised it as "a profound and valuable work." [31]

The importance Jung gave to unconscious racial elements in the creative process also appealed to James Oppenheim. *The Seven Arts'* editor had been treated by Dr. Beatrice Hinkle, a Jungian analyst, who translated the 1916 edition of Jung's *Psychology of the Unconscious.* Although *The Seven Arts* rarely mentioned Jung's name, his ideas were implied in the periodical's call for a new indigenous arts and letters directly related to the American experience. Emerson, Whitman, and contemporary European cultural movements influenced the staff, but the ideas of Jung also lurked behind Oppenheim's editorial pronouncements. The writer's prewar poetry on such themes as racial consciousness, the Oedipus complex, and the psychoanalytic conversion experience reflected a similar interest. After World War I he became a professional Jungian analyst and published three books on psychology.[32]

The social critics thus used the new psychology, as they did many other ideas, to overturn outdated tradition in many areas of American life. As a group they were extremely conscious of the inhibiting factors in society preventing personal and artistic freedom. The Villagers, however, were never wild bohemians but serious rebels with a strong sense of moral commitment to social and artistic change. Freud's ideas justified their social criticism and confirmed their belief that a less provincial society was more conducive to artistic creativity. Jung's theories also inspired *The Seven Arts'* cultural nationalists to call for a new indigenous art and literature. Taking both a humorous, serious, and positive approach, the writers popularized the new psychology in their work and prepared the way for the wider dissemination of psychoanalysis during the next decade.

NOTES

1. Floyd Dell, *Homecoming* (New York: Farrar & Rinehart, Inc., 1933), pp. 245-46; Louis Untermeyer, *From Another World, The Autobiography of Louis Untermeyer* (New York: Harcourt, Brace and Company, 1939), p. 42.

2. Caroline F. Ware, *Greenwich Village 1920-1930, A Comment on American Civilization in the Post-War Years* (New York: Harper Colophon, 1965), pp. 94-95; Charles Grand Pierre, *Rambling Through Greenwich Village* (New York: Greenwich Village Weekly News, 1935), p. 29; Anna Alice Chapin, *Greenwich Village* (New York: Dodd, Mead & Company, Inc., 1917), p. 294; Frederick C. Howe, *Confessions of a Reformer* (New York: Charles Scribner's Sons, 1925), pp. 240-41; Malcolm Cowley, *Exile's Return, A Literary Odyssey of the 1920's* (New York: Compass Books, 1965), pp. 59-61.

3. See Albert Parry, *Garrets and Pretenders* (New York: Dover Publications, Inc., 1960), pp. 268-69; Edmund T. Delaney, *New York's Greenwich Village* (Barre, Mass.: Barre Publishers, 1968), p. 107; Harold E. Stearns, *The Street I Know* (New York: Lee Furman, 1935), pp. 99, 126; Hutchins Hapgood, *A Victorian in the Modern World* (New York: Harcourt, Brace and Company, Inc., 1939), p. 358; Jo Davidson, *Between Sittings, An Informal Autobiography of Jo Davidson* (New York: Dial Press, 1951), p. 126; Louis Sheaffer, *O'Neill, Son and Playwright* (Boston: Little, Brown and Company, 1968), pp. 332-35.

4. Quoted from a newspaper article by Hutchins Hapgood, entitled "A Promoter of Spirit" in "Scrapbook of Articles on Mabel Luhan," Mabel Dodge Luhan Collection, Beinecke Library, Yale University. For a description of Luhan's villa see Gertrude Stein, *The Autobiography of Alice B. Toklas* (New York: Modern Library Paperback, n.d.), pp. 129-35; Gertrude Stein, "Portrait of Mabel Dodge at the Villa Curonia," *Camera Work,* special no. (1913), 3-5. Her Greenwich Village apartment is described in Mabel Dodge Luhan, *Intimate Memoirs,* vol. 3: *Movers and Shakers* (New York: Harcourt, Brace and Company, 1936), p. 8.

5. *Movers and Shakers,* p. 83.

6. William Zorach, *Art Is My Life* (New York: World Publishing Co., 1967), passim; Orrick Johns, *Time of Our Lives; The Story of My Father and Myself* (New York: Stackpole Sons, 1937), pp. 217-19. Alyse Gregory, "Randolph Bourne, Life and Selected Letters," unpublished MS., Beinecke Library, Yale University; her autobiography, *The Day is Gone* (New York: E. P. Dutton & Co., Inc., 1948), passim; Jerome Mellquist and Lucie Wiese, eds., *Paul Rosenfeld, Voyager in the Arts* (New York: Creative Age Press, 1948), p. 23.

7. Lawrence Langner, *The Magic Curtain* (New York: E. P. Dutton & Co., Inc., 1951), pp. 67-73; Gregory, *The Day Is Gone,* p. 99; Hapgood, p. 277; Charles Grand Pierre, *The Legend of Free Love in Greenwich Village, A Badly Misinterpreted Phase of the Fascinating History of Its Bohemia* (New York: Greenwich Village News, 1937), p. 4; and his *Rambling Through Greenwich Village,* p. 40; Parry, pp. 269-72; Keith Norton Richwine, "The Liberal Club: Bohemia and the Resurgence in Greenwich Village, 1912-1918," Ph.D. dissertation, Department of American Civilization, University of Pennsylvania, 1968.

8. Quoted from a Liberal Club letterhead found on a piece of stationery in the Mabel Dodge Luhan Collection, Beinecke Library, Yale University; Langner, *The Magic Curtain,* p. 72.

9. Zorach, p. 54; Parry, p. 277; Lloyd Morris, *Incredible New York, High Life and Low Life of the Last Hundred Years* (New York: Bonanza Books, 1951), p. 308; Richard Drinnon, *Rebel in Paradise, A Biography of Emma Goldman* (Chicago: University of Chicago Press, 1961), pp. 147-48.

10. *New York World,* December 27, 1914; clipping found in the "Stuart Davis Scrapbook," Archives of American Art, New York City, N.Y.

11. Parry, pp. 275-77; Delaney, pp. 106-7; Arthur Young, *On My Way: Being the Book of Art Young in Text and Picture* (New York: Liveright Publishing, 1928), pp. 127-29; as well as John Sloan's account in "Comments on Etchings (1945)"–an unpublished MS. in the John Sloan Trust, Delaware Art Center, Wilmington, Delaware.

12. Guido Bruno, "Little Talks by the Editor," *Greenwich Village,* I (January 20, 1915),`5; Hippolyte Havel, "The Spirit of the Village," *Greenwich Village,* I (January 20, 1915), 1-2.

13. John Reed, *The Day in Bohemia* (New York; privately printed, 1913), p. 49.

14. Dell, *Homecoming,* p. 272; Floyd Dell, "The Rise of Greenwich Village" and "The Fall of Greenwich Village" in *Love in Greenwich Village* (New York: George H. Doran Company, 1926).

15. Floyd Dell, "Alcoholiday," *The Masses,* VIII (June 1916), 30; *Homecoming,* p. 148.

16. Max Eastman, *Enjoyment of Living* (New York: Harper & Brothers, 1948), pp. 417-18; *Love and Revolution; My Journey Through an Epoch* (New York: Random House, Inc., 1964), p. 4.

17. Letter of Randolph Bourne to Esther Cornell, August 10, 1917, in the Bourne Collection, Columbia University, New York City.

18. H. L. Mencken, "Our Literary Centers," in *H. L. Mencken's Smart Set Criticism,* ed. William H. Nolte (Ithaca: Cornell University Press, 1968), p. 12 (first published in *The Smart Set,* November 1920).

19. See John C. Burnham, "Psychoanalysis in American Civilization before 1918," unpublished Ph.D. dissertation, Stanford University, 1958, passim; F. H. Matthews, "The Americanization of Sigmund Freud: Adaptations of Psychoanalysis before 1917," *Journal of American Studies,* I (April 1967), 39-62; Celar B. Slender, "New Ideas for Old: How Freudianism Was Received in the United States from 1900-1925," *Journal of Education Psychology,* XXXVIII (April 1947), 193-206; Frederick J. Hoffman, *Freudianism and the Literary Mind* (Baton Rouge: Louisiana University Press, 1945), passim; Nathan Hale, *Freud and the Americans, The Beginnings of Psychoanalysis in the United States, 1876-1917* (New York: Oxford University Press, 1971), pp. 397-404.

20. A. A. Brill, "The Introduction and Development of Freud's Work in the United States," *American Journal of Sociology,* XLV (November 1939), 323.

21. Max Eastman, *Great Companions: Critical Memoirs of Some Famous Friends* (New York: Farrar, Straus & Cudahy, 1959), p. 172.

22. Max Eastman, "A New Journal," *The Masses,* V (April 1914), 9; "Exploring the Soul and Healing the Body," *Everybody's Magazine,* XXXII (June 1915), 741-50; "Mr. Er-Er-Er Oh! What's His Name?," *Everybody's Magazine,* XXXIII (July 1915), 95-103.

23. Sherwood Anderson, *Sherwood Anderson's Memoirs* (New York: Harcourt, Brace and Company, Inc., 1942), p. 243.

24. Floyd Dell, "Speaking of Psychoanalysis: The New Boon for Dinner Table Conversationalists," *Vanity Fair,* V (December 1915), p. 53.

25. See *Homecoming,* pp. 291-94; Floyd Dell, *Love in the Machine Age* (New York: Farrar & Rinehart, Inc., 1930).

26. Barnes's cartoon appeared in *The Masses,* IX (October 1917), 22. *Suppressed Desires* is published in George Cram Cook and Frank Shay, eds. *The Provincetown Plays* (New York: D. Appleton & Company, Inc., 1921), pp. 11-44.

27. Walter Lippmann, *A Preface to Politics* (New York: Ann Arbor Paperback, 1962), pp. 42, 60 (first published New York, 1913).

28. Alfred Booth Kuttner, "A Note on Forgetting," *New Republic* I (February 28, 1914), 15-17; "The Artist," *The Seven Arts,* I (February 1917), 406-12; "The Artist (A Communication)," *The Seven Arts,* I (March 1917), 549-52.

29. Quoted from "The Advent of Psychoanalysis" in *H. L. Mencken's Smart Set Criticism,* p. 148.

30. See the use Bourne makes of sublimation in his article ".The Puritan's Will to Power," in *The Seven Arts,* I (April 1917), 631-37. On Brooks see his autobiography, *Days of the Phoenix, The Nineteen-Twenties I Remember* (New York: E. P. Dutton & Co., Inc., 1957), p. 21; Claire Sprague's introduction to *Van Wyck Brooks, The Early Years, A Selection from His Works, 1908-1921* (New York: Harper Torchbooks, 1968), pp. x-xi; William Wasserstrom, *Van Wyck Brooks* (Minneapolis: University of Minnesota Press, 1968), pp. 23-25. On Frank see Waldo Frank, "Sigmund Freud," *Virginia Quarterly Review,* X (October 1934), 529-39; Paul J. Carter, *Waldo Frank* (New York: Twayne Publishers, 1967), pp. 27-29; Hoffman, pp. 260-62.

31. Louis Untermeyer, "Twenty Books," *The Masses,* VIII (June 1916), 3; Floyd Dell, "The Science of the Soul," *The Masses,* VIII (July 1916), 30-31. See Dr. C. G. Jung, *Psychology of the Unconscious, A Study of the Transformation and Symbolism of the Libido,* trans. Dr. Beatrice M. Hinkle (New York: Moffat, Yard, 1916).

32. For a sample of Oppenheim's poetry see *War and Laughter* (New York, 1916) and *The Book of the Self* (New York, 1917). Oppenheim's books on psychology were *The Psychology of Jung* (Gerard, Ks.: Haldeman, 1925); *Behind Your Front* (New York: Harper & Brothers, 1928); *American Types: A Preface to Analytic Psychology* (New York: Alfred A. Knopf, Inc., 1931).

CHAPTER SIX

Feminism

Like their belief in the new psychology, educational reform, and socialism, the social critics' adherence to the women's rights movement was motivated by a desire to change the nature of American society and culture. Militant feminism, they felt, challenged the strict morality of nineteenth-century sexual standards and struck at the foundations of genteel culture. They viewed the past century's literature and art as sentimental and restrictive in subject matter. According to most painters and writers, artistic creativity and personal happiness derived from the uninhibited expressions of the emotions. Some participants consequently joined the feminist bandwagon hoping to end the restrictions society placed on the arts and sexual relationships.

Feminism was a popular issue during the prewar years and a time of change in women's rights and morality. With its many women's rights organizations, New York City was an important center of the suffrage movement. Here many feminists took a militant position that went well beyond the question of the vote by demanding complete economic and social equality. Although freer sexual standards did not become widespread until the 1920s, a change in morals occurred during the prewar period, particularly in wealthy urban society. The Victorian precepts governing women's role in marriage, the home, and the family were also gradually breaking down. Partly responsible for this development was the country's increased urbanization and industrialization permitting more leisure time and economic opportunity for women. Disgruntled with her role as housewife and consumer, many women became increasingly independent of men by gaining employment outside the home. During the prewar period the sacrosanct institution of marriage began to be questioned, and divorce rates increased dramatically. Women sometimes smoked and drank in public, defied convention by wearing a tight slit "hubble skirt," and danced such suggestive dances as the Turkey Trot, Bunny Hug, and Grizzly Bear. Thus the artists' and writers' call for a freer morality was part of a growing contemporary development.[1]

The radicals' commitment to the feminist cause was integrally related to their Socialist beliefs. Certain left-wing feminists, influenced by the writing of Friedrich Engels and August Bebel, viewed marriage as an economic institution exploiting women and attacked capitalism for perpetuating sexual inequality through the patriarchial system. Although the Socialist party supported women suffrage and ran women candidates for office, most moderate Socialists were hesitant to support changes in morality. More militant in this respect was Emma Goldman, who criticized marriage as an institution exploiting women as property and urged free love based on mutual equality. Participants who were attracted to anarchism and left-wing socialism were generally supporters of feminism.

A major voice of radical feminism during the Little Renaissance was *The Masses* magazine. The editors printed feminist articles attacking the double standard, discriminatory divorce laws, and job discrimination. During 1915 they issued a woman's citizen number containing essays by Dell and Eastman backing woman suffrage. Stuart Davis portrayed a woman riding a subway on the issue's cover (Fig. 8) and poked fun at antisuffragists in three other illustrations. One cartoon by Maurice Becker criticized the image of the "doll-baby" glamour girl by depicting a pseudo-sophisticated society woman at the dressmaker.[2]

Dell was among the most dedicated feminists on *The Masses*. His interest in women's rights had first developed in Chicago literary circles, where, Dell remembered, "feminism was in the air as well as in my mind—men and women were thinking about it, and eager to read about it. The criticism of existing society in literature, which had gone some distance along economic lines, was turning toward sexual arrangements." The influential works of Edward Carpenter, Ellen Key, and Havelock Ellis arguing for women's independence and a freer morality stimulated his desire to support the feminist movement. While in Chicago he began to write a series of newspaper articles on important feminists and woman reformers, which were published in book form in 1913.

Fig. 8. Woman's Citizenship Number, *The Masses* (November 1915).
Reproduced by permission of The Huntington Library, San Marino,
California.

These biographical sketches praised the whole spectrum of the women's rights movement from Jane Addams to Emma Goldman and proved that the author was an avid male feminist before coming to New York.[3]

In Manhattan's radical circles Dell's feminism became more militant. He spoke and debated at suffrage meetings and actively backed Margaret Sanger's birth control movement. Once after visiting an antisuffrage office, he wrote a humorous article for *The Masses* poking fun at the "antis." Dell's support of suffrage was partly based on the idea that women's involvement in politics would make her a more wordly companion for men. Women's liberation, he argued, would end tedious dull marriages in which wives were confined to the home. Socialism and feminism were viewed as copartners in the struggle for economic and sexual changes. The feminist movement, he asserted, was a "revolt of women and men against the type of women created by . . . [economic] conditions." In *Love in the Machine Age* (1930), Dell later interpreted marriage as an economic institution and blamed capitalism for perpetuating repressive moral standards and outdated patriarchal family arrangements.[4]

Another active male feminist on *The Masses* was Eastman, who once called the women suffrage movement "the big fight for freedom in my time." Family influence played a strong role in first attracting him to the feminist cause. He greatly admired his mother, who, as a Congregational minister and educator, epitomized the successful independent professional woman. The editor was also very close to his sister Crystal and no doubt her activities drew him into the feminist movement. As a result Eastman made *The Masses* a leading voice of left-wing feminism and contributed editorials and articles in the magazine backing woman suffrage. As cofounder and secretary of the New York Men's League for Woman Suffrage, he also wrote pamphlets, spoke at suffrage meetings, and marched in parades.[5]

Eastman's arguments for women's rights derived from the ideas of democratic egalitarianism and Socialist thought. Like many suffragettes, he insisted that denying women the ballot was undemocratic and violated the country's traditional principles of equality. Eastman insisted that the vote would make women more responsible citizens and an interesting companion, and that their increasing employment outside the home demanded political representation. He also lashed out at genteel society's false ideals of woman-hood and attacked the double standard. He criticized the antisuffragists for arguing that women's involvement in politics would destroy their virtue. Why, he asked, does society idealize women's purity while allowing men sexual freedom? What society needed were sexual relationships based on equality rather than hypocrisy.[6]

In the pages of *The Masses* the editor praised Margaret Sanger's efforts in arguing "clearly and quietly for popular education in the means of preventing conception." Noticing that the publication and dissemination of birth control material violated obscenity laws, Eastman declared that if Sanger "goes to court in this fight, we must go too and stand behind her and make her martyrdom—if martyrdom it must be—the means of that very publicity she is fighting to win." On another occasion he protested her husband's arrest for distributing birth control literature. Linking the struggle for birth control with the Socialist movement, Eastman suggested that the population explosion caused poverty and took away the worker's propensity for revolt:

> The unskilled worker is never free, but an unskilled worker with a large family of half-starving children *cannot even fight for freedom.* That for us is the connection between birth control and the working class struggle. Workingmen and women ought to be able to feed and rear the children they want—that is the end we are seeking. But the way to that end is a fight; a measure of working-class independence is essential to that fight; and birth control is a means to such independence.[7]

One reason *The Masses* staff supported birth control was because they were personally acquainted with Margaret Sanger. She and her husband William, an architect and painter, entertained Socialist intellectuals and creative writers and artists at their uptown Manhattan apartment. Mrs. Sanger avidly read *The Masses,* attended the Luhan salon, and was associated with the Modern School. As a member of the Socialist party she was involved in the same radical movements as the participants. Her first articles on sexual hygiene and population control were serialized in the Socialist *New York Call* during 1912 and 1913, and her magazine *The Woman Rebel,* published during 1914, exuded a rebellious anarchistic tone that reflected the mood of the Little Renaissance. Articles on birth control, women's emancipation, and radicalism appeared in the fiery journal, which was eventually suspended by the Post Office for its "obscene" material.

The participants rallied to Sanger's defense because the birth control issue also revolved around the question of free speech and dissent. Feeling that the suppression of birth control information was unjust censorship, Dell spoke out against laws preventing the dissemination of literature. He believed he had a moral right to give out such information and informed readers where to obtain material on population control. Dell had no second thoughts concerning this action: "My law-breaking was in accordance with the implicit oath which I had taken as a rebel against tyranny, it made America a little better, and it gained me only the approval of my conscience." *The Masses* also advertised Sanger's pamphlets, and helped raise money to defend her husband when he was arrested for distributing literature. Reed also wrote an article denouncing Margaret Sanger's arrest and criticizing the censorship of her ideas. When Emma Goldman was arrested for lecturing on birth control he spoke on her behalf at a Carnegie Hall protest meeting. Thus Reed and Dell advocated birth control partly because it was related to the value of individual freedom.[8]

The New Republic magazine joined *The Masses* in backing birth control and suffrage, but the editors of the liberal reform journal stated their arguments in a more moderate progressive framework. A special supplement in 1915 devoted to woman suffrage urged that giving women the vote was an extension of the democratic process. Herbert Croly, the editor, represented their opinion that suffrage would make women better citizens and "add to the bonds of passion and affection the bond of a joint responsibility for the political welfare of society." Lippmann was the most dedicated moderate feminist among *The New Republic* writers. In *A Preface to Politics,* the author stated that feminism should be seen not only in terms of political representation but also as a realignment of sexual and economic relationships. Women "are looking for a readjustment of their relations to the home, to work, to children, to man, to the interests of civilized life," he declared. The following year, in *Drift and Mastery,* Lippmann's idealism seemed to wane as he criticized the feminist movement for having irresponsible leadership and slipshod planning. Turning to a more conservative viewpoint, he suggested that women were better off at home than in offices or factories, but he still believed that they could no longer be dominated by men and treated as second-class citizens.[9]

Unlike Lippmann, Bourne's dedication to the feminist movement was based more on an emotional commitment. His interest in women's rights began when he became excited by the English suffrage movement in Europe and attended feminist meetings in Paris. Discovering that the French were less hypocritical in sexual relationships, Bourne wrote home that "American attitudes toward women were so belittling . . . and so far from the genuine instinctive feeling of equality, which I should think should be the possession of every modern man or women." Upon his return he wrote a nostalgic sketch of a beautiful French student he had met in Paris, a feminist and a symbol of youth. In New York, he made friends with several radical women who swayed him to their cause. Bourne thrived on friendships with the opposite sex, writing once that woman was a "heaven-sent companion and the blessedest gift of the gods." According to the social critic, America was dominated by men and their materialism; women, he felt, could assuage male competitiveness through their innate sensitivity and understanding. Bourne also spoke out for equal economic opportunity for women and such measures as divorce and birth control. In one unpublished essay he protested a discriminatory law segregating men and women on New York's ferryboats. Bourne also once thought of writing a book on American women, but he never completed the project.[10]

Mencken was another participant interested in the subject of feminism. His book, *In Defense of Women* (1918), criticized outdated moral standards and society's idealistic view of women. Looking at women honestly he hoped would make "men . . . consider them anew, not as romantic political and social invalids, to be coddled and caressed, but as free competitors in a harsh world." According to the author, women's innate intelligence and aesthetic sense made them far superior to men, who, by contrast, were naive and sentimental. He accused men of exploiting the female sex and appreciating women only "in proportion as she is dependent." The institution of marriage was a lot of "romantic fol-de-rol," a form of barter in which the female exchanges "her sexual charm for a lion's share in the earnings of one man." More often than not a husband never lives up to his wife's ideals, and she ends up either hating or pitying him. The married man, on the other hand, sells his life for domesticity and regimentation. Since monogamy destroys passion and love, he advised his readers to remain bachelors, a state in which one is free from the "sentimentalism of his sex." [11]

Despite his attack on sexual stereotypes and roles, Mencken had an ambivalent attitude towards the feminist movement. Women suffrage would bring a measure of rational intelligence into political life, he declared, and mark the "real beginning of an improvement in our politics, and, in the end, in our whole theory of government." He accused the suffragettes, however, of being obsessed with their cause, sexually frustrated, and envious of men. As for birth controllers, they were "simply women who have done their utmost to snare men, and failed." The feminist movement also caused women to shirk their duties as competent housewives. The conservative Mencken was obviously not ready to grant women complete emancipation from domestic responsibilities. More important to him was a freer morality and an end to sexual repression. Women, he declared, still "suffer from a suppressed revolt against the inhibitions forced upon them by our artificial culture." Virginity before marriage was a hypocritical double standard; premarital sex, by contrast, was educational. Mencken's lively work linked the issue of women's rights to the outdated genteel tradition.[12]

The participants felt that most nineteenth-century literature avoided the subject of sex and tried to preserve the image of women's purity. A more honest open attitude towards sexual relationships would reduce censorship and permit more freedom of expression. Dell once noted that the subjects of fiction were changing because nineteenth-century morals were gradually breaking down.[13] Novelists such as Dreiser, he commented, were unafraid to treat sex openly in their work. The view that women's emancipation would lead to a more honest American literature was another important reason why so many participants supported the feminist crusade.

The new modern woman often appeared as the major protagonist in Little Renaissance writing. Neith Boyce, the wife of Hutchins Hapgood, wrote many stories concerning tragic heroines who fail to find satisfying sexual relationships based on mutual equality. The independent woman searching for self-identity was often a central character in Susan Glaspell's plays. Male novelists were likewise fascinated with the topic of the liberated woman. Oppenheim's *Idle Wives* (1914) concerns the self-sufficient wife who demands her right to work outside the home, while Alfred Kreymborg's novella *Edna Vitek* (1914) depicts an independent woman who refuses to marry any of her lovers. Just before his death, Bourne was planning an autobiographical novel, contrasting an honest relationship of youthful lovers with the "scruples and righteous hypocrisies of the older generation." [14]

The subject of free love and modern marriage was taken up by Dell in several one-act plays and novels. He wrote, "The Village quite understood this attitude; it wanted its most serious beliefs mocked at; it enjoyed laughing at its own convictions." Despite their humor, the plays suggest that free love, sexual freedom, and tolerance of extramarital affairs were difficult to practice in reality. His heroes and heroines preach feminism, but when it comes to acting out their beliefs jealousy often intervenes. The plays reveal that moral qualms often tempered or even shattered the feminists' ideals. After the war Dell turned to writing numerous novels depicting "the break-up of the old patriarchal family institution in contemporary America." Although he wrote these novels after 1917, their plots often take place in the prewar period when feminism was at its height. *The Briary Bush* (1921), for example, is about the breakup of a modern marriage due to jealousy and incompatibility. The new independent woman rebelling against small-town morality is the subject of *Janet March* (1923) and *This Mad Ideal* (1925). Dell might admire the new woman, but he basically feared the consequences of her independence, and many novels end with the heroine adjusting to society through marriage and domesticity. Their conclusions show the effects of Dell's psychoanalysis and his postwar conservatism.[15]

Another familiar figure in Little Renaissance writing was the prostitute. Most radical artists and writers denounced the practice as a manifestation of the double standard and sympathetically viewed her as a victim of the capitalist system. *The Masses* staff attacked the white slave traffic by dramatizing her predicament in words and pictures. One drawing by Art Young suggested that there was direct relationship between prostitution and "Commercial Greed." (See Fig.2.) The prostitute as both victim and hero was depicted in Untermeyer's poem "Any City" and Reed's moving short story, *A Daughter of the Revolution*. When Sloan attended a trial of streetwalkers at a police night court, he became indignant over the way they were mistreated and sentenced indiscriminately. A drawing depicting his experience blamed society for both causing and penalizing the practice of prostitution. One solution to the problem, according to *The Masses'* contributors, was less covert restrictions on sexual relations.[16]

The new woman who defied genteel society was celebrated in the Little Renaissance community. One of the most popular figures was the dancer Isadora Duncan. Sloan was captivated by her exhilarating personality and once drew her dancing the "Marche Militaire" for *The Masses* (Fig. 9). Dell called her performance "terrific and blinding; it recreated the soul anew with its miraculous loveliness, the loveliness of youth and joy. . . . It is not enough to throw God from his pedestal, and dream of superman and the co-operative

Fig. 9. John Sloan, *Isadora Duncan in the "Marche Militaire," The Masses* (May 1915). Courtesy, Tamiment Library, New York University, New York City.

commonwealth: one must have *seen* Isadora Duncan to die happily." Duncan represented to the participants such prewar ideals as women's emancipation, sexual liberation, artistic freedom, and political protest. Her expressive dancing to revolutionary songs and her love of Greek civilization perfectly matched the era's political rebellion and mood.[17]

Greenwich Village was the home of "the new woman" who was active in the militant feminist movement and in her own private life demanded respect and independence. A good representative was the high school teacher Henrietta Rodman, who wore bobbed hair and dressed in sandals and a "meal-sack" gown. A radical feminist and disciple of Charlotte Gilman, Rodman attacked the New York City Board of Education for discriminating against the hiring of married women teachers and prohibiting maternity leaves. She also organized the Feminist Alliance in 1914 to fight for equality in all areas of American life. Her pet project was the establishment of a large cooperative apartment house with a communal kitchen and a child-care center.

Two other important radical feminists in the Village were Crystal Eastman and Ida Rauh. Crystal, the sister of Max Eastman, was a multitalented professional woman dedicated to social reform. A lawyer-sociologist by profession, she was hired by governmental agencies to investigate factory hazards in Pittsburg and to help write New York's workmen's compensation law. As an active member of the National American Woman Suffrage Association, she managed the 1911 suffrage amendment campaign in Wisconsin. Influenced by Gilman and Socialist politics, her concept of equal rights for women went well beyond the vote. She later joined Alice Paul's more militant Congressional Union and cofounded the New York Woman's Peace Party. Crystal's sister-in-law, Ida Rauh, who married Max Eastman in 1911, was another Socialist-feminist. She was actively involved in the birth control movement and once was arrested in Union Square for distributing a pamphlet on family planning. Rauh, Eastman, and Rodman supported legal means such as an equal rights amendment to improve women's status. They also shared the feeling that sexual roles were economically and culturally determined, and that full equality would occur only through a Socialist revolution and a new consciousness on the part of American men.[18]

Another important representative of the new woman was Mabel Dodge Luhan. Her attire and bobbed hair gave her the appearance of a liberated woman well before the 1920s (Fig. 10). She worshiped the qualities of intuition and will

Fig. 10. Mabel Dodge Luhan. Courtesy, Collection of American Literature, Beinecke Rare Book and Manuscript Library, Yale University,
New Haven, Connecticut.

power largely because of her admiration for Bergson and Nietzsche. Once she concluded an article on the role of women with these stirring lines:

> Melt, You Women!
> Melt to August–grow ON and Ripen
> Give Yourselves Up!
> That is the only way to be Alive,
> That is what you want, isn't it?
> To be alive?
> Life lies in The Change,
> Try it and see.[19]

Her flamboyant personality made her the most captivating femme fatale in Little Renaissance circles.

Her vivacious emotional qualities and insatiable appetite for life both attracted and repelled her friends and lovers. Married four times, she divorced her second husband Edwin Dodge because he was "an insulator that stood between me and a new fire of life" and "blocked my growth and my need for new ideas." Her third husband, the artist Maurice Sterne, found her passionate, self-indulgent, vindictive, and extremely jealous. He described her eyes as

> cool, dark gray pools, shaded with long black lashes. They reflected her complex emotions spontaneously and honestly, they could flare up with fury, be lucid with pleasure, or glow with rapture. But I loathed their flashes of cruelty. There was something inhuman in that particular look of hers! In contrast, her voice was like a viola, soft, caressing, mellow, with confidential overtones.

Luhan's stormy love affair with Reed was a subject of constant gossip. Her domineering personality caused Reed to tell Hutchins Hapgood that "Mabel is wonderful, I love her, but she suffocates me, I can't breathe." In his poem "Epitaph for Mabel," he called her a "keen, cold, amorous" woman always demanding continuous change and excitement.[20]

Reed's love affair eventually went sour suggesting that the participants' attraction to liberated women often decreased rather than increased their enthusiasm for the feminist cause. The male Villagers wanted honest sexual relationships, but often they discovered that militant feminists refused to be confined to one permanent relationship and if married wanted complete independence. According to Dell, there was an inseparable difference between male feminists like himself who wanted a mutual companionship and radical female feminists who thought this was another form of inferiority. This attitude among ultrafeminists eventually made Dell less interested in supporting women's rights. The male feminists might argue for women's independency as an ideal but once involved in a relationship they discovered that their ideas of free love and mutuality were difficult to practice.

The male feminists sometimes accused the liberated woman of being anti-masculine. Because of Bourne's emotional commitment and romantic view of the female sex, he was especially vulnerable to disenchantment with the women's rights movement. Bourne experienced a crisis when he became romantically involved with a Greenwich Village feminist who wanted complete independence from any emotional and serious relationship with men. Angry and hurt, he called her a "life denying woman, who in the name of a career and her pride and the sacred independence of woman destroys not only you but herself." He then wrote a vicious portrait of a "woman's woman" who hates men and marriage. The problem was that the male and female feminists were at odds over goals. The new woman looked on the women's rights movement as a serious struggle demanding full commitment, while to the less dedicated male Villagers it was only one of many reforms in the fight for social change.[21]

Although the participants often demanded free love, they were never a licentious group. What they meant by this term was not unlimited sexual license but a mutual comraderie based on the ideals of equality and honesty. Many sought one enduring relationship rather than a series of light love affairs. A sexual attachment was not viewed as a fling but as a serious involvement representing personal values. No doubt some Village artists and writers had mistresses. O'Neill carried on a relationship with Reed's wife while *The Masses* writer was recovering from a kidney operation in a hospital. Unbeknown to anyone, the painter Arthur Davies lived a double life as a married man and keeper of a mistress. Many couples lived together for economic reasons sharing food and rent, while others married because they found living together an uncomfortable situation.

The participants' love affairs were often consummated in marriage. Once Luhan took a stranger as a lover in order to find out if sexual freedom really worked in practice but she was repulsed by the thought of having relations with him. Sterne referred to his wife as

a very respectable bourgeois, though like an impulsive adolescent in rebellion against custom mainly because of exhibitionism. However, when the initial impetus was spent, she always had middle-class scruples about her misdemeanors *against convention.* This is why her love affairs eventually had to be sanctified. She felt she had to pay her debt to society by marriage, like a good Buffalo Christian.

Luhan's case was not exceptional for after living together with Louise Bryant for a year Reed insisted that they marry. Eastman once wrote that marriage was "utterly romantic" and "'husband' and 'wife' among the most distasteful words in the language." Despite his progressive views, he married Ida Rauh in order to placate convention and his parents. Eastman nonetheless called his union a modern marriage, put his wife's maiden name on the mail box, and urged her to pursue a career. Even the most rebellious writers were thus susceptible to social and moral pressures.[22]

Despite an overblown reputation as a Greenwich Village lover, Dell also sought one permanent relationship and avoided light love affairs. He called his relationship with a woman photographer a "companionship of two artists which we knew might not last long, but which we hoped would last forever."[23] Before this affair he had experienced a modern marriage with Margaret Curry, a school teacher, in which both partners treated each other as equals. Despite their liberal views, Dell's extramarital affairs led to a divorce that made him skeptical about freedom in marriage. In 1919, he remarried, and finding himself exceedingly happy began extolling the virtues of matrimony. Although his old feminist friends criticized him for his sudden conservatism, Dell's prewar experience revealed that there were limits to his and the other Villagers' views on sexual liberation. A strong moral conscience thus tempered their feminist beliefs as it had their bohemianism.

The social critics supported the feminist crusade, as they did other movements, partly because it was directly related to their aspirations to create a new culture. Their avid interest in feminism, socialism, bohemianism, progressive education, and the new psychology created a tradition of iconoclastic social criticism that formed a major part of the new literature they were so eager to develop. As a result of this social criticism, the situation for the American artist and writer was much better in 1917 than it was in 1908. By the era's end many critics were remarking that their iconoclasm had been relatively successful. "The rock of ages, in brief, had been blasted for us," proclaimed Lippmann in 1914. "Those who are young to-day are born into a world in which the foundations of the older order survive only as habits or by default." Before he died in 1918, Bourne commented that "the indictment of the Victorian Age . . . has almost driven the Victorian from the field." Contributing to the critics' optimism were current movements in modern poetry, painting, and theater that were overturning genteel aesthetics and creating new forms in the arts that revolutionized American culture.[24]

NOTES

1. James R. McGovern, "The American Woman's Pre-World War I Freedom in Manners and Morals," *Journal of American History,* LV (September 1968), 315-30; Sidney Ditzion, *Marriage, Morals, and Sex in America* (New York: Bookman Associates, 1953), p. 367; Aileen S. Kraditor, *The Ideas of the Woman Suffrage Movement, 1890-1920* (New York: Columbia University Press, 1965), passim; Christopher Lasch, *The New Radicalism in America (1884-1963), The Intellectual as a Social Type* (New York: Vintage Books, 1967), pp. 46-47, 62-65; William L. O'Neill, *Divorce in the Progressive Era* (New Haven, Conn.: Yale University Press, 1967), pp. 20, 89-90, 164, 203, 257-58; William E. Carson, *The Marriage Revolt* (New York: Hearst's International Library, 1913), pp. 34-35; Alan C. Valentine, *1913, America between Two Worlds* (New York: The Macmillan Company, 1962), pp. 75-84.

2. See *The Masses,* VII (October-November 1915). The early *Masses* also had a feminist number in the December 1911 issue.

3. Floyd Dell, *Women as World Builders: Studies in Modern Feminism* (Chicago: Forbes, 1913), p. 55. Dell's 1912 articles appeared in the *Friday Literary Review,* a literary supplement of the *Chicago Evening Post.*

4. Floyd Dell, "Socialism and Feminism," *The New Review* (June 1914), 349. See also Floyd Dell, "Adventures in Anti-Land," *The Masses,* VII (October-November 1915), 5-6; "Feminism for Men," *The Masses,* V (July 1914), 19-20; *Love in the Machine Age* (New York: Farrar & Rinehart, Inc., 1930).

5. Max Eastman, *Enjoyment of Living* (New York: Harper & Brothers, 1948), p. 306. See also Max Eastman, "Confession of a Suffrage Orator," *The Masses,* VIII (October-November 1915), 7-9; "Early History of the Men's League," *The Woman Voter,* III (October 1912), 17-18.

6. Max Eastman, *Is Woman Suffrage Important?* (New York: Men's League for Woman Suffrage, 1912), passim; Max Eastman, *Woman Suffrage and Sentiment* (New York: Equal Franchise Society, 1913), passim.

7. Max Eastman, "The Woman Rebel," *The Masses,* V (May 1914), 5. See also Max Eastman, "Revolutionary Birth Control," *The Masses,* (July 1915), 22; "Is the Truth Obscene?," *The Masses,* VI (March 1915), 5-6; *Enjoyment of Living,* p. 419; Margaret Sanger, *My Fight for Birth Control* (New York: Farrar & Rinehart, Inc., 1931), pp. 80-81.

8. Floyd Dell, *Homecoming* (New York: Farrar & Rinehart, Inc., 1933), p. 253. See also Floyd Dell, "Criminals All," *The Masses,* VI (October-November 1915), 20; John Reed, "Comments on Margaret Sanger's Arrest," [1915?], unpublished MS., Reed Collection, Houghton Library, Harvard University, Cambridge, Massachusetts.

9. Herbert Croly, "The Obligation of the Vote," part II of *The New Republic,* IV (October 9, 1915); Walter Lippmann, *A Preface to Politics* (Ann Arbor: Ann Arbor Paperbacks, 1962, first published New York, 1913), p. 73; *Drift and Mastery: An Attempt to Diagnose the Current Unrest* (Englewood Cliffs, N.J.: Prentice-Hall, Inc., 1961, first published New York, 1914), p. 125.

10. Letter of Randolph Bourne to Alyse Gregory, April 10, 1914, Bourne Collection, Columbia University, New York City, N.Y.; Van Wyck Brooks, *Fenollosa and His Circle* (New York: E. P. Dutton and Co., Inc., 1962), p. 268; "Mon Amie," *Atlantic Monthly,* CXV (March 1915), 354-59; "The Excitement of Friendship," *Youth and Life* (New York: Houghton Mifflin Company, 1913), pp. 135-51; "Sex and Ferryboats," unpublished MS. in the Bourne Collection.

11. H. L. Mencken, *In Defense of Women,* rev. ed. (New York: Garden City Publishing Company, 1922, first published New York, 1918), pp. 189, 47, 90, 66, 84.

12. Ibid., pp. 137, 59, 158.

13. Floyd Dell, "Changes in American Life and Fiction," *The New Review,* III (May 1, 1915), 13-15.

14. Ilse Dusoir, "The History of the *Seven Arts,*" unpublished Master's thesis, New York University, New York City, N. Y., 1940, p. 11; Alfred Kreymborg, *Erna Vitek, The Glebe,* vol. 1, no. 6 (1914). Quoted from Randolph Bourne, "Outline of a Proposed Autobiographical Novel," unpublished MS. dated December 1918 in the Bourne Collection.

15. *Homecoming,* pp. 261, 362; Floyd Dell, *King Arthur's Socks and Other Village Plays* (New York: Alfred A. Knopf, Inc., 1922); *The Briary Bush* (New York: Alfred A. Knopf, Inc., 1921); *Janet March* (New York: Alfred A. Knopf, Inc., 1923); *This Mad Ideal* (New York: Alfred A. Knopf, Inc., 1925).

16. Art Young, "Defeated," *The Masses,* IV (May 1913), 10-11; Louis Untermeyer, "Any City," in William L. O'Neill, ed., *Echoes of Revolt: The Masses 1911-1917* (Chicago: Quadrangle Books, 1966), p. 187; John Reed, "The Daughter of the Revolution," *The Masses* (February 1915); Lloyd Goodrich, *John Sloan* (New York: Whitney Museum of American Art, 1952), pp. 41-44; John Sloan, "Before Her Makers and Her Judge," *The Masses,* IV (August 1913), 11-12.

17. John Sloan, *John Sloan's New York Scene; from the Diaries, Notes, and Correspondence, 1906-1913,* ed. Bruce St. John (New York: Harper & Row, 1965), p. 352; John Sloan, "Isadora Duncan in the 'Marche Militaire,'" *The Masses,* VI (May 1915); Floyd Dell, "Who Said That Beauty Passes Like a Dream," *The Masses,* VIII (October 1916), 27.

18. June Sochen, *The New Woman in Greenwich Village, 1910-1920* (New York: Quadrangle Books, 1972), pp. 11-18, 26-34, 47-60, 65-73, 96-117, 120-25, 141-47.

19. From an untitled article found in a "Scrapbook of Articles by Mabel Luhan," Mabel Dodge Luhan Collection, Beinecke Library, Yale University, New Haven, Conn.

20. Mabel Dodge Luhan, *Intimate Memoirs,* vol. 3: *Movers and Shakers* (New York: Harcourt, Brace and Company, Inc., 1936), p. 13; Maurice Sterne, *Shadow and Light, The Life, Friends, and Opinions of Maurice Sterne,* ed. Charlotte Leon Mayerson (New York: Harcourt, Brace and Company, Inc., 1965), p. 14; Hutchins Hapgood, *A Victorian in the Modern World* (New York: Harcourt, Brace and Company, Inc., 1939), p. 353.

21. Letter of Randolph Bourne to Alyse Gregory, November 19, 1916, in the Bourne Collection; Randolph Bourne [Max Coe], "Karen, a Portrait," *The New Republic,* VIII (September 23, 1916), 187-88.

22. *Shadow and Light,* p. 124; Eastman, *Enjoyment of Living,* pp. 356, 380.

23. *Homecoming,* p. 249.

24. Lippmann, *Drift and Mastery,* p. 16; Randolph Bourne, "An Examination of Eminences," *The Dial,* LXV (December 18, 1918), 603-5.

PART TWO

Modernism:
New Forms in Poetry, Painting, and
Theater

CHAPTER SEVEN

The *Others* Group

"There had been a break somewhere, we were streaming through, each thinking his own thoughts, driving his own designs towards his self's objectives," reminisced William Carlos Williams about the prewar years. "Whether the Armory Show in painting did it or whether that also was no more than a facet—the poetic line, the way the image was to lie on the page was our immediate concern." [1] As Williams suggests, there was a major breakthrough in culture during the Little Renaissance as modern painters and writers began to create new experimental forms in poetry, painting, and drama. Rejecting what they considered to be the old-fashioned literary and artistic standards of the past century, the modernists wanted to forge new styles expressive of the twentieth century. As an aesthetic philosophy and cultural movement, modernism was another manifestation of the participants' revolt against the genteel tradition.

According to the new poets, most nineteenth-century poetry was sentimental and suffered from brooding introspection and noble thoughts. Why, they asked, did a poet have to follow set rules of meter and rhyme and be confined to certain subjects? The modernists found it difficult to publish their work because most magazine editors were reluctant to accept experimental verse. The genteel poetic tradition was represented institutionally by the Poetry Society of America, formed in 1910. On one occasion the experimental poet Alfred Kreymborg was invited by Joyce Kilmer to attend a society meeting and found himself uncomfortable in the staid smug environment. "The whole affair," he wrote, "was as smooth as one of Mr. Howells' editorials in *Harper's,* one of the papers in *The Atlantic Monthly,* one of the sermons of Henry Van Dyke." [2]

In New York and Chicago young poets were revolting against the trite sentimentality and formalities of conventional verse by writing imagist poetry. Amy Lowell defined imagist poetry as a new technique relying on vivid images and clear and colloquial language to describe experience. According to Ezra Pound, the new verse conveyed a sense of spontaneous freedom because of its method of invoking reality through impressions. Imagism thus fit in well with the prewar spirit of individual liberation and emphasis on emotional experience. Most New York poets either went through imagist phases or partly applied the new ideas to their own styles, but poets exclusively devoted to imagism were a rarity in Manhattan, for it was only one technique among many used by the Little Renaissance poets to forge a modern movement. [3]

One of the most prominent figures in New York poetry circles was Wallace Stevens. At this time, Stevens was an insurance company executive in New York, and during nights or on weekends diligently wrote poetry. As an undergraduate at Harvard College, Stevens had published some early verse in the *Advocate,* but not until 1914, at the age of thirty-five, did he begin to find an outlet for his current work. A major breakthrough occurred in September when *Trend* magazine, a commercial current events journal, printed "Carnet de Voyage." *Trend*'s editor, Pitts Sanborn, a classmate of Stevens at Harvard, was no doubt responsible for the publication. Sanborn resigned as editor shortly after the poem's appearance and was replaced by Carl Van Vechten, who had been writing theater criticism for the magazine. Impressed by "Carnet de Voyage," Van Vechten requested Sanborn to ask the author to send more contributions; consequently, the November *Trend* carried two poems by Stevens. [4]

Stevens and Van Vechten soon became members of a small literary coterie which played a major role in the development of modern poetry. The four other members were the poets Walter Arensberg, Donald Evans, Allen Norton, and Kreymborg. Van Vechten called the group a "post-decadent" circle, while Kreymborg referred to them as a "light band of esthetes, satirists, dandies, poets, dilettanti." Attuned philosophically to the spirit of the fin de siècle, they shared an enthusiasm for the work of the French symbolists and the writing of Gertrude Stein. Because of his retiring personality and business interests, Stevens did not share the group's dilettantism, but he was stimulated by their literary interests and work, especially the poetry of Donald Evans. This minor

poet, a close friend of Van Vechten and a copy reader on the *New York Times,*
wrote sonnets that showed the influence of the French symbolists, Oscar Wilde,
and Gertrude Stein. Although Evans's work never matched Stevens's, the
subject matter and color imagery of Evans's poems closely resembles the more
famous poet's work.[5]

In 1915, the coterie founded *Rogue* magazine for the purpose of publishing
their own poetry. Evans and Arensberg had been thinking of a journal for some
time, and when *Trend* magazine folded in late 1914 because of financial
difficulties, Van Vechten joined them in their plans. Although *Rogue* was issued
irregularly only for one year, it had a successful short life. The editor Allen
Norton put a smart-looking checkerboard design on the cover, and published
clever drawings imitative of Aubrey Beardsley and amusing commentaries on
contemporary politics and society. Kreymborg was correct when he wrote that
its flippant satirical tone smacked of the decadent carefree air of the 1890s. The
poetry in *Rogue* was exceptional, especially two contributions by Stevens: "Cy
Est Pourtraicte, Madame Ste Ursule, et Les Unze Mille Vierges" and
"Disillusionment of Ten O'Clock." In the latter poem the poet effectively uses
imagism and color symbolism to capture the banal atmosphere of a small town:

> People are not going
> To dream of baboons and periwinkles,
> Only, here and there, an old sailor
> Drunk and asleep in his boots,
> Catches tigers
> In red weather.

Stevens's connections with the postdecadent group had given him a timely
outlet for his work, and it would eventually lead to further publications.[6]

One of the coterie's most influential members was Alfred Kreymborg. Born
in New York in modest surroundings, the poet had been forced early in his
career to earn a living as a newspaper reporter, a reader for publishing houses,
and as a professional chess player. During leisure hours he wrote experimental
verse plays, novellas, and short imagist poems called *Mushrooms.* The talented
Kreymborg cofounded *The Glebe* magazine whose history is important for
understanding the further development of the New York poetry movement.
The idea for *The Glebe* originated during 1913 when Kreymborg and the modern
painters Man Ray and Samuel Halpert shared a summer cabin in Grantwood,

New Jersey, an attractive suburban artists' colony. Encouraged by the founding of Chicago's *Poetry* magazine, Kreymborg spoke to Ray about his desire to create a New York journal devoted to discovering unknown American writers. Ray urged him to carry out the project and offered to design the first cover, while Kreymborg convinced the Boni brothers to finance the magazine. *The Glebe* was actually a series of inexpensive editions of poems, plays, and novels by relatively unkown writers, what Kreymborg called "one-man shows in the American magazine field." [7]

The first anthology of imagist poetry in America was published under *The Glebe* imprint. The editor had written the poet John Cournos in London asking him to send some contributions to *The Glebe*. Cournos related the request to Pound who promptly forwarded the anthology's manuscript to Kreymborg. The package arrived special delivery and was covered in what "resembled the stout paper butchers use for wrapping meat." Inside was a windfall—"an exotic manifestation of something alive and beautiful," wrote Kreymborg. "Nearly all of the pieces moved without rhyme or a traditional metre." [8] *Des Imagistes, An Anthology* contained important experimental poems by Pound, Richard Aldington, Hilda Doolittle, F. S. Flint, Ford Madox Hueffer, Skipwith Cannéll, Allen Upward, John Cournos, James Joyce, Amy Lowell, and William Carlos Williams. Because the magazine had limited circulation, the anthology failed to popularize the imagist movement, but it was avidly read by a select circle of New York poets and intellectuals. This groundbreaking collection secured *The Glebe*'s reputation as an important magazine in the early development of modern American poetry. The journal, however, had a short existence. Kreymborg wanted to make *The Glebe* strictly a periodical promoting American writing, but the Bonis desired also to publish European literature. As a result of this dispute the editor quit and the journal soon folded.

The quarrel proved beneficial to Kreymborg because he next became connected with a more ambitious project. One afternoon in 1915 he met Stevens and Arensberg in Norton's apartment. The meeting with Arensberg proved prophetic: "A friendship arose which laid the foundation of another experiment in poetry," recalled Kreymborg. Not long after their first meeting, Arensberg suggested to Kreymborg that "what was needed in America was a poetry magazine . . . dedicating its energies to experiment." *Rogue* magazine had its limitations, said Arensberg; it "would never do, couldn't last." He suggested that the new journal "begin with" Wallace Stevens and Mina Loy, while

Kreymborg agreed that these two poets alone "would create the paper we have in mind."[9]

Appointed the new journal's editor, Kreymborg drew up a manifesto: "The old expressions are with us always, and there are always others." The "old" represented outdated genteel literary tradition; "others" stood for the new and experimental. Thus Kreymborg decided "others" would be an appropriate title. The magazine's purpose, the editor declared, was to

> print the work of men and women who were trying themselves in the new forms. A principle of rigid privacy was determined upon. There was to be in no sense of the word a group. Poets as yet unknown were to be asked to submit material alongside poets of repute. There would be no financial inducement for contributing; and the editors had no idea or concern as to whether the paper would sell or not.[10]

Others soon became New York's most important modern poetry journal as crucial to the Little Renaissance as *Poetry* magazine was to the Chicago movement. Issued on a monthly basis from July 1915 to May 1919, *Others* cost fifteen cents a copy and had a subscription list numbering approximately 300 readers. Its contents had a wider circulation due to Alfred A. Knopf, who published two anthologies of the magazine's verse. *Others* offered young poets the opportunity to rally together against poetic tradition and to share a feeling of creative excitement. At first the journal's headquarters were in Grantwood where on Sunday afternoons contributors and friends gathered for a round of picnicking, poetry readings, and engaging conversations on the subjects of modern poetry and painting. These meetings gave the poets and painters a sense of comraderie and feeling of "joyous bewilderment in the discovery that other men and women were working in a field they themselves felt they had chosen in solitude."[11]

The poets in *Others* were given complete freedom to experiment with line, meter, rhyme, and subject matter. Among its most famous contributors were Ezra Pound, T. S. Eliot, Richard Aldington, John Gould Fletcher, Amy Lowell, and Conrad Aiken. Issues were sometimes organized around a particular movement or theme. A Chicago number included poems by Sherwood Anderson and Carl Sandburg; a women's issue featured the work of Harriet Monroe and Hilda Doolittle, while one edition was devoted to the Spectrist

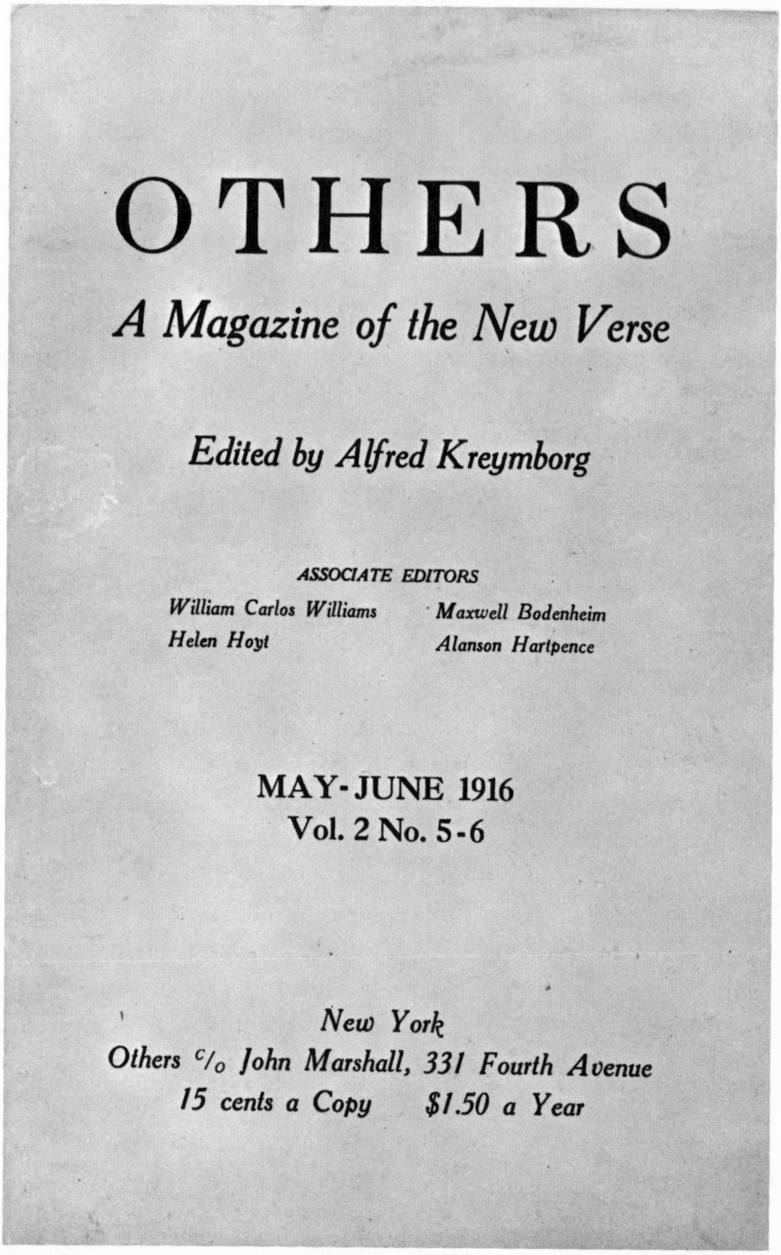

OTHERS

A Magazine of the New Verse

Edited by Alfred Kreymborg

ASSOCIATE EDITORS

William Carlos Williams · *Maxwell Bodenheim*
Helen Hoyt *Alanson Hartpence*

MAY-JUNE 1916
Vol. 2 No. 5-6

New York
Others c/o John Marshall, 331 Fourth Avenue
15 cents a Copy $1.50 a Year

Fig. 11. Cover of *Others* poetry journal. Reproduced by permission of the Huntington Library, San Marino, California.

school of poetry, a group whose main purpose was to parody the imagists. Besides Kreymborg, many minor poets often published in *Others,* including Arensberg, Orrick Johns, Mary Carolyn Davies, Skipwith Cannéll, Helen Hoyt, Maxwell Bodenheim, and Mina Loy. As the most experimental poet in this group, Loy daringly avoided punctuation marks and left spaces between lines.

The founding of *Others* turned out to be an important turning point in Stevens's career. Although he never attended the Grantwood colony's Sunday afternoon meetings, the poet was well acquainted with the *Others* crowd. His main contact with the group came in the city where he drew inspiration from the staff and began to develop self-confidence in his writing. Prompted by his friend Arensberg, who helped finance *Others,* Stevens published eighteen poems in the journal.[12] Among them were some of his best prewar work, including the famous "Peter Quince at the Clavier." Stevens had stuffed the poem into Kreymborg's pocket with the admonition: "I must ask you not to breathe a word about this. Print it if you like, send it back if you don't." [13] "Peter Quince at the Clavier" deals with the theme of physical desire versus aesthetic beauty or reality versus the imagination—a subject that continued to occupy Stevens throughout his career. The fine little epigram "Bowl" and the exquisite "Thirteen Ways of Looking at a Blackbird" also describe the process of artistic creativity. Kreymborg further published "Domination of Black" and "Le Monocle de Mon Oncle," two of Stevens's most successful early poems. Largely due to his poems in *Others,* Stevens was beginning to emerge as a major modern poet by the end of the Little Renaissance.

Others magazines also helped develop William Carlos Williams's reputation as a leading modern poet. The poems in his first published volume were in regular meter and on grandiose themes such as love, God, and beauty, but between 1909 and 1913, Williams's verse slowly began to break loose from the genteel manner. "This was a period of finding a poetry of my own," he remembered. "I wanted order, which I appreciate. The orderliness of verse appealed to me—as it must to any man—but even more I wanted a new order. I was positively repelled by the old order which, to me, amounted to restriction." Under the influence of Pound, he began to experiment with such structural innovations as direct objective short lines, the use of colloquial language and monologue, and letting the line arrangement reflect the poem's rhythm. "I was beginning to turn away from the romantic," he declared. "It may have been my studies in medicine; it may have been my intense feeling of Americanism;

anyhow I know that I wanted reality in my poetry and I began to try to let it speak." [14]

During this important experimental period the poet found an outlet for his avant-garde work in *Others*. Pound had written Kreymborg to contact his friend Williams—"my one remaining pal in America . . . old Bull—he lives in a hole called Rutherford, New Jersey." A practicing physician in this small town outside New York, Williams wrote poetry between medical calls and during the weekends. On Sundays the poet-doctor would drive over to the nearby Grantwood colony in a "battered, two-seated Ford" and "looking like Don Quixote de la Mancha driving the rusty Rosinante." Kreymborg convinced Williams to submit his poetry and also enlisted him to help with the layout work, read manuscripts, and occasionally edit a few issues. "Whenever I wrote at this time, the poems were written with *Others* in mind," Williams admitted. "I made no attempt to get publication anywhere else; the poems were definitely for *Others.*" The magazine was "individually useful to many of us; it gave a hearing to us in the face of the universal refusal to publish and pay for the available new work by young poets. It helped break the ice for further experimentation." [15]

In *Others*, Williams broke away from genteel precedents to find new subject matter in the American scene. One poem concerns a street cleaner—an "old man who goes about / gathering dog lime," and whose walk "is more majestic than / that of the Episcopal minister." In another work Williams describes a dilapidated house with its "yards cluttered / with old chicken wire, ashes." Such objects, he suggests, are a source for poetry and carry an intrinsic beauty. Williams's admiration for uninhibited sensuality is evident in "Danse Russe," in which a husband finding himself alone dances nakedly before a mirror. These poems forecast the themes, subject matter, and technique of his later work.[16]

Others was also an important early outlet for the poetry of Marianne Moore. After teaching for four years in an Indian school in Carlisle, Pennsylvania, she and her mother moved to her brother's house in Chatham, New Jersey, in late 1915 or early 1916. This was an important turning point in her career for now she was living close to New York and could easily associate with the *Others* group. As a young writer she must have drawn inspiration from the editorial staff, who published seven of her poems. Later, she remarked that she was grateful to Kreymborg for doing "all he could to promote me." [17]

Her best poem in *Others*, "Critics and Connoisseurs," was an experiment in subject matter and technique. In the poem she criticizes the "unconscious fastidiousness" of nineteenth-century verse and urges the use of everyday objects as poetic subject matter. Animals would make especially good material, perhaps a pup eating "his meat from the plate" or an "ant carrying a stick north, south." [18] Moore also utilizes several innovative technical devices such as the enumeration of objects, avoidance of capitalization, and the use of conversation. "Critics and Connoisseurs" typified the many fine works published during the Little Renaissance that were inspired by a reaction against outdated standards and in themselves were part of the era's new literature. Compared to Stevens and Williams, her contributions to *Others* were minor, and her total body of prewar work never matched the output of her two colleagues. Her *Others* verse suggested nonetheless that she was beginning to discover her own style by 1917.

Moore, Stevens, and Williams thus broke new ground in poetic form and subject matter during this period. Stevens's work was much more impressionistic than the other two poets, but the three shared much in common. Rejecting the romantic tradition, they used realistic subject matter and were interested in clear precise language. Partly influenced by the imagist movement, they adapted its principles to fit their own unique styles. As a result of their similar poetic interests and association during the prewar years, the trio became close colleagues in the modern poetry movement. After World War I they further increased their reputations as three of America's leading modern poets, but the root of their success dates back to the Little Renaissance and *Others* magazine.

The early work of poets such as Williams, Moore, and Stevens received a hostile reception from both genteel critics and certain participants. For those brought up on the aesthetics of the nineteenth century, modern poetry challenged traditional standards. According to Kreymborg, the first issue of *Others* caused "a small-sized riot. . . . Travesties, bullyragging, every conceivable form of ridicule, appeared far and wide." One angry critic labeled the journal "the little yellow dog." Mencken, who had an ambivalent attitude toward experimental verse, called *Others* a manifestation of superficial Greenwich Village dilettantism. Untermeyer likewise found many selections in *Others* eccentric and criticized Stevens's poetry as overly intellectual. The magazine's "honesty," he complained, "is lost in pages of intellectual pretense where platitudes are unable to disguise themselves as iconoclasm." In *The New Republic*

Lippmann debated Amy Lowell and Leo Stein on the merits of imagism. To Lippmann, modern poetry was second-rate and incomprehensible, reminding him "of the art collections which museums put in the basement." [19]

The new experimental poetry thus created dissension in the Little Renaissance community. Many radical writers felt that the modernists lacked social awareness and were too interested in technique. Although certain Socialists like Dell and Oppenheim defended the new poetry, others such as Eastman had conservative literary tastes and condemned the modern verse as sloppy formless writing. The antimodernists' views were biased because certain new poets like Williams poignantly depicted the problems of urban industrial America. Social realism, however, was not the main objective of the modernists. Although Williams contributed to *The Masses,* he remarked that the magazine "cares little for poetry unless it has some beer stenches upon it." [20] Except for a shared feeling of revolt from the genteel tradition, the era's two movements of socialism and modernism remained aesthetically at odds.

The modern poets, painters, and dramatists, however, found encouragement among themselves because they were a closely knit community participating in similar activities. The Little Renaissance movements in poetry, painting, and the theater were integrally related. Kreymborg, Williams, and Stevens, for example, were involved with the new theater and wrote experimental verse plays. In autumn 1916, the Provincetown Players staged Kreymborg's *Lima Beans,* a one-act "scherzo play" poking fun at marriage. Williams acted in the production while the sculptor William Zorach, who took a small part, helped design the sets and costumes. Because the Provincetown directors were reluctant to stage experimental verse plays, Kreymborg eventually formed his own group called The Other Players but after staging one production they folded because of financial reasons. [21]

Besides their involvement with the avant-garde theater, the *Others* group was closely associated with the modern painting movement. This was not a coincidence since both modern poetry and painting had many similarities. Imagist poets and impressionist painters interpreted their surroundings through the symbolic use of color, while vorticism in poetry and futurism in painting recreated the dynamic technology of the twentieth century. The artists Man Ray, William Zorach, and Marsden Hartley published their poetry in *Others.* Hartley introduced Kreymborg to Alfred Stieglitz's circle of painters at Gallery 291. The poet admired the sense of comradeship among the Stieglitz group and was stimulated by the photographer's charismatic personality. Noticing that the new experimental poetry shared many similarities with modern art, Kreymborg wrote "that the lines of painting and sculpture complemented the lines of music and poetry; that, without drawing needless parallels, one could readily trace a relationship proving that many artists of the age, no matter what their medium, were seeking similar fundamentals and evolving individual forms." Another important link between the modern painting and poetry movements was Arensberg, who was an avid art collector. His apartment on West Sixty-seventh Street was an important salon where modern poets and painters mingled. The French Dadaists, Marcel Duchamp, Francis Picabia, and Albert Gleizes, often attended his parties, as did other artists, including Man Ray, Joseph Stella, Charles Demuth, Charles Sheeler, and Morton Schamberg.[22]

Stevens, who often visited Arensberg's home, greatly admired French impressionism and Flemish and Dutch art. Cognizant of the relationship between painting and poetry, Stevens wrote that the "problems of poets are the problems of painters, and poets must often turn to the literature of painting for a discussion of their own problems." [23] Some critics find a definite influence of cubism and impressionism on Stevens's work. The lush scenery and descriptions in "Sunday Morning" (1915) suggest an impressionistic painting, and like the expressionists he often uses color for symbolic-dramatic effect. "Thirteen Ways of Looking at a Blackbird" reflects the cubist method of interpreting an object from different angles, while the cubist subject matter of guitars and mandolins are often found in his poetry.

Another *Others* contributor influenced by modern art was William Carlos Williams. Like Kreymborg, he often visited Stieglitz's gallery and the Arensberg salon. Charles Demuth, an old student friend, stimulated his interest in painting and directly influenced his work at this time. A few early poems portray the geometric relationships between objects, a subject Demuth also treats on canvas.[24] Both the objectivism of Williams's later poetry and the precisionist technique of Demuth rely on the use of precisely rendered objects. In 1928, Demuth based his famous painting *I Saw the Figure 5 in Gold* on one of Williams's poems.

If some new poets found inspiration in painting, a few modern artists such as Marsden Hartley and Max Weber wrote experimental poetry. Hartley began writing free verse in 1908 and published four volumes of poetry during his life. Several poems like "Fisherman's Last Supper" and "Portrait of Albert Pinkham

Ryder" reflect the subject matter of his oils. In his imagist free verse he often uses broken lines and color imagery to create similar effects as in his paintings. A talented amateur, Hartley would have become a major poet if he had devoted more time to poetry. This is also true of Max Weber, who in his *Cubist Poems* (1914) attempted to apply cubism to poetry. Through free verse, repetition, and short broken lines he strove to create a staccato effect by reproducing the fast pace of modern life. Weber's and Hartley's poetry proved the close alliance between the modern poetry and painting movements. The poets and painters were together breaking down the older aesthetic tradition and creating a new American culture. Like the *Others* group, the Stieglitz circle of modern artists stood in the forefront of this rebellion.[25]

NOTES

1. William Carlos Williams, *The Autobiography of William Carlos Williams* (New York: New Directions Paperbooks, 1967), p. 138.

2. Alfred Kreymborg, *Troubadour: An American Autobiography* (New York: American Century, 1957), p. 121.

3. Ezra Pound, "A Few Don'ts by an Imagiste," *Poetry,* I (March 1913), 200-1; Amy Lowell, "The New Manner in Modern Poetry," *New Republic,* VI (March 4, 1916), 124-25; and "A Consideration of Modern Poetry," *North American Review,* CCV (January 1917), 103-17.

4. Biographical and publishing facts have been gathered from Wallace Stevens, *Letters of Wallace Stevens,* ed. Holly Stevens (New York: Alfred A. Knopf, Inc., 1966), passim; Samuel French Morse, et al., *Wallace Stevens Checklist and Bibliography of Stevens Criticism* (Denver: Swallow Press, 1963); Wallace Stevens, "Carnet de Voyage," *Trend,* VII (September 1914), 743-46; "From a Junk" and "Home Again," *Trend,* VIII (November 1914), 117.

5. Carl Van Vechten, "Rogue Elephant in Porcelain," *Yale University Library Gazette,* XXXVIII (October 1963), 46; Alfred Kreymborg, *Our Singing Strength, An Outline of American Poetry (1620-1930)* (New York: Coward-McCann, Inc., 1929), p. 407. See Carl Van Vechten's article on Evans entitled "The Origins of the Sonnets from the Patagonian," *Hartwick Review,* III (Spring 1967), 50-57. For a sample of Evans's work see *Sonnets from the Patagonian: The Street of Little Hotels* (New York: Claire Marie Press, 1914).

6. Wallace Stevens, "Cy Est Pourtraicte, Madame Ste Ursule, et Les Unze Mille Vierges," *Rogue,* I (March 15, 1915), 12; "Disillusionment of Ten O'clock," *Rogue,* II (September 15, 1915), 7.

7. *Troubadour,* p. 162; Man Ray, *Self Portrait* (Boston: Little, Brown, and Company, 1963), pp. 29-44.

8. *Troubadour,* pp. 156-57.

9. Ibid, pp. 162, 171-72. See also Alfred Kreymborg, "An Early Impression of Wallace Stevens," *Trinity Review,* VIII (May 1954), 12-16.

10. *Troubadour,* p. 172.

11. Ibid, p. 188.

12. They were: "Peter Quince at the Clavier," "The Silver Plough-Boy" (August 1915), 31-34; "Domination of Black," "Tattoo," "The Florist Wears Knee-Breeches," "Song," "Six Significant Landscapes," "Inscription for a Monument," Bowl" (March 1916), 171-77; "The Worms at Heaven's Gate" (July 1916), 6; "Thirteen Ways of Looking at a Blackbird," "Valley Candles," "The Wind Shifts," "Gray Room," "Meditation" (December 1917), 25-28; "Le Monocle de Mon Oncle" (December 1918), 9-12, "Life is Motion," "Earthy Anecdote" (July 1919), 14.

13. *Troubadour,* p. 187.

14. William Carlos Williams, *I Wanted to Write a Poem, The Autobiography of the Works of a Poet,* ed. Edith Head (Boston: Beacon Press, 1958), pp. 17-18.

15. *Troubadour,* pp. 157, 186; Williams, *Autobiography,* pp. 141-42; *I Wanted to Write a Poem,* p. 19. The poems in *Others* were "Pastoral," "Pastoral," "The Ogre," "Appeal" (August 1915); "Metric Figure," "Tract," "Toriche," "To a Solitary Disciple," "Epigramme" (February 1916); "Drink" (July 1916); "Keller Gegen Dom," "Love Song," "The Old Man," "The Young Housewife," "Portrait of a Woman in Bed," "Major K," "McD," "Spring Strains," "El Hombre," "New Prelude," "Danse Russe," "Ballet Good," "Night," "Spring Song," "Fire Spirit," "Pastoral" (December 1916).

16. Williams, "Pastoral," *Others,* I (August 1915), 23; William Carlos Williams, "Pastoral," *Others,* I (August 1915), 24; "Danse Russe," *Others,* III (December 1916).

17. "Interview with Donald Hall," in Marianne Moore, *A Marianne Moore Reader* (New York: The Viking Press, Inc., 1965), p. 158.

18. Marianne Moore, "Critics and Connoisseurs," *Others,* III (July 1916), 4-5; reprinted in *The Complete Poems of Marianne Moore* (New York: The Macmillan Company, 1967), pp. 38-39.

19. *Troubadour,* p. 183; H. L. Mencken, "The New Poetry Movement," *Prejudices: First Series* (New York: Alfred A. Knopf, Inc., 1919), pp. 83-85; Louis Untermeyer, "Others," in *The New Era in American Poetry* (New York: Henry Holt and Company, 1919), p. 328; Walter Lippmann, "Miss Lowell and Things," *New Republic,* VI (March 11, 1961), 179.

20. William Carlos Williams, "America, Whitman, and the Art of Poetry," *The Poetry Journal,* VIII (November 1917), 35. Williams published two poems in *The Masses,* "Sick African" and "Chinese Nightingale," IX (January 1917), 42.

21. *Troubadour,* pp. 238-52; William Zorach, *Art Is My Life* (New York: World Publishing Co., 1967), pp. 55-56; William Carlos Williams, *Autobiography,* pp. 138-40; *I Wanted to Write a Poem,* p. 59; Alfred Kreymborg, "Lima Beans," *Representative One-Act Plays by American Authors* (Boston: Little, Brown and Company, 1919) pp. 256-67.

22. *Troubadour,* p. 128. See also Alfred Kreymborg's letters to Stieglitz in the Alfred Stieglitz Collection, Beinecke Library, Yale University, New Haven, Connecticut and "What 291 Is to Me," *Camera Work,* no. 47 (1914), 29. See William Zorach's untitled poem in *Others,* I (December 1915), 113; Man Ray, "Three Dimensions," *Others,* I (December 1915), 108; Marsden Hartley, "Scaramouche," *Others,* V (February 1919), 16.

23. Wallace Stevens, *Opus Posthumous* (New York: Alfred A. Knopf, Inc., 1957), p. 160;

reprinted from a paper Stevens read at the Museum of Modern Art in 1951, entitled "The Relations between Poetry and Painting." See also Michel Benamou, "Wallace Stevens: Some Relations between Poetry and Painting," in *The Achievement of Wallace Stevens,* eds. Ashley Brown and Robert S. Haller (New York: J. B. Lippincott Company, 1962), pp. 232-48.

24. Williams's "To a Solitary Disciple," *Others* (February 1916) has as its subject the geometric relationship of a church's steeple with a rising moon; a scene quite similar to one of Demuth's Bermuda watercolors executed about this time.

25. See Hartley's *Selected Poems* (1945); *Twenty-Five Poems* (1922); *Androscoggin* (1940); *Sea Burial* (1914). See also Jerome Mellquist, "Marsden Hartley, An American Painter Who Wrote Exceptional Poetry," *Perspectives U.S.A.,* no. 4 (Summer 1953), 62-77; Elizabeth McCausland, *Marsden Hartley* (Minneapolis: University of Minnesota Press, 1952), pp. 14-16, 23; Max Weber, *Cubist Poems* (London: Elkin Mathews, 1914).

CHAPTER EIGHT

The Stieglitz Group

The year 1908 is highly significant in the history of American painting. During this year two events took place in New York that were crucial to the development of twentieth-century art. One was the famous Eight Show held at the Macbeth Gallery. Another was the first exhibition of modern art in America at Stieglitz's Gallery 291 when he displayed fifty-eight drawings by Auguste Rodin. Both the 291 modern artists and The Eight rebelled against the outdated traditions of the National Academy of Design and wanted to broaden the base of American painting. Compared to The Eight, the Stieglitz group was much more revolutionary, and went beyond representational painting to experiment in color, form, and design.

Before opening his famous Photo-Secession Gallery, Stieglitz had already made a name for himself as a leading modern photographer. Born in Hoboken, New Jersey, in 1864, Stieglitz had received his training in photography at the Berlin Polytechnic. Returning to New York in 1890, he had entered the photo-engraving business, and during the next decade he gained a reputation as a talented experimental photographer. In highly original photography, Stieglitz captured the multifarious life of New York City from poor immigrants to fashionable Fifth Avenue. His sensitive portraits also probed beneath the surface of the subject. (See Fig. 12.) He was especially interested in pictorial effects, including the technical features of texture and tonal qualities and the contrast between light and shade. Whether a driving snowstorm or a sensuous nude, his photographs reflect a sense of drama and mood.[1]

Stieglitz and other pioneers in the Photo-Secession movement wanted a

Fig. 12. Alfred Stieglitz, *Self-Portrait* (1910). Photograph reproduced by permission of the Dorothy Norman Collection.

permanent place to exhibit their work. The photographer Edward Steichen knew of a vacancy in a brownstone he was living in at 291 Fifth Avenue and convinced Stieglitz in 1905 to rent two small rooms on the fourth floor. At the Little Galleries of the Photo-Secession or Gallery 291 Stieglitz presented ground-breaking shows of modern photography. In late 1908 or early 1909, the photographer moved the gallery into two rooms across the hall from his first headquarters. Actually the new gallery was now at 293 Fifth Avenue, a wall having been broken down between the two buildings. The exhibition room in the new 291 was small and intimate, measuring only 12 by 15 feet. The walls were covered with a light gray burlap material and in the center stood a large brass bowl of flowers on a square platform.

As early as October 1905, Stieglitz had written the Photo-Secession members that the gallery would also stage painting exhibitions. The first show occurred in January 1907 when Stieglitz exhibited the paintings of the American realist Pamela Colman Smith. Responsible for the famous 1908 Rodin Exhibition was Edward Steichen, who sent the artist's drawings to Stieglitz from Paris. Steichen's crucial role cannot be overestimated because he was influential in obtaining the work of Cézanne, Brancusi, Picasso, and Marin for other 291 exhibitions. In early 1908, Steichen brought to the United States Matisse's fauve paintings. Their exhibition at 291 shocked academic art critics and newspaper reporters, who called his work incomprehensible and ugly. Matisse's distortion of form and radical use of color also offended the general public's sensibilities and revealed that modern art would gain slow acceptance in America.[2]

Ignoring the critics, Stieglitz continued to present modern European painting exhibitions between 1909 and 1917. During 1911, Cézanne and Picasso had their first one-man American shows at Gallery 291. Like the furor over Matisse's works, Picasso's drawings and watercolors received a hostile reception from academic critics.[3] Henri Rousseau, Francis Picabia, and Gino Severini were also given their first American one-man shows at 291. Stieglitz also exhibited the sculpture of Matisse, Brancusi, and Manolo and presented the first American exhibition of African sculpture in 1914. During the Little Renaissance 291 became an indispensable center for introducing the work of leading European modern artists.

Stieglitz was also interested in creating an indigenous American modern art movement. At this time it was extremely difficult for modern artists to find a

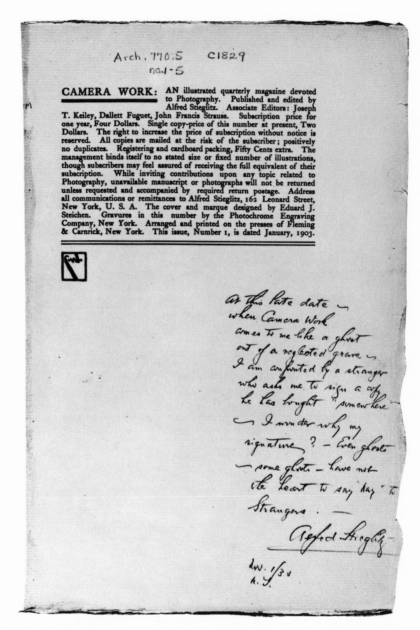

Fig. 13. First number of *Camera Work* signed by Alfred Stieglitz. Architecture and Fine Arts Library, University of Southern California, Los Angeles, California.

Fig. 14. John Marin, *Brooklyn Bridge* (1910). The Metropolitan Museum, Alfred Stieglitz Collection, 1949.

gallery willing to show their work. Max Weber called the situation for the
experimental painter in New York "bleak." "The academy was at its greatest,
highest strength," he said. "They were the ruling ... powers of the art of
America.... It was very difficult to gain a footing for a young man with new
thoughts, new ideas, and aspirations." Breaking with this tradition, Stieglitz
held a "Younger American Painters" exhibition (1910), featuring the
avant-garde work of Weber, Arthur Dove, John Marin, Alfred Maurer, and
Marsden Hartley—all of whom would become leading members of the Stieglitz
circle. Modern art critics praised the event as signaling the birth of a new
painting movement in the United States. During the era Stieglitz also presented
various one-man shows featuring the work of Abraham Walkowitz, Oscar
Bluemner, Elie Nadelman, and S. Macdonald-Wright, but most 291
exhibitions centered around the painting of Marin, Hartley, and Dove.[4]

Marin was the oldest artist among the trio. Born in Rutherford, New Jersey,
in 1870, he had first studied art under Thomas Anshutz at the Pennsylvania
Academy of Fine Arts and at the Art Students League in New York. From 1905
to 1910, he had made several trips to Europe where he had come under the
influence of European moderns. Marin's most important prewar show was his
1913 exhibition of watercolors. Through the use of surging lines and
fragmented planes Marin's New York watercolors caught the dynamic speed of
urban civilization. Under Marin's pen, Brooklyn Bridge (Fig. 14) and the
Woolworth Building were broken up into disjointed fragments toppling in
space. Although these city scenes showed the influence of cubism, futurism,
and the French artist Robert Delaunay, he successfully fused these schools into
his own expressionistic style. Several genteel critics, however, found his work
"topsy turvy," including Cass Gilbert, the architect of the Woolworth
Building. By contrast, most reviewers receptive to modern art agreed that the
painter had successfully captured the turbulent life of urban America. Marin
interpreted this work as essentially an emotional response to his environment:

> I see great forces at work; great movements; the large buildings and the
> small buildings; the warring of the great and the small; influences of one
> mass on another greater or smaller mass. Feelings are aroused which give
> me the desire to express the reaction of these "pull forces," those influences
> which play with one another; great masses pulling smaller masses, each
> subject in some degree to the other's power.

In life all things come under the magnetic influence of other things, the bigger assert themselves strongly, the smaller not so much, but still they assert themselves, and though hidden they strive to be seen and in so doing change their bent and direction.

While these powers are at work pushing, pulling, sideways, downwards, upwards, I can hear the sound of their strife and there is great music being played.

And so I try to express graphically what a great city is doing. Within the frames there must be a balance, a controlling of these warring, pushing, pulling, forces. This is what I am trying to realize. But we are all human.[5]

Like Marin, Hartley was also creating a unique style to express the twentieth century. Born in Lewiston, Maine, in 1877, he had first studied painting in Cleveland, Ohio, and at the New York School of Art. His early lyrical landscapes drenched in rich colors reflected the work of Cézanne, the Italian impressionist Segantini, and the somber mystical moods of Albert Ryder's oils. Hartley's first trip to Europe in 1912 was the major turning point in his career. He became captivated by the painting of Cézanne, Picasso, and Matisse at several exhibitions and at Gertrude Stein's Paris apartment. He wrote Stieglitz from Europe "that the importance of my having come here is incalculable. It has done more for clarity of ideas and sensations than I could have done at home in years." [6]

Later, he visited Munich and became acquainted with Wassily Kandinsky and the German *Blaue Reiter* school. This group's expressive use of color, including Kandinsky's pioneer linear abstractions, impressed the young painter. After a short trip to America in 1913, Hartley returned to Europe and lived in Berlin for two years. Under the influence of the German expressionists, Hartley painted richly decorative geometric patterns, signs, and symbols such as his famous 1914 *Portrait of a German Officer* (Fig. 15). These studies when shown at 291 stupefied academic critics but his colleagues praised them as daring experiments in form and design.[7] With his brilliant expressive "German" work, Hartley had reached the apex of his early career.

Arthur Dove was also one of America's first practitioners in semiabstract art. Born in Canandaigua, New York, in 1880, he had first worked as a commercial artist in New York. After residing in Paris for two years, he returned to take up farming in Westport, Connecticut, where he raised chickens and did occasional

Fig. 15. Marsden Hartley, *Portrait of a German Officer* (1914). The Metropolitan Museum, Alfred Stieglitz Collection, 1949.

lobster and crab fishing. An imaginative artist, Dove experimented in various painting techniques and by 1910 was breaking new ground in his art. That year he executed a series of six abstractions that made him an early pioneer in nonobjective painting. At his 1912 show at 291 he exhibited several abstract pastels, what he called "experiments in . . . decorative designs." [8] Although conservative critics found Dove's innovative paintings incomprehensible, his early work was never purely abstract but always contained a suggestion of natural forms, including plants, flowers, and animals. (See Fig. 16.) By 1917 Dove had already found a personal style that would make him a forerunner in American abstract art.

During the prewar period Georgia O'Keeffe, another 291 artist, was also beginning to paint in a semiabstract manner. Born in Sun Prairie, Wisconsin, in 1887, O'Keeffe had first studied art at several schools in Chicago and New York. A major turning point in her career came between 1914 and 1916, when she studied under Arthur Wesley Dow, head of the Department of Fine Arts at Columbia University. A pupil of the Orientalist Ernest Fenollosa, Dow was an influential instructor who stressed harmonious design in painting. Under his influence O'Keeffe began using thin delicate lines and organic forms in her work. Unbeknown to the artist, a friend of O'Keeffe sent her charcoal sketches and watercolors to Stieglitz in 1916. "Finally a woman on paper," the photographer exclaimed on seeing her work.[9] He immediately exhibited ten drawings and a year later staged a show exclusively devoted to her work. This latter exhibition included exquisite sensual studies of flowers and other organic forms that suggest themes in her later oils. (See Fig. 17.) After World War I she joined Marin, Hartley, and Dove as an important member of the Stieglitz group.

This circle of artists formed a closely knit community drawing inspiration from the gallery owner's magnetic personality and leadership. The group revered the older Stieglitz as a father and viewed 291 not only as an art gallery but also as a spirit and philosophy symbolizing noncommercialization and artistic freedom. In an important issue of Stieglitz's magazine *Camera Work* approximately fifty artists and writers wrote short interpretations of 291 as a stimulating cultural oasis for the lonely artist and a laboratory of experimentation. In an untitled poem Marin called 291 "a place electric, a place alive," while Hartley wrote that it was an indispensable force in bringing modern art to America. Many Little Renaissance writers who visited his gallery were also stimulated by the photographer and contributed to the issue. Hutchins Hapgood declared that

Fig. 16. Arthur Dove, *Cow* (1914). The Metropolitan Museum, Alfred Stieglitz Collection, 1949.

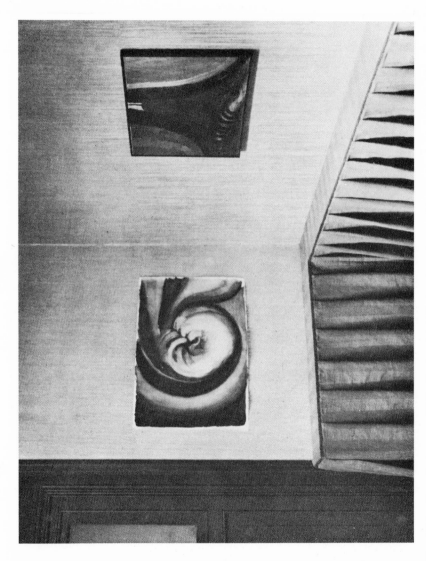

Fig. 17. Alfred Stieglitz, *Paintings, O'Keeffe, 291 Exhibition* (1916-17). Photograph reproduced by permission of the Dorothy Norman Collection.

" '291' to me is a 'Salon,' a laboratory, and a refuge—a place where people may exchange ideas and feelings, where artists can present and try out their experiments." Hippolyte Havel called Stieglitz "an iconoclast in the realm of art" and 291 "a battlefield for new ideas." Besides celebrating the virtues of 291 in a poem, Mabel Luhan admitted in her autobiography that Stieglitz "helped me to See—both in art and in life." The photographer was an important link between the modern art movement and the literary side of the Renaissance.[10]

Stieglitz was also greatly admired by *The Seven Arts* writers, particularly Paul Rosenfeld and Waldo Frank. A friend of the gallery owner, Rosenfeld once lauded him as a magnanimous individual whose concept of art was "a bridge to consciousness of self, to life, and through that, to new life and new creation again." In *Our America,* Frank glowingly celebrated 291 as a religious "altar at which life was worshipped above the noise of a dead city. Here was a refuge, certain and solitary, from the tearing grip of industrial disorder." Both Stieglitz and *The Seven Arts* writers believed in the idea of a community of artists working together for aesthetic change and in the ability of art to improve society. After World War I Frank and Rosenfeld continued to be among the leading literary admirers of Stieglitz.[11]

Besides feeling a common purpose in belonging to 291, the Stieglitz artists shared similar aesthetic views. Modern art to them meant not only a concern with the basic elements of structure in a painting but also a philosophy and a faith. Modernism implied a revolt from outdated academic standards and a commitment to change and experimentation. Like the *Others* group, the Stieglitz circle shared the iconoclastic spirit of the Little Renaissance, and demanded the freedom to express through art their own private vision of contemporary society. As the new poets they wanted to be emancipated from the past and to break up the old aesthetic formulas.

Subjective expressionism through the use of the senses was the credo of the Stieglitz group. Their art was not primarily motivated by intellectual theories but by intuitive feelings. The group's aesthetic philosophy reflected the influence of Henri Bergson and his idea that the act of artistic creativity derived from the *élan vital* or the "life force." According to Bergson, art was motivated by the spontaneous instinctive response of an artist toward his subject. Hartley, who was attracted to his theories, wrote Stieglitz from Paris that he was "convinced of the Bergson argument in philosophy, that the intuition is the only vehicle for art expression and it is on this basis that I am proceeding."

Stieglitz also admired the French philosopher and printed extracts from Bergson's *Laughter* and *Creative Evolution* in *Camera Work*. Kandinsky's writing and Italian futurist manifestos also helped shape Hartley's and Marin's aesthetic views, but Bergson was the most profound European influence on the Stieglitz group.[12]

Hartley, Marin, and Dove often pointed to the instincts as the major source of artistic creativity. In the catalogue of his 1914 exhibition, Hartley wrote that "it is the artist's business to select forms suitable to his own specialized experience, forms which express naturally the emotions he personally desires to present." A painting, according to Hartley, derived from an artist's momentary response to his subject. Modernism to him meant a romantic philosophy implying a new and ever-changing relationship to nature. Like Hartley, Marin called his prewar paintings in the 1916 Forum Exhibition "constructed expressions of the inner senses, responding to things seen and felt." Rejecting intellectual theories, Dove also stressed subjective sensations and the importance of the inner consciousness in the creative act.[13]

The most important modern art theorist in the prewar Stieglitz group was the painter Max Weber. A native of Russia, Weber and his parents had emigrated in 1891 to Brooklyn where he had first studied art under Arthur Wesley Dow at the Pratt Institute. In 1905, he went to Paris where he worked with Henri Matisse and developed a highly eclectic style based on the French impressionists, cubists, and fauvists. Because his painting seemed daringly progressive when he returned to America in 1909, critics attacked his first one-man show at the Haas Gallery. Shortly after this exhibition, Weber joined the Stieglitz circle and even resided at the gallery for a short period. Because of his travels abroad he served as an ambassador of modern art to the group, informing them of the newest developments in European painting. Stieglitz admitted that "it was through the closeness of Weber and myself and my study of his work—living with it—that gave me an opportunity to enlighten myself in a way in which I couldn't have otherwise in America." [14]

Weber's affiliation with the group was nevertheless short-lived. During his one-man show in January 1911 he quarreled with Stieglitz because the gallery owner wanted him to be present during the exhibition to explain his work to visitors. Weber thought his attendance was unnecessary since his work was self-explanatory, but he agreed to the photographer's request. When he arrived late on the fourth day, Stieglitz admonished him for his tardiness. Weber then walked out of the gallery in anger and severed his relationship with the photographer. Because of this experience Weber was one of the few people who downgraded Stieglitz's importance in the development of modern art.[15]

Like the other Stieglitz artists, Weber aimed to render momentary impressions on a canvas through perceptions and feelings. Modern art portrayed a new realm of the imagination, what he called the "fourth dimension" or "the consciousness of a great and overwhelming sense of space–magnitude in all directions at one time." In his informative *Essays on Art* (1916), a book derived from his lectures on art history and appreciation at the New York White School of Photography, the painter defined the act of artistic creativity as the contact between the artist's senses and the outside world. He called on both artists and laymen to cultivate their intuitions and ability to communicate with their surroundings. "Culture will come," he remarked, "when people touch things with love and see them with a penetrating eye." As a result, "man would value man more. The wonder of and the faith in other human beings would kindle a new and spiritual life." Like other participants, Weber believed that art could improve the human condition and redeem society. He also thought that the artist should create new forms to express the twentieth century. There were artistic precedents in classicism, the painter wrote, yet "we cannot express our 'modern' emotions in the terms and means of the ancients. Indeed we must invent new means." Weber's *Essays on Art* was a highly significant document expressing the aesthetics of the prewar modern art movement.[16]

Another important modern art spokesman was Willard Huntington Wright. After leaving *The Smart Set* in 1914, the ubiquitous Wright became an art critic for the *Forum* magazine. During his tenure he proved to be a perceptive critic by attacking academic art and praising modern artists. His excellent study, *Modern Painting, Its Tendencies and Meaning* (1915), was a very original historical and interpretive analysis suggesting that the new painting derived partly from primitive and classical art. Although his objectivity was somewhat marred by a bias in favor of his brother, Stanton Macdonald-Wright, and his synchromist painting, Wright's book established him as a leading authority on the subject of modern art.

An important feature of Stieglitz's magazine *Camera Work* was the perceptive art criticism of Charles H. Caffin, Sadakichi Hartmann, Benjamin de Casseres, and Marius de Zayas. Caffin was a professional art critic, de Zayas a caricaturist for the *Evening World,* and Hartmann and de Casseres established poets and essayists. This quartet and the 291 artists formed a close coterie, often meeting for luncheon discussions at the Holland House restaurant or the Prince George Hotel dining room where they plotted the downfall of representational painting. Their pieces in *Camera Work* were written in a colorful impressionistic style, smacking of fin de siècle aestheticism. Finding the old art formulas dated, they vigorously attacked academic painting and called for a new art reflecting the twentieth century. These critics made *Camera Work* the most important modern art journal of the Little Renaissance.[17]

Founded by Stieglitz in 1903, the quarterly had first gained fame as an important photographic magazine containing the new pictorial photography of the Photo-Secession group. Around the time of the first art shows at 291, *Camera Work* began to devote more space to European painting. The magazine often printed reproductions of the work of leading European modern artists, including Matisse, Rodin, Picasso, Van Gogh, and Cézanne. Also published were essays on the 291 group and reprinted newspaper and magazine reviews of the gallery's shows. *Camera Work* also included literary material, including poetry, the selected letters of Vincent Van Gogh, and the writings of Shaw, Maeterlinck, and Bergson.

During 1915 and 1916, de Zayas and three other associates of Stieglitz (Agnes Ernst, Katherine Rhoades, and Paul Haviland) published the magazine *291*. In essence a Dadaist magazine, *291* was experimental, satirical, and arty in tone. The French artist Francis Picabia, whose work was often exhibited at 291, was its most important contributor. Several of his Dadaist drawings mocked technology; one, a camera, represented Stieglitz; another, a spark plug, was titled "A Young American Girl in the State of Nudity." Besides Picabia, the magazine was mainly built around the clever satirical drawings of Katherine Rhoades and Marius de Zayas. Inside its covers could also be found poetry, current art news (often in French), and "Ideogrammes" by Guillaume Apollinaire. *291* was heavily influenced by French art magazines and the Dadaist movement; indeed, when Picabia returned briefly to Europe in 1916 he founded a journal called *391* based on the Stieglitz periodical.[18]

At this time Dadaism was beginning to burgeon in several art capitals, including New York City. Besides Picabia, the European war caused the temporary migration of two other French modern artists to Manhattan, Albert Gleizes and Marcel Duchamp. Dazzled by the country's mechanization and urban development, these three artists painted the American scene. At

Arensberg's salon they met several American artists, including Sheeler, Schamberg, Demuth, and Ray, all of whom fell under their influence. Arensberg and his French Dadaist friends published *The Blind Man,* an arty irreverent journal that stood for advancing avant-garde culture. One number featured a cover drawing by Duchamp, poetry by Arensberg, and a short story by Mina Loy. Issued only sporadically during 1917, the journal later became a collector's item.

One reason for the Dadaists' immediate acceptance and popularity in the New York art community was that their revolt against conventionality perfectly matched the Little Renaissance spirit of iconoclasm and modernism. Picabia's wife was correct when she wrote that the prewar years in New York "turned out to be an exceptionally favorable climate for the development of a certain revolutionary spirit in the domain of the arts and letters which, later on, became crystalized under the name of *Dada.*" Two amusing incidents occurring during the 1917 Independent Show best reveal the relationship between Dadaism and the Little Renaissance. When the exhibition's hanging committee refused to accept Duchamp's entry, a urinal entitled *La Fontaine,* the artist angrily resigned from the Society of Independent Artists, the show's sponsors, and accused them of not staging an "open" show. His urinal sculpture, he declared, was not "immoral" but "an ordinary article of life," which had lost "its useful significance . . . under the new title and point of view." The second incident involved Arthur Cravan, poet, amateur boxer, and confessed burglar, who was scheduled to deliver a lecture on the Dadaist movement at the Independent Show. Cravan showed up drunk and began shouting obscenities at the audience. When he started taking his clothes off he was immediately arrested by the police.[19]

The appearance of the Dadaists proved that partly due to Stieglitz New York had become an important world art capital by 1917. Compared to 1908, when Stieglitz first showed Rodin's work, America's artistic climate was somewhat freer. The exhibitions at 291 had certainly helped pave the way for the gradual acceptance of modern art. Hartley, Marin, O'Keeffe, Dove, and Weber had created ground-breaking work during the Little Renaissance period. The Stieglitz group, however, was limited to a select circle, and even the number of people who visited his gallery was relatively small. What was needed to accompany the 291 exhibitions was a larger and more widespread independent movement in American painting which would vindicate Stieglitz's far-sighted modern art shows.

NOTES

1. For biographical facts on Stieglitz and the Gallery 291 exhibitions see the appendix in *America and Alfred Stieglitz: A Collective Portrait,* eds. Waldo Frank et al. (Garden City, N.Y.: Doubleday, Doran, 1934), pp. 311-22; Dorothy Norman, ed., *Stieglitz Memorial Portfolio, 1864-1946* (New York: Twice-a-Year Press, 1947), p. 61. On Stieglitz's photography see Robert Doty, *Photo-Secession, Photography as a Fine Art* (Rochester, N.Y.: George Eastman House, 1960), passim; Doris Bry, *Alfred Stieglitz, Photographer* (Boston: October House, 1965), passim; Carl Zigrosser, "Alfred Stieglitz," *Twice-a-Year,* nos. 8-9 (1942), 137-45.

2. For reviews of the Matisse show see *Camera Work,* no. 23 (1908), 10-13.

3. For reviews of the Picasso show see ibid., no. 36 (1911), 49-54, 65, 68.

4. Max Weber, "The Reminiscences of Max Weber," pp. 77-80, unpublished MS. in the Max Weber Collection, Oral History Research Office, Columbia University, New York City, N.Y. "'The Younger American Painters' and the Press," *Camera Work,* no. 31 (1910), 47-50.

5. Marin's statement is printed in *Camera Work,* nos. 42-43 (1913), 18.

6. Letter of Marsden Hartley to Alfred Stieglitz, [Oct. 31], 1912, in the Alfred Stieglitz Collection, Beinecke Library, Yale University, New Haven, Connecticut.

7. *Camera Work,* no. 45 (1914), 19-22.

8. Ibid., no. 38 (1912), 43-44.

9. Daniel Catton Rich, *Georgia O'Keeffe* (Chicago: Art Institute of Chicago, 1943), p. 18.

10. Quoted from *Camera Work,* no. 47 (1914); Mabel Dodge Luhan, *Intimate Memoirs,* vol. 3: *Movers and Shakers* (New York: Harcourt, Brace and Company, Inc., 1936), p. 78.

11. Paul Rosenfeld [Peter Minuet], "291 Fifth Avenue," *The Seven Arts,* I (November 1916), 64. Waldo David Frank, *Our America* (New York: Boni and Liveright, 1919), p. 184. Paul Rosenfeld, "Alfred Stieglitz," in *Port of New York* (Urbana: University of Illinois Press, 1966), pp. 237-79, which also contains articles on Marin, Dove, Hartley, and O'Keeffe.

12. Letter of Marsden Hartley to Alfred Stieglitz, December 1912, in the Stieglitz Collection. Henri Bergson, "What Is the Object of Art?" *Camera Work,* no. 37 (1912), 25, reprinted from Bergson's *Laughter.* An extract from *Creative Evolution* also appeared in *Camera Work,* no. 36 (1911), 20-21.

13. Hartley's remarks are reprinted in *Camera Work,* no. 45 (1914), 17. Marin's and Dove's statements are in *The Forum Exhibition of Modern American Painters* (New Yokr: Mitchell Kennerley, 1916), n.p.

14. Holger Cahill, *Max Weber* (New York: Downtown Galleries, 1930), passim; "The Reminiscences of Max Weber," pp. 36, 58-59, 62. Quoted from Dorothy Norman, "Alfred Stieglitz; From Writings and Conversations," *Twice-a-Year,* no. 1 (Fall-Winter 1938), 83.

15. "The Reminiscences of Max Weber," pp. 82-91, 100-7; Stieglitz's letter to Weber, January 17, 1911, in the Stieglitz Collection.

16. Max Weber, "The Fourth Dimension from a Plastic Point of View," *Camera Work,* no. 31 (1910), 25; *Essays on Art* (New York: W. E. Rudge, 1916), pp. 32, 55, 17.

17. For examples of their work see Benjamin de Casseres, "Modernity and the Decadence," *Camera Work,* no. 37(1912), 17-19; Sadakichi Hartmann, "Structural Units," *Camera Work,* no. 36 (1911), 18-20; and his review of the "Younger American Painters" show in *Camera Work,* no. 31 (1910), 47-49.

18. Alfred Stieglitz, "Four Happenings," *Twice-a-Year,* nos. 8-9 (1942), 131-36; letter of Stieglitz to Hartley, May 4, 1915, in the Stieglitz Collection; "'291'–A New Publication," *Camera Work,* no. 48 (1916), 62-65.

19. "The European Art Invasion," *The Literary Digest,* LI (November 27, 1915), 1224-25; Gabrielle Buffet-Picabia, "Arthur Cravan and American Dada," *Transition* (April-May 1938), 314; "Duchamp Resigns from Independents," *American Art News,* XV (April 14, 1917), 1.

CHAPTER NINE

The Independent Movement

The independent movement was not really an official organization but a shared desire among many progressive painters to create art exhibitions free from the jurisdiction of the National Academy of Design. Like other Little Renaissance movements, it was inspired by the attempt to overturn genteel culture, in this case to break the control of the Academy over American painting. There were several academies in major cities at the turn of the century, yet New York's National Academy, founded in 1826, was the largest and most powerful. The Academy's officials defined set standards for a painting and were largely opposed to experimentation. Academic art generally meant painting in a style imitative of the French Barbizon School and the Düsseldorf School; consequently, thousands of rather stilted pastoral landscapes and unimaginative portraits flooded the art market. Slashing brushwork, technical proficiency, and a desire to evoke beauty and sentiment were the Academy's guidelines for a good painting. One generally had to follow this style in order to join the Academy and to exhibit in their shows, which were ruled over by a jury system accepting only conventional art. The Eight artists, particularly Sloan and Henri, opposed the use of juries and prizes and called for independent exhibitions open to all artists.

Their movement was basically a reaction against academic art or what Sloan called "high-class American pot-boilers." The Eight wished to broaden the scope of subject matter by painting everyday reality. "Draw what you see around you," Sloan once told his art students, while his colleague Henri advised his pupils to paint common people, for "art cannot be separated from life."

According to Everett Shinn, The Eight "looked beyond the outposts of society where people were real by default of riches—to saloons where periled the dreams of change and expansion, to alleyways and gutters, train yards, night courts, dives, docks, dance halls and park benches." By the end of the nineteenth century the realists were hard at work revolutionizing American art.[1]

The arrival of The Eight artists in New York was a momentous event that helped make Manhattan a center of artistic revolt. During the late nineteenth century, Henri, Sloan, Shinn, George Luks, and William Glackens had worked as newspaper illustrators in Philadelphia where they had been close associates. In 1896, Luks and Glackens had obtained jobs as artist-reporters on New York newspapers. Four years later Henri had settled permanently in the city and was followed by Sloan in 1904. Here they continued their close friendship by assembling together on Tuesday and Thursday evenings at Henri's midtown studio and Gramercy Park home and at Mouquin's French restaurant, a famous meeting place for other artists and newspapermen.[2]

They also rendezvoused at Petitpas's Chelsea boarding house run by three French sisters, which became popular in 1908 when the Irish painter John Butler Yeats, father of the poet, began residing here. Because he was already an established painter and more worldly than the group, he often gave them advice and counsel. Sloan, Glackens, Shinn, Henri, Bellows, and Brooks often joined Yeats for dinner at Petitpas's. The young aspiring artists would sit around a long table presided over by the elderly Yeats and enjoy his witty conversation while eating a good inexpensive French table d'hôte dinner. On fine summer days they dined in the garden. These pleasant occasions were captured in Sloan's famous 1910 painting *Yeats at Petitpas'* (Fig. 18) and a drawing by Bellows. The five ex-Philadelphian artists were an amicable group united by friendship and similar attitudes toward art.[3]

As early as 1901, Henri had sponsored an independent show of progressive painters at New York's Allan Gallery, which included his and Glackens's work. Henri's hanging methods had defied the Academy's procedure of giving favorite painters eye-level position and better lighting. He had instead arranged the exhibits in two well-placed lines with the best lighting distributed equally among the exhibitors. A more important forerunner of the 1908 show had been Henri's organization of an exhibition at the National Arts Club in 1904, which included the work of six members of The Eight: Sloan, Henri, Luks, Glackens,

Fig. 18. John Sloan, *Yeats at Petitpas'* (1910). Collection of the Corcoran Gallery of Art, Washington, D.C. From left to right: Van Wyck Brooks, J.B. Yeats, Alan Seeger, Dolly Sloan, Ann Squire, John Sloan, and Fred King.

Maurice Prendergast, and Arthur B. Davies. This show and the Allan Gallery exhibit commenced the revolutionary independent movement.[4]

Important events in 1907 precipitated the realists' final break with the Academy. Disagreement erupted when works by Luks, Glackens, and Shinn were rejected by the Academy for their spring 1907 exhibition. When Henri's paintings were also classified as doubtful participants and given secondary ranking, he withdrew them from the competition. In April, several artists, including Davies and Lawson, failed to get elected to the Academy which they had hoped to liberalize through membership. Henri was also offended because he had not been reappointed to the Academy's jury selection committee. He was now convinced that the conservative organization was utterly opposed to experimentation and that the avant-garde must hold their own shows.

As a result the realists decided on immediately staging an independent exhibition. Davies, Luks, Glackens, Sloan, and Lawson met in Henri's studio to plan the organization. Henri was assigned the correspondence and press relations, Sloan was appointed secretary and treasurer, and Davies was put in charge of the catalogue and the task of finding a suitable art gallery. Davies's involvement with the preparations for The Eight Show proved to be valuable training for organizing the Armory Show five years later. He contracted the Macbeth Gallery, where he once had a one-man show, to stage the exhibition. Founded in 1892 by William Macbeth, the gallery was one of the few places in New York willing to exhibit the work of progressive painters.[5]

The Eight Show, which opened on February 3, created considerable controversy as approximately 7,000 people attended the exhibition during its two-week engagement. Some conservative academic critics, finding the new subject matter of urban life tasteless and vulgar, called the realists the "Black Gang" and the "Apostles of Ugliness." Other reviewers correctly interpreted the show as a revolution in American art. The newspaper critics Frederick James Gregg and Charles Fitz Gerald praised the realists for breaking new ground in subject matter. Another commentator, Mary Fanton Roberts, suggested that the group was developing an indigenous American scene painting. Besides signifying the birth of a new realism, The Eight Show helped break the Academy's control.[6]

Compared to the Stieglitz circle, The Eight had a tenuous relationship that dissolved shortly after the 1908 exhibition. The show traveled to several cities in the East and Midwest, but after this tour the artists never exhibited together.

There were several reasons for this. First, they were only an informal body to begin with and not a permanent organization. Despite their shared antipathies toward the Academy, each artist painted in a different style, and the group was split between realists and postimpressionists.

The realists differed themselves in technique, influences, and subject matter. Although Henri occasionally painted the urban scene, he was equally adept at painting bucolic landscapes and handsome portraits in a manner deriving from Hals, Velázquez, Goya, and Manet. Both Luks and Shinn were interested in other subjects besides the city. Under the influence of Hals, Luks became known for his dramatic paintings of athletes, while Shinn drew the theater world in a style reminiscent of Degas. Of an entirely different nature was the work of Davies, who painted decorative neoclassical scenes in the Pre-Raphaelite manner. Only Sloan's work seemed to fit the "Ash-Can" label.

As postimpressionists, Glackens, Prendergast, and Lawson were the most modern among the group. By 1905, Glackens had abandoned social realism for an impressionist style based on Renoir. Both he, Prendergast, and Lawson used bright colors in comparison to the dark palette of their realist colleagues. Glackens's subject matter ranged from scenes of Central Park to ladies' boudoirs, while Lawson gained fame for his sparkling suburban landscapes and river scenes. Prendergast, who painted richly luminiscent oils, had been under the influence of Cézanne and Bonnard since the 1890s. These three would remain in the forefront of American painting after the Armory Show.

If The Eight never again showed their work as a group, their exhibition set off an impetus for further independent shows. The first was the 1910 Exhibition of Independent Artists, an event initiated by several artists, including Jerome Myers and Walt Kuhn. The organizers wanted this exhibition to be independent of the Academy and open to all for a nominal fee. Breaking with tradition, they declared the exhibition a jury and prize-free show in which exhibits would be hung alphabetically. Davies suggested that the exhibition be international in scope, but it was decided to make the show exclusively American. Henri, Sloan, and Kuhn took charge of the arrangements and rented a large vacant building at 29-31 West Thirty-fifth Street. On April 1, the Exhibition of Independent Artists opened to the public for four weeks. Due to curiosity and free admission, 2,000 people showed up on the first day. Unable to handle the large crowds, the organizers kept 500 people standing outside in the cold and the police had to be summoned to keep order. Despite the large attendance throughout the month, the exhibition was not a financial success and few works were sold.[7]

Although there were nearly 500 works by 104 artists, most paintings were representational and did not reflect the newest European developments. All The Eight except Luks contributed to the show, but the Stieglitz artists were noticeably absent. Some exhibitors like Jerome Myers, Walt Kuhn, George Bellows, and Rockwell Kent were well known, but there were too many apprentice pieces by students of Henri. James Huneker, a staunch defender of avant-garde art, called the gigantic exhibition a carnival, and inconsequential compared to the Younger American Painters show occurring simultaneously at the 291 Gallery.[8] Huneker was partly right, for compared to the Stieglitz show the 1910 Exhibition of Independent Artists was tame; nonetheless, Myers, Kuhn, and Davies gained valuable experience in organizing the exhibition.

A more important show, signaling a change in leadership in the independent movement, occurred the following year. One requirement for submitting work to the 1911 Independent Show was that an exhibitor must completely boycott the Academy's exhibitions. This was too stringent a requirement for Henri, who had continued to show his work at the Academy. Consequently, he, Bellows, Sloan, Shinn, and Glackens refused to submit their work to the 1911 event, and the show's organization was taken over by Davies and Rockwell Kent. With the 1911 Independent Show, Henri began to lose his position as the most important figure in American art. His leadership of the independent movement passed to artists such as Davies, Kuhn, and Walter Pach, who looked more favorably toward European modern art. Although Henri admired the work of Matisse and Picasso, he was rather ambivalent toward impressionism and cubism. The 1913 Armory Show completely diminished Henri's leadership and made the art of The Eight realists look passé.

Ironically, the idea for the Armory Show was initiated not by American modernists but by a group of realist painters: Henry Fitch Taylor, Walt Kuhn, Jerome Myers, and Elmer MacRae. They first proposed the project in December 1911 at the Madison Gallery and later at Myers's midtown studio where they discussed "the possibilities of organizing a society for the purpose of exhibiting the works of progressive and live painters, both American and foreign; favoring such work usually neglected by current shows and especially interesting and instructive to the public." In a following meeting the originators and fourteen other artists formed an organization called the American Painters and

Sculptors; later incorporated as the Association of American Painters and Sculptors. According to the constitution, its purpose was "to provide adequate place for, and to hold periodically, national and international exhibitions of the best examples procurable of contemporary art in New York or wherever else the Association may hereafter designate." The Association was thus founded to exhibit both modern European and American art.[9]

There were few modern artists among the Association's first twenty-five members. J. Alden Weir, a member of the Ten American Painters group, was elected president; the sculptor Gutzon Borglum, vice-president; Elmer MacRae, treasurer; and Walt Kuhn, secretary. All The Eight artists were members of the A.A.P.S., except for Davies and Glackens, who were in charge of the American section, yet the others played a small role in organizing the 1913 exhibition.[10] The Association was instead controlled by an inner circle of men led by Kuhn and Davies. When Weir resigned as president in January 1912 because of the Association's outspoken opposition to the National Academy, Davies was chosen as his successor.

The selection of Davies was paramount to the Armory Show's development and success. He was an able fund raiser, a talented administrator, and a man of incredible energy. Enthusiastic about modern European painting, Davies aimed to introduce the American public to international modern art. In an "Explanatory Statement" describing the Armory Show's purpose, Davies wrote: "The time has arrived for giving the public here the opportunity to see for themselves the results of new influences at work in other countries. . . . Its sole object is to put the paintings, sculptures, . . . on exhibition so that the intelligent may judge for themselves by themselves." His plan was to model the exhibition on the current 1912 Cologne Sonderbund, a large contemporary European art show. For this purpose he sent the Sonderbund catalogue to Kuhn with a note saying, "I wish we could have a show like this." [11]

Immediately after receiving Davies's note, Kuhn left for Europe to visit the Cologne exhibition and to acquire works in other foreign art capitals. Arriving on the last day of the Sonderbund show, he was excited by the display. From Cologne he went to the Hague, Berlin, and Munich, where he contacted art dealers and made arrangements to send paintings to New York. Kuhn and Davies also traveled to London to see the modern art exhibit at the Grafton Galleries where they obtained some Matisse works. Paris turned out to be the most important place on Kuhn's tour. The American painter Alfred Maurer introduced him to the famous art dealer Monsieur Vollard. Kuhn also contacted the painter Walter Pach whose knowledge of the Parisian art scene was a crucial factor in the Armory Show's success. Pach introduced Kuhn and Davies to many French painters, art dealers, and collectors and took them to see Gertrude and Leo Stein's art collections. After Kuhn and Davies returned to New York, Pach was put in charge of obtaining more European art. His important acquisitions made him, along with Davies and Kuhn, one of the three principal organizers behind the Armory Show.[12]

Once back in New York, Kuhn and Davies, excited about the exhibition's prospects, completed the final preparations. Kuhn wrote Pach in December that "we want this old show of ours to mark the starting point of the new spirit in art as far as America is concerned." For $5,500 a month they rented the Sixty-ninth Regiment Armory located at Twenty-fifth Street and Lexington Avenue. Several prominent socialites interested in the arts helped finance the show. Gertrude Vanderbilt Whitney contributed $1,000 toward decorating the Armory, while Mabel Luhan put her limousine and chauffeur at the Association's disposal. The International Exhibition of Modern Art opened with considerable fanfare on February 17, 1913. John Quinn, the Association's lawyer, inaugurated the four-week exhibition with a stirring speech, and a band played in the balcony as students handed out free buttons stamped with the show's official emblem—the pine tree flag of the American Revolution. Except for the opening day, when approximately 4,000 visitors crowded the auditorium, few attended the exhibition during its first two weeks. When several popular magazines criticized the exhibits, thousands of curious visitors decided to attend and on the closing day 10,000 people jammed the Armory.[13]

The auditorium was divided into eighteen separate rooms containing approximately 1,300 works by 300 artists, including paintings, drawings, prints, and sculpture. (See Fig. 19.) Davies divided the exhibits into three categories: classicists, realists, and romanticists. The foreign section was purposely hung to trace the development of modern art beginning with Goya, Ingres, and Delacroix and running through impressionism, postimpressionism, orphism, fauvism, and cubism. A few artists' works were displayed in more than one category, while Cézanne, Van Gogh, Redon, and Gauguin were assigned separate rooms. The cubists were represented by Picasso, Braque, Léger, Picabia, Gleizes, and Duchamp, and the fauve group by Matisse, Rouault, Derain, Vlaminck, and Raoul Dufy. French modern art clearly dominated the European section since

Fig. 19. Photograph of exhibitions, Armory Show, 1913. Archives of American Art, Smithsonian Institution, Washington, D.C.

only a few German expressionists contributed work and the Italian futurists, who had wanted their own room, boycotted the exhibition.

There were several reasons why the American section looked weak compared to the Europeans, despite the fact that over two-thirds of the exhibits were from the United States. The country's modern art movement was just beginning in 1913 and lagged behind European developments. The American section was also a heterogenous collection, containing work of academicians, urban realists, and modernists. All The Eight except Shinn contributed to the exhibition, but the American modernists were underrepresented. Hartley and Marin submitted exhibits, but the works of Dove, Demuth, and S. Macdonald-Wright were missing. Weber did not submit his work because the organizing committee had restricted him to two entries, and he believed that they were favoring European artists over American.[14]

The publicity given to the foreign art invasion bothered certain Association members. Henri, an avid cultural nationalist, felt that there were too many European paintings. Glackens believed that the American section looked "tame" compared to the Europeans, but he hoped that the show would set off an artistic renaissance at home. Jerome Myers complained later that the Armory Show had done little for American art. "Davies had unlocked the door to foreign art and thrown the key away," he wrote. "Our land of opportunity was thrown wide to foreign art, unrestricted and triumphant; more than ever before, our great country had become a colony; more than ever before, we had become provincials." There was an obvious split between nationalists and internationalists in the Association's ranks, a conflict that would soon lead to the organization's demise.[15]

Severe criticism of the show also came from the general public and academic critics. The sudden invasion of modern art shocked Americans who were largely unaware of European developments and found the new painting incomprehensible. The *New York Herald* reported that on the exhibition's first day "amazement mixed with amusement was written on the faces of bystanders. The comments most frequently heard were those of censure." Reactions to the show took various forms. Cartoons in newspapers and magazines poked fun at modern art while jokes, jingles, and anecdotes were coined ridiculing the exhibits. Duchamp's *Nude Descending a Staircase,* the show's sensation, was called "an explosion in a shingle factory" and "Rude Descending a Staircase." A New York Vice Commission representative was sent to investigate the amount of nudity in

Duchamp's cubist painting and returned befuddled. Students of the Chicago Art Institute protested the show by burning effigies representing Matisse and Pach.[16]

Three leading genteel art critics, Kenyon Cox, Frank Jewett Mather, and Royal Cortissoz led the critical attack. As defenders of academic painting, they called the new art formless and immoral and representing socialism and revolution. "I have no fear that this kind of art will prevail, or even that it can long endure," exclaimed Cox. "But it may do a good deal of harm while it lasts." Theodore Roosevelt, whose views on art were not as progressive as his politics, felt that some of the modern paintings had been executed by lunatics. For the academic critics and the conservative general public, the Armory Show represented an assault on the fundamental laws of art, morality, and society.[17]

By contrast, the participants interpreted the event as a momentous occasion signifying a break with the past. As an iconoclastic revolt from outdated tradition, the exhibition represented many of the rebels' beliefs. After viewing the traveling exhibition in Chicago, Dell called it "an emotional experience which led to a philosophical and moral revaluation of life." Mabel Luhan interpreted the show as a revolutionary event equivalent to the signing of the Declaration of Independence. Stieglitz wrote a few weeks before the exhibition that the "dry bones of a dead art are rattling as they never rattled before. The hopeful birth of a new art that is intensely alive is doing it." Realizing the show justified his work at 291, he later congratulated Davies for striking "a vital blow" for modernism. The difference of opinion between the genteel art critics and the participants revealed the wide generation gap between the two groups.[18]

Despite the intense controversy, the Armory Show did introduce the American public to the new painting and the concept of modernism. Suddenly, words like "futuristic," "cubistic," and "modernistic" became part of the national vocabulary, while department stores commenced advertising colorful dresses in cubist and futurist patterns. The audience for modern art created by the Armory Show was nevertheless a limited one; indeed, the majority of the public remained unconverted. The exhibition tended to divide the American art world and artistic taste into two camps: realists and modernists. Nonetheless, thanks to the Armory Show, modern art was here to stay and would gain gradual acceptance over the years.

The exhibition also had an impact on the work of certain American artists, especially some realists who were forced to change their style to meet the new trends. The Stieglitz group was already well aware of avant-garde art either through the 291 exhibitions or by living in Europe; consequently, the Armory Show had little effect on their work. This was likewise true of other leading modernists such as Weber, Joseph Stella, and Charles Demuth, who had been to Europe and whose work already reflected foreign influences. For the young *Masses* artist, Stuart Davis, the Armory Show was a major turning point in his career. Before 1913, Davis was mainly a social realist who had been influenced by his teacher Henri, but the new art at the Armory Show caused him suddenly to experiment with form and color. As a result he went on to become one of America's most outstanding modern artists.[19]

The Armory Show also had a disruptive effect on the realistic style of The Eight painters. Henri became more involved with the problems of technique and less interested in subject matter, while Sloan, influenced by Van Gogh, Cézanne, and Renoir, brightened the color in his work and attempted to develop a three-dimensional form for his paintings. The impressionists among The Eight, Glackens, Prendergast, and Lawson, were already under the influence of European art and seemed to adapt more successfully to the new trends. All told the Armory Show made The Eight realists look old-fashioned, and the Stieglitz group consequently replaced The Eight as leaders of the progressive forces in American art. Ironically, the independent movement, which The Eight had first sponsored, led to their demise.

Mainly due to John Quinn, the Armory Show also changed the nature of the commercial art market. Besides playing an instrumental role in the exhibit, Quinn was a wealthy dilettante who enjoyed dabbling in the arts and owned valuable literary manuscripts and paintings. As a modern art collector, he adamantly opposed the provision in the 1909 Tariff Act levying a 15 percent duty on art less than twenty years old. The Association's leading members also wanted the tariff reduced, and as their attorney he argued successfully before the House Ways and Means Committee to abolish the duty. Quinn, who was also an influential Democratic party member, convinced his friend Oscar Underwood, the Committee's chairman, that a repeal would create a healthful competition between European and American modern art and improve the quality of art education at home. Museums, he declared, would then be more willing to purchase the new foreign art, and students would not have to go abroad to see modern European paintings. Because of Quinn's convincing arguments and Underwood's support, the 1913 Underwood-Simmons Tariff Act exempted imported contemporary art.[20]

The Armory Show also stimulated private and public art collecting. Quinn purchased works by Redon, Derain, Duchamp, Villon, Matisse, Brancusi, and Segonzac at the Show. Lillie P. Bliss bought two Redon lithographs, and her large collection eventually became the nucleus for starting New York's Museum of Modern Art. Other collectors who purchased paintings included Arensberg, Arthur Jerome Eddy, and Dr. Albert C. Barnes. Museums, which heretofore were reluctant to purchase twentieth-century painting, now began to take an interest in modern art. An important breakthrough occurred when Bryson Burroughs, the curator of the Metropolitan Museum of Art, bought Cézanne's *Colline des Pauvres* at the Armory Show. A few months after the exhibition the Newark Museum displayed seventeen works by Max Weber—the first one-man show of a native modernist in an American museum.[21]

This sudden interest in modern painting led to the opening of several new galleries in New York between 1913 and 1915. Before the Armory Show only a few places, outside of 291, were willing to risk showing modern art. The most important new gallery was the Daniel on West Forty-seventh Street, which opened in December 1913. Its owner, Charles Daniel, was a former café and hotel operator, whose interest in avant-garde painting had been stimulated by visiting Stieglitz's 291. He put together an outstanding list of American modernists: Man Ray, Charles Demuth, William Zorach, Marsden Hartley, Stuart Davis, Ernest Lawson, Samuel Halpert, Rockwell Kent, and Preston Dickinson. Another place to see the new art was the Carroll Gallery, which was noted for exhibiting the work of contemporary French artists and the synchromists. With the financial aid of Stieglitz and Arensberg, the artist Marius de Zayas opened his Modern Gallery on Fifth Avenue where he exhibited the work of Van Gogh, the French cubists, and the Dadaists. The New Yorker could also see contemporary painting at several other places, including the Liberal Club, the MacDowell Club, and the Modern School. By 1917 experimental artists had several outlets for their work.[22]

Another influential art gallery started during the Little Renaissance was that owned by the sculptor Gertrude Vanderbilt Whitney, the eldest daughter of Cornelius and Alice Claypoole Vanderbilt. In 1907 she converted an old stable on MacDougal Alley in Greenwich Village into an art studio where she exhibited the work of prominent artists. Later, in 1914, she expanded the premises by purchasing an adjoining building on Eighth Street. The Whitney Club, as it was now called, put on a variety of exhibitions, including topical shows such as "The Immigrant in America" and "To Whom Shall I Go for My Portrait." The latter exhibition featured portraits by Luks, Davies, Henri, and Bellows as well as the photography of Stieglitz and Steichen. Whitney was especially interested in exhibiting The Eight, and she gave Sloan his first one-man show at the Whitney Club in January 1916. Compared to the 291 exhibitions, the Whitney Club shows were rather tame, but her studio proved important for future developments. In 1915, she formed the Friends of the Young Artists in order to give aspiring American painters an opportunity to exhibit their work in nonjury and prize-free exhibitions. Whitney's aims were clearly inspired by the independent movement and the need to free art from academic restrictions. In 1918, she moved her art gallery to West Fourth Street where she and the gallery's director, Julianna Force, staged many major exhibitions during the 1920s.[23]

If the Armory Show had a widespread effect on the development of American art, its organizers, the Association of American Painters and Sculptors, had a short existence. Approximately a year after the show, the institution began to break up when some members revolted against the organization, including Henri, Sloan, Luks, Myers, and Bellows. One reason for their dissatisfaction was that they resented the fact that a small clique led by Davies controlled the Association. The conflict ripened when Henri and his associates failed in April 1914 to be elected to the board of directors. The Henri group was also more interested in exhibiting American art and disliked the internationalism of Davies that had led to the Armory Show. Believing that the Association's finances had been poorly managed, they resented the fact that no treasurer's report on the Armory Show's financial losses had been presented. These issues led Henri, Luks, Bellows, and Sloan to resign from the Association during 1914. Their resignations no doubt contributed to the organization's disbandment in August 1916.[24]

A new group, called the Society of Independent Artists, was formed that year to continue the independent movement. Modeled after the Parisian *Société des Artistes-Indépendants* (1884), it was organized by both American modernists and realists as well as Marcel Duchamp and Francis Picabia. The Society's purpose was to organize annual art exhibitions open to all artists for a nominal fee and without juries or prizes. Its first exhibit took place during 1917 at the Grand Central Palace where over 2,500 works by approximately 1,300 artists were shown. This large successful show was one of the biggest exhibitions ever held in America, and it brought to a climax the prewar independent movement. The Society went on to create a broad base for the future of American art by holding shows open to all artists until 1941.[25]

By World War I the Academy had lost its powerful position because of the insurgency of the independent movement and experimental artists could now more easily exhibit their work. Beginning in 1908 with The Eight Show, the independent movement had first fostered the development of realism. Then, with the Armory Show, the independents helped pave the way for the emergence of modern painting. The tradition of American modern art had first evolved at Stieglitz's 291 Gallery, but it was the independent movement and the Armory Show that broadened the range of its development. By 1917 modernism rivaled realism as an important movement in American art. That year the stage designer Lee Simonson could safely proclaim in *The Seven Arts* that "modern painting has won its character of freedom" and that "the insularity of our critics and our museums has been destroyed at a blow." [26]

NOTES

1. John Sloan, *New York Times,* April 12, 1907, clipping in the John Sloan Archives, Museum of Modern Art Library, New York City, N. Y.; John Sloan, *Gist of Art, Principles and Practise Expounded in the Classroom and Studio* (New York: American Artists Group, 1939), p. 81; Robert Henri, "My People," *Craftsman,* XXVII (February 1915), 459-69; Everett Shinn, "Recollections of the Eight," in *The Eight* (Brooklyn: Brooklyn Museum Press, 1943), p. 13.

2. William Innes Homer, *Robert Henri and His Circle* (Ithaca, N.Y.: Cornell University Press, 1969), pp. 150-51; Charles H. Morgan, *George Bellows, Painter of America* (New York: Reynal & Company, Inc., 1965), pp. 145-46; Ira Glackens, *William Glackens and the Ashcan Group* (New York: The Universal Library, 1957), pp. 54, 84.

3. Van Wyck Brooks, *John Sloan; A Painter's Life* (New York: E. P. Dutton & Co., Inc., 1955), pp. 102-3; and his *Scenes and Portraits, Memories of a Childhood and Youth* (New York: E. P. Dutton & Co., Inc., 1954), pp. 170-71; B. L. Reid, *The Man from New York, John Quinn and His Friends* (New York: Oxford University Press, 1968), pp. 39, 57-58, 84; letter of John Sloan to Elizabeth Yeats, February 7, 1922, in J. B. Yeats, *Letters to His Son W. B. Yeats and Others, 1869-1922* (London: Faber & Faber, Ltd., 1924), p. 289. Bellows's drawing was entitled "At Petitpas'," *The Masses,* VIII (July 1916).

4. Homer, pp. 106, 115-16; Glackens, pp. 49, 77.

5. Homer, pp. 126-30.

6. William Innes Homer, "The Exhibition of 'The Eight,' Its History and Significance," *American Art Journal,* I (Spring, 1969), 60-64; Homer, *Henri,* pp. 128-30, 137, 141; Sam Hunter, "The Eight–Insurgent Realists," *Art in America,* XLIV (Fall 1956), 58; *New York Realists, 1900-1914* (New York: Whitney Museum of American Art, 1937), p. 8. For reviews see *New York World,* February 2, 1908, clipping in the John Sloan Scrapbook, Library of the Museum of Modern Art; Mary Fanton Roberts [Giles Edgerton], "The Younger American Painters: Are They Creating a National Art?," *Craftsman,* XIII (February 1908), 523-31.

7. Catalogue, *The Fiftieth Anniversary of the Exhibition of Independent Artists in 1910* (Wilmington: Delaware Art Center, 1960).

8. James Huneker, " 'The Younger American Painters' and the Press," *Camera Work,* no. 31 (1910), 50.

9. Quoted from the "Minute Book of Meetings" and the "Constitution" in the Walt Kuhn Collection, Armory Show Papers; a Collection of Correspondence, Photographs, Catalogues, and Scrapbooks Relating to the American Association of Painters and Sculptors and the Exhibition of Modern Art, 1913; in the Archives of American Art, New York City, N.Y. See also Jerome Myers, *Artist in Manhattan* (New York: American Artists Group, 1940), p. 34; Milton W. Brown, *The Story of the Armory Show* (New York: New York Graphic Society, 1963), pp. 29-30.

10. The membership list in the Kuhn Collection lists all The Eight as members, including Bellows.

11. Arthur B. Davies, "Explanatory Statement," *Arts and Decoration* (Special Armory Show Exhibition Number), III (March 1913), 149; Walt Kuhn, *The Story of the Armory Show* (New York: Walter Kuhn, 1938), p. 8.

12. For Kuhn's trip see his *Story of the Armory Show,* passim. For the important role of Walter Pach see Brown, pp. 49-51.

13. Letter of Walt Kuhn to Walter Pach, December 12 [?], in the Kuhn Collection; Brown, pp. 71-75, 89-95; Mabel Dodge Luhan, *Intimate Memories,* vol. 3: *Movers and Shakers* (New York: Harcourt, Brace and Company, Inc., 1936), pp. 25-38; "Extreme Art Draws Crowd at Opening," *New York Herald,* February 13, 1913, clipping in the "Scrapbook of Catalogs and Clippings on Modern Art in America, 1912-1934," Museum of Modern Art Library, New York City, N.Y.

14. Max Weber, "The Reminiscences of Max Weber," pp. 273-74, unpublished MS. in the Max Weber Collection, Oral History Research Office, Columbia University, New York City.

15. William J. Glackens, "The American Section, The National Art," *Arts and Decoration,* III (March 1913), 162; Myers, p. 36.

16. "Extreme Art Draws Crowd at Opening." On criticism of the show see Brown, pp. 52-57, 83-87, 107-15, 126-49; Walter Pach, *Queer Things, Painting* (New York: Harper & Brothers, 1938), p. 195; Meyer Schapiro, "Rebellion in Art," *America in Crisis,* ed. Daniel Aaron (New York: Alfred A. Knopf, Inc., 1952), p. 209.

17. Cox's statement is from Barbara Rose, ed., *Readings in American Art Since 1900, A*

Documentary Survey (New York: Frederick A. Praeger, Inc., 1968), p. 85; reprinted from Kenyon Cox, "The 'Modern' Spirit in Art," *Harper's Weekly* (March 15, 1913). Theodore Roosevelt, "A Layman's View of an Art Exhibition," *Outlook* (March 29, 1913), 718-20.

18. Floyd Dell, *Homecoming* (New York: Farrar & Rinehart, Inc., 1933), p. 238; letter of Mabel Dodge to Gertrude Stein, January 1913, in *Flowers of Friendship, Letters Written to Gertrude Stein* (New York: Alfred A. Knopf, Inc., 1953), pp. 70-71; Alfred Stieglitz, *New York American,* January 26, 1913, clipping in "Scrapbook of Catalogs and Clippings on Modern Art in America, 1912-1934," Museum of Modern Art Library; letter of Stieglitz to Arthur Davies, February 18, 1913, in the Alfred Stieglitz Collection, Yale University, New Haven, Connecticut.

19. James Johnson Sweeney, *Stuart Davis* (New York: Museum of Modern Art, 1945), pp. 9-13; Stuart Davis Memorial Exhibition Catalogue (Washington D.C.: National Collection of Fine Arts, 1965), p. 17; Stuart Davis's interview in Katherine Kuhn, ed., *The Artist's Voice; Talks with Seventeen Artists* (New York: Harper & Row, 1962), pp. 65-66.

20. Reid, pp. 152, 157-60. Quinn's brief is in the Kuhn Collection.

21. Reid, pp. 149-50, 198, 207-8; Brown, pp. 96-106; Aline B. Saarinen, *The Proud Possessors, The Lives, Times, and Tastes of Some Adventurous Collectors* (New York: Random House, Inc., 1958), pp. 216-17.

22. Brown, pp. 205-13; Elizabeth McCausland, "The Daniel Gallery and Modern American Art," *Magazine of Art,* XLIV (November 1951), 280-85; " '291' and the Modern Gallery," *Camera Work,* no. 48 (1916), 63.

25. *The Whitney Museum and Its Collection, History, Purpose, and Activities* (New York: Whitney Museum of American Art, 1954), passim; Doty Healy, "A History of the Whitney Museum of American Art, 1930-1954," unpublished Ph.D. dissertation, New York University, School of Education, 1960; "Gertrude Vanderbilt Whitney," unpublished collection of papers in the library of the Whitney Museum of American Art, New York City, N.Y.

24. Brown, pp. 192-204; John Sloan, "1950 Notes," unpublished MS. in the John Sloan Trust, Delaware Art Center, Wilmington, Delaware, pp. 64, 181.

25. *Society of Independent Artists, Catalogue of the First Annual Exhibition, 1917* in the John Sloan Trust; John Sloan, "The Independent, An Open Door," *The Arts,* XI (April 1927), 187-88; William Glackens, "The Biggest Art Exhibition in America and Incidentally War," *Touchstone,* I (June 1917), 164-73.

26. Lee Simonson, "The Painters' Ark," *The Seven Arts,* II (June 1917), 204-5.

CHAPTER TEN

The Little Theater Movement

In 1908 the commercial standards of Broadway dominated the American theater. Sometimes a New York theatergoer could see a good European import by George Bernard Shaw or watch Sarah Bernhardt act in a classic, but generally the young aspiring playwright with new ideas found it almost impossible to get his plays produced. Broadway producers, indifferent to staging serious drama or experimental plays, selected plays having box office appeal. The standard fare on "The Great White Way" between 1912 and 1917 mostly consisted of mediocre plays and entertaining musicals. Romantic love plays such as Edward Sheldon's *Romance* (1913) and sentimental comedies like J. Hartley Manners's *Peg O' My Heart* (1912) were popular with Broadway audiences. Bayard Veiller's melodramas sold out nightly as well as a large selection of entertaining musical comedies and revues catering to the tired businessman. The Ziegfeld Follies and musicals by Irving Berlin, including *Watch Your Step* (1914) and *Stop! Look! Listen!* (1915), were box ofice smashes. Famous stars such as George M. Cohan, Billie Burke, Cornelia Otis Skinner, and Ethel Barrymore drew large audiences, while the productions of Charles Frohman and David Belasco became synonymous with Broadway success.[1]

While the general public delighted in Broadway's bill of fare, the social critics and young dramatists reacted in disgust. Mencken, who reviewed Broadway plays for *The Smart Set,* called the theater a commercial bore. "Why waste a whole evening, once or twice a week, in a stuffy and over-red theater, breathing zymotic air, sniffing discordant perfumery, looking at idiotic scenery, listening to the bleeding English of ignorant and preposterous actors," he stated. Important people in the Little Renaissance little theater movement such as George Cram Cook and Eugene O'Neill also criticized the commercial Broadway productions. Eugene's father, James O'Neill, was a famous actor well known for his leading role in *The Count of Monte Cristo*. The playwright felt that the plays his father performed were trite and sentimental, and *The Count of Monte Cristo* an artificial melodrama. He saw so many of his father's plays that he became repelled by their false cliché plots.[2]

The New York little theater movement attempted to emancipate the theater from Broadway's powerful influence. Rejecting theatrical tradition, the young dramatists, directors, and set designers wanted to create new forms and subject matter. Like the Stieglitz painters and the *Others* group, they were motivated by a spirit of iconoclasm and modernism. "The new spirit that has come into the dramatic world is the spirit of change—of experiment," wrote the critic Sheldon Cheney, a leading exponent of the little theater movement. "It is the spirit of dissatisfaction with traditional forms, which has entered not only into the arts but into every activity of civilization."[3] By contrast, David Belasco, a leading producer of the polished Broadway play, castigated the new drama as dangerous radical experimentation.

An important characteristic of the movement was the creation of small inexpensive intimate theaters for the production of plays. Unlike the Broadway star system, the performers and playwrights were rarely paid and were generally part of a repertory company. The producers usually sold annual subscriptions and memberships and often let the public select plays. The little theater specialized in presenting rotating bills of one-acters that gave performers the needed experience of playing several parts. The one-act plays were inexpensive to produce and a form conducive to experimenting with subject matter or mood. The little theaters also initiated new lighting methods and stagecraft designs by doing away with lavish scenery and using simple impressionistic stage sets. Often little theaters were associated with a particular community or university; indeed, the performers, designers, directors, and dramatists thought of themselves as a closely knit group working together to create a new American theater.[4]

Like so many other Little Renaissance movements, these innovations derived from changes in European culture. Experimental playwriting and production methods began on the Continent around the end of the nineteenth century when the first little theater, André Antoine's Théâtre Libre, opened in Paris in

1887. The movement quickly spread to other European capitals, including Moscow where Konstantin Stanislavsky began his famous Art Theatre in 1890. Other important new drama troupes were Max Reinhardt's Deutsches Theatre, Jacques Copeau's Théâtre du Vieux Colombier, and Dublin's famous Abbey Players. These theaters experimented with modern lighting and scenery and staged the work of Europe's new playwrights, including Ibsen, Strindberg, Hauptmann, and Shaw.

Some Americans were directly influenced by European developments. The stage designer Robert Edmond Jones learned of the new stagecraft while studying under Reinhardt in Berlin. Jones first applied the new techniques in 1915 when he designed the sets for Anatole France's *The Man Who Married a Dumb Wife*. Alice and Irene Lewisohn, the founders of the Neighborhood Playhouse, visited several art theaters in 1914, and eventually adopted the European innovations in their own company. O'Neill was impressed by the experimental Abbey Players when they staged the plays of J. M. Synge, W. B. Yeats, and Lady Gregory in New York during November 1911. One evening the Irish-Americans in the audience threw stink bombs and eggs at the actors because they disliked the way Synge treated their countrymen in *The Playboy of the Western World*. Despite the hostile reception, the visit of the Abbey Players influenced the development of the native little theater movement. Cook, who saw them perform in Chicago, modeled his Provincetown Players on the Irish troupe.[5]

The American little theater movement started in 1912 when Mrs. Lyman Gale organized the Toy Theater in Boston and Maurice Browne formed the Little Theatre in Chicago. Browne's theater played an important role in the Chicago Renaissance by staging contemporary European dramas and standard classics. Many other little theaters sprung up in the Midwest during the prewar period both in large cities such as Cleveland, Detroit, and Indianapolis and in smaller towns like Lake Forest, Illinois, and Madison, Wisconsin. By 1917 there were over fifty experimental theaters in American cities, small towns, and seashore villages. At first New York lagged behind the Midwest but due to the founding of the Neighborhood Playhouse, the Washington Square Players, and the Provincetown Players, Manhattan soon became the major center of experimental activity in the drama.[6]

Even before the formation of these three important companies, there were signs in New York of a theatrical renaissance. In 1912 the New York Stage

Society was founded to produce quality foreign and domestic plays. The Stage Society later helped finance the Provincetown Players and sponsored the important 1914 Exhibition of the Arts of the Theatre, a display featuring the work of modern stage designers. The first attempt to establish a major independent theater occurred in autumn 1909 when Winthrop Ames's New Theatre opened. Since the company was privately endowed by several wealthy New Yorkers, the directors hoped that the New Theatre would be free from the commercial pressures of Broadway and serve as a national theater similar to the Comédie Française. A large ornate auditorium occupying an entire block on Central Park West was built in Renaissance style to house the company.[7]

Responsible for the New Theatre's limited success was its young talented director Winthrop Ames. Favoring ensemble acting rather than the star system, he developed the New Theatre into an excellent repertory company. Under his guidance the troupe performed many classical and contemporary European plays, including works by Shakespeare, Maeterlinck, and Galsworthy. During its two-year existence the company staged only three new American dramas, and only one, Edward Sheldon's *The Nigger,* on- Southern race relations, was noteworthy. Since Sheldon was already an established dramatist, the theater failed to discover any new playwrights.

There were other reasons why the New Theatre failed to become a leading national company. Some mediocre productions were hastily put together and actors were often miscast. Ames also compromised his ideas by sometimes hiring stars to perform major roles. Another drawback was that the auditorium was badly constructed and too large for some plays. Conflicts also erupted over budgetary costs and production methods between Ames, the financially conservative governing board, and Lee Shubert, the business manager. Loss of money and lack of enthusiasm finally forced the founders to give up the enterprise in spring 1911. The failure of the New Theatre showed that the American public was not yet ready for a large resident stock company. What was needed were smaller less elaborate theaters in which artistic production and financial management were controlled by performers, playwrights, and directors.

Several minor Greenwich Village theaters were organized in this manner. One was the Thimble Theatre run by Charles Edison, the inventor's son, who produced plays by Strindberg and Chekhov. The poet Harry Kemp later took over the theater for the purpose of presenting his verse plays. During 1911 the painter Everett Shinn staged his own plays in the courtyard behind his Greenwich Village studio. His theater, called the Waverly Place Players, accommodated about fifty-five people and only four actors could fit on the tiny proscenium stage. Members of The Eight often acted in Shinn's satirical parodies of nineteenth-century melodramas. Although the theater lasted only a year, his skits became standard repertory pieces in European vaudeville houses.[8]

The most important new little theater on the Lower East Side was the Neighborhood Playhouse. In early 1912 certain members of the Henry Street Settlement House formed a dramatic group called The Neighborhood Players and performed plays in the local area for the residents. Three years later the troupe converted a simple red brick building on Grand Street into a theater complex. The Neighborhood Playhouse, as it was called, included a spacious auditorium, scenery and costume workshops, a carpenter shop, classrooms for acting, and rehearsal rooms. "It was our task," wrote Alice Lewisohn, "to develop a point of view toward the coordination of acting, setting, costume, among the group."[9] The Neighborhood Playhouse was both a community theater serving the Lower East Side and a dedicated group of performers and directors working together to improve the American theater.

Under the direction of Helen Arthur, Agnes Morgan, and the Lewisohn sisters, the Players staged various types of productions. The troupe specialized in original music and dance dramas based on religious themes and classical legends as well as contemporary European plays by such writers as Shaw and Chekhov. A few new American plays were presented before 1917, but only Susan Glaspell's *The People* was noteworthy. The Playhouse's auditorium was also used to show motion pictures and for special events such as poetry readings and song recitals. More known for its experimental production methods than for introducing new writers, the Neighborhood Playhouse continued to be a leading little theater after World War I.

The second most important prewar theatrical group was the Washington Square Players. This little theater derived from the one-act plays staged by several Greenwich Village writers at the Liberal Club. These performances proved such a success that they decided to create a permanent theater company. Behind the decision was Lawrence Langner, a successful New York patent lawyer and playwright. After attending Maurice Browne's Little Theatre, he thought of starting a similar company in New York. Inspired also by the successes at the Liberal Club, he organized the Players in late 1914 with the help of Albert Boni,

Edward Goodman, Josephine A. Meyer, Lucy Huffaker, Philip Moeller, Helen Westley, and Ida Rauh. The idea of a group of actors, playwrights, and designers harmoniously working together was stressed at the beginning. The players thought of themselves as a noncommercial organization

> of individuals who believe in the future of the theatre in America . . . that a higher standard can be reached only as the outcome of experiment and initiative. . . . We believe that hard work and perserverance, coupled with ability and the absence of purely commercial considerations, may result in the birth and healthy growth of an artistic theatre in this country.
>
> We have only one policy in regard to plays which we will produce—they must have artistic merit. Preference will be given to American plays, but we shall also include in our repertory the works of well-known European authors which have been ignored by the commercial managers.[10]

With these purposes in mind the Players began to stage important American and European plays, first at the Bandbox Theatre on East Fifty-seventh Street and then at the Comedy Theatre on West Thirty-eighth Street. The company relied heavily on selling subscriptions and subscribers were entitled to attend private performances and lectures. A typical season consisted of from five to seven bills of four one-act plays performed two or three nights a week. Comedy, serious drama, verse plays, and historical satire were often on the same program. The Players became noted for producing fine European plays by such writers as Schnitzler, Maeterlinck, Strindberg, Wedekind, Ibsen, and Chekhov. John Reed's *Moondown,* Theodore Dreiser's *The Girl in the Coffin,* and Susan Glaspell's *Trifles* highlighted the American productions, but its best success was the 1917 premier production of O'Neill's war play, *In the Zone.*

The Washington Square Players helped launch the careers of several dramatic performers and stage designers. Although nonprofessionals often acted in their plays, the Players mostly used professionals and formed their own acting school and traveling company. Katherine Cornell began her illustrious career with the Players in 1916 when she first appered in a one-act Japanese play. Other important members were the performers Helen Westley, Ida Rauh, Roland Young, and Glenn Hunter. The stage designer Lee Simonson received some of his first commissions from the Players. A familiar figure in Little Renaissance circles, Simonson was a frequent visitor to Luhan's salon and an art critic for *The New Republic.* Influenced by contemporary European stagecraft, he was interested in dramatizing the mood of a play through bright impressionistic colors.[11] His set designs contributed to the company's success, and this early training was important for the development of his brilliant career. Thus the Washington Square Players helped create a new American theater by rejecting commercial standards and allowing actors, playwrights, and designers freedom of expression.

Another important little theater in the New York Renaissance was George Cram Cook's Provincetown Players. Before coming to New York in 1913, Cook had spent much of his life in Davenport, Iowa, where he was born in 1873. Here had had met his future wife, the playwright Susan Glaspell, and his lifelong friend Floyd Dell, who had given him a job as associate editor on the *Chicago Evening Post's Friday Literary Review*. The Davenport trio of Cook, Glaspell, and Dell would later be among the original organizers of the Provincetown Players.

There were several crucial factors behind Cook's creation of the troupe, one of which was his aspirations for American culture. Besides being a Socialist and Nietzschian individualist, Cook worshiped ancient Greek civilization. He wanted the United States to imitate the rich cultural life of Greece by creating a climate conducive to artistic growth. An elite group of artists and writers, he wrote, should work together to forge a cultural renaissance:

> An American Renaissance of the Twentieth Century is not the task of ninety million people, but of one hundred. Does that not stir the blood of those who know they may be of that hundred? Does it not make them feel like reaching out to find each other—for strengthening of heart, for the generation of intercommunicating power, the kindling of communal intellectual passion.
>
> I call upon the vital writers of America to attain a finer culture, to develop in themselves and in each other more depth and fire—truth felt more blazingly; to be finer soils and finer voices, to make themselves strong as caryatides, prepared to bear together each of the hundredth part of our Renaissance.[12]

The idealist Cook believed that the best way to create a renaissance would be by establishing a group organized around the principles of a Greek community theater, in which writers, actors, and directors would work together to create new forms in the dramatic arts. Disliking the Broadway stage, Cook envisioned his troupe as noncommercial in spirit and dedicated to artistic freedom.

When Cook and Glaspell arrived in New York, they immediately became more interested in the theater. Together they wrote the comedy *Suppressed Desires,* which the Washington Square Players refused to stage because of its unusual subject matter. This action bothered Cook, who accused the company of conservatism and presenting too many foreign works. He then decided to organize his own group in 1915. The first productions were staged in Provincetown, Massachusetts, then a quiet quaint Cape Cod fishing village where several Greenwich Village painters and writers lived during the summer. The initial performance took place during July in Hutchin Hapgood's home where they staged *Suppressed Desires* and Neith Boyce's *Constancy,* a one-act comedy spoofing the Reed-Luhan love affair. Later that summer the group converted an old wharf fish-house owned by Mary Heaton Vorse into a small theater seating about ninety people on hard wooden benches. For the Wharf Theatre's opening the group repeated the first bill and two new one-acters.[13]

After another successful summer season at Provincetown during 1916, Cook and Reed prompted the group to continue their presentations in New York. Before leaving, the company met in the Wharf Theatre where they decided to officially call themselves the Provincetown Players and elected Cook president. A constitution was drawn up by Cook, Reed, Eastman, and the actor Frederick Burt and signed the following day by twenty-nine members. There were only four professional theater people among the signers, including Burt and O'Neill. Reed, Eastman, Dell, and Vorse were associated with *The Masses;* Hapgood was a journalist, while Cook, Glaspell, and Boyce were primarily fiction writers. Among the original members were the artists William and Marguerite Zorach, Charles Demuth, and Bror Nordfelt. The involvement of the painters and *The Masses* writers revealed the close alliance between Little Renaissance movements.[14]

The company was formed mainly for the purpose of challenging the commercial restrictions of the Broadway stage and to discover the works of new American dramatists. A resolution passed during a meeting on September 5, 1916, summarized its goals:

> That it is the primary object of the Provincetown Players to encourage the writing of American plays of real artistic, literary and dramatic—as opposed to Broadway—merit.
>
> That such plays be considered without reference to their commercial value, since this theater is not to be run for pecuniary profit.

That in attaining the results wished for the Provincetown Players do not necessarily limit their choice of plays to those written by active members.

That it shall be the duty of active members to discover and encourage new plays and playwrights.[15]

Freedom of artistic expression, rejection of past traditions, and cultural nationalism were three typical Little Renaissance values expressed in this important resolution. In contrast to the autocratic nature of the Broadway stage, the constitution stipulated that plays would be selected by a majority vote at meetings in which the proposed play would be read aloud to the entire membership. Playwrights were given control over production, and members were counseled not only to write plays but to involve themselves in other aspects of production, including scenery, costume, and lighting. The Players were thus organized around Cook's ideal of a community of artists working together to create an American theatrical renaissance.

Inspired by these goals, the troupe converted the parlor floor of a Greenwich Village brownstone on MacDougal Street into a theater. The apartment was divided into two sections, the rear used for the stage, while visitors sat in the front where brown wooden benches, accommodating about 150 customers, were laid out in tiers. Admittance to the Playwrights' Theatre, legally a private club, was by subscription only in order to avoid the city's housing and fire regulations for commercial theaters. The playhouse opened with considerable fanfare on November 3, 1916, with O'Neill's *Bound East for Cardiff,* Louise Bryant's *The Game,* and Dell's *King Arthur's Socks.* Cook and O'Neill played leading roles in *Bound East for Cardiff,* while Reed and Zorach starred in Bryant's one-act morality play. Since only a few professional performers appeared in the early plays, a considerable amount of amateurishness weakened the first productions.[16]

The Players made up for the uneven quality of their presentations by staging some excellent plays by new American writers. A stardard Provincetown bill consisted of both amusing and serious one-acters performed three nights a week and rotated every two or three weeks. Some early noteworthy plays were Pendleton King's *Cocaine* concerning a drug addict's desire to commit suicide, and Reed's *Freedom,* a satire on four prisoners attempting to escape from jail. Many of Dell's comedies mocked sexual relations in Greenwich Village, including the fantasy *The Angel Intrudes* (1917), which starred Edna St. Vincent Millay. The Provincetown Players helped launch Susan Glaspell's playwriting career by staging two early works. The one-acter, *Trifles,* dealing with a sheriff's investigation of a homicide on a midwestern farm, brilliantly conveyed the drudgery of farm life and the author's talent for recreating mood and writing dialogue. Lighter in vein was her humorous one-acter *The People,* which starred Cook as the editor of a radical little magazine. After 1920, she continued to write for the company, and gradually developed into one of the country's finest dramatists, receiving the 1931 Pulitzer Prize for *Alison's House.*[17]

Although Eugene O'Neill was the major playwright who made the Provincetown Players famous, he had already begun writing plays before joining the company. After dropping out of Princeton University in 1907, he took up a series of odd jobs in New York. Then for two years he lived the life of a sailor and beachcomber, making trips to Argentina and Honduras for gold prospecting. After returning from South America in 1911, O'Neill resided in a flophouse above "Jimmy-the Priest's" waterfront bar on Fulton Street, where he met many seamen and longshoremen who would later serve as models for characters in his plays. A year later O'Neill moved to New London, Connecticut, where he became a newspaper reporter, a career that was cut short when he was forced to spend six months in a nearby tuberculosis sanitarium. Around this time he turned to writing plays after having first dabbled in short stories and poetry. In a surge of inspiration during 1913-14, he wrote at least eight apprentice one-act plays and two longer works. His first play was probably *A Wife for a Life* (1913), a one-act melodrama concerning miners, which remained unpublished until 1950. Daring for its open treatment of sex was *Abortion* (1914) dealing with a student who commits suicide. Two other longer works, *Servitude* (1914) and the still unpublished "Bread and Butter" (1914), were overly melodramatic and badly constructed.[18]

O'Neill's talent as a dramatist was more evident in the five plays he published in 1914 foreshadowing themes in his later work. O'Neill's identification with the dispossessed was evident in *The Web,* which features a consumptive prostitute who becomes involved in a gangland murder. Two other plays in the volume, *Thirst* and *Fog,* depict one of his favorite subjects, the individual trapped by fate. *Thirst* concerns three people—a dancer, a gentleman, and a mulatto sailor—who are adrift on a raft after a shipwreck. When the mulatto sailor wants to drink the blood of the dead dancer, the gentleman prevents him by throwing her body into the sea; the sailor then stabs him and both fall into the shark-infested waters. In *Fog,* a poet, businessman, and a Polish peasant woman on a lifeboat are rescued by the wailing cries of the woman's dying child. The quarrel between the poet and the businessman symbolizes a confrontation between artistic creativity and commercialism—a familiar theme in O'Neill's later plays. No doubt these apprentice plays with their forced suicide endings were overly theatrical, but their naturalism, mood, poetic language, and subject matter departed radically from standard Broadway fare.[19]

O'Neill's association with the Players began during the summer of 1916 when he and a friend, Terry Carlin, were residing near Provincetown. When Glaspell asked Carlin for a play for her group, he told her that he had none but that O'Neill had several. The playwright then submitted *Bound East for Cardiff,* a moving one-act drama about a dying seaman who dreams of giving up seafaring for farming. The Players gathered in Cook's house to hear the play read out loud. Excited about what they heard, the group decided to include it in the second bill of their 1916 summer season with Cook taking the leading role of Yank and O'Neill playing a minor part. The play was an immediate success, but when it opened in New York's Playwrights' Theatre the following November, most critics were generally too busy reviewing Broadway shows to take notice. A well-written mood play and character study, *Bound East for Cardiff* was nonetheless an important turning point in O'Neill's career. (See Fig. 20.)

The playwright's success with this play and his association with the Provincetown Players proved prophetic. The group gave him carte blanche to write anything he wanted at a time when he was beginning to find himself as a dramatist. Since he had few friends among the Players, his relationship with the group was mainly professional. He preferred the company of sailors, gangsters, prostitutes, and longshoremen at the Greenwich Village "Hell Hole" saloon. With its wooden tables, nickelodeon, aroma of stale beer, and sawdust on the floor, the "Hell Hole" served as the model for Harry Hope's saloon in *The Iceman Cometh.* For the Players he completed during 1917 two more important one-act sea plays dealing with the ship S.S. *Glencairn. Bound East for Cardiff* had taken place on the S.S. *Glencairn* and he used the ship again for the plots of *The Moon of the Caribbees* and *The Long Voyage Home.* Actually the S.S. *Glencairn* was the fictional name for the S.S. *Ikala,* a British tramp steamer on which O'Neill had served as a sailor. An impressionistic play emphasizing atmosphere and characterization, *The Moon of the Caribbees* was a major break with theatrical

Fig. 20. Members of the Provincetown Players arranging scenery for Eugene O'Neill's *Bound East for Cardiff*, Playwrights' Theatre, New York City, November 1916. Courtesy, the Museum of the City of New York. Standing on the ladder is O'Neill, while seated on the bench is the Anarchist Hippolyte Havel. At the far right, holding a pole, is George Cram Cook.

traditions. Provincetown productions of *The Long Voyage Home* (1917) and *The Moon of the Caribbees* (1918) were well received and helped establish him as a new talented American playwright.[20]

O'Neill's sudden success ironically brought to a close the early years of the Provincetown Players. In 1920, the Players staged perhaps their greatest production, O'Neill's *The Emperor Jones,* with Charles Gilpin in the lead. The play was so successful that it moved uptown to the Princess Theater, while a Provincetown production of O'Neill's *Diff'rent* also went to Broadway the same year. These successes worried Cook, who feared that the group was beginning to cater to Broadway and was losing its original purpose as a small community theater. Devoted to noncommercialism, Cook was hesitant about moving any productions uptown. Because other influential members favored Broadway productions, dissension soon occurred within the group. In early 1922, Cook resigned from the Players because he felt that the company had become too commercial. Shortly thereafter he and his wife sailed for Greece, where they lived until Cook died in 1924. Sadly, he wrote Mary Vorse that the community spirit behind the Players had dissolved into selfish commercialism: "We have not, as we hoped, created the community of life-givers." [21]

Despite Cook's pessimism, the Players did reform the Broadway stage and the American theater in general. In 1923, the Players were reorganized under the direction of O'Neill, Robert Edmond Jones, and Kenneth MacGowan, and the theater renamed the Provincetown Playhouse where the group continued to stage some of the best plays of the postwar era. O'Neill and Glaspell came to brighten Broadway with their works and the new stagecraft began to be adopted on "The Great White Way" due to Simonson's and Jones's designs. The Broadway theater no doubt remained primarily commercial but the New York little theater movement at least improved the quality of its productions. The American stage was far better in 1920 than in 1908, because of the new playwrights, performers, directors, and designers developed by such little theaters as the Provincetown Players.

The members of the little theater movement joined the Little Renaissance modern poets and painters in creating new forms representative of the twentieth century. They shared with the *Others* group and the Stieglitz circle the spirit and philosophy of modernism. Nor were these groups entirely exclusive since experimental poets also wrote plays and were influenced by modern painting, while some painters practiced free verse and belonged to the new theater movement. If the modern poets, painters, and playwrights remained aloof from the politics of the Little Renaissance, the modernists still had much in common with the social critics. Both were motivated by a spirit of iconoclasm and revolt against the genteel tradition. For the avant-garde poets, painters, and playwrights, iconoclasm took the form of modernism, a philosophy and artistic method implying a rejection of the old and the creation of novel ways of expression. If the critics developed a new literature of social protest as a result of their revolt, the modernists' rebellion also led to new forms in the arts, best exemplified by the experimental poems in *Others,* the semiabstract painting of the Stieglitz group, and the moving one-act plays of O'Neill:

NOTES

1. Edmund M. Gagey, "The Great White Way, 1912-1917," *Revolution in American Drama* (New York: Columbia University Press, 1947), pp. 1-19.

2. H. L. Mencken, "Getting Rid of the Actor," in *H. L. Mencken's Smart Set Criticism,* ed. William H. Nolte (Ithaca, N.Y.: Cornell University Press, 1968), p. 54; reprinted from *The Smart Set,* September 1913; Susan Glaspell, *The Road to the Temple* (New York: Frederick A. Stokes, 1927), p. 148; Arthur and Barbara Gelb, *O'Neill* (New York: Harper and Brothers, 1962), p. 306; Louis Sheaffer, *O'Neill, Son and Playwright* (Boston: Little, Brown and Company, 1968), p. 205; Doris Alexander, *The Tempering of Eugene O'Neill* (New York: Harcourt, Brace & World, Inc., 1962), pp. 184-85.

3. Sheldon Cheney, *The New Movement in the Theatre* (New York: Mitchell Kennerley, 1914), p. 14.

4. Thomas H. Dickinson, *The Insurgent Theatre* (New York: B. W. Huebsch, 1917), pp. 76-81; Constance D'Arcy Mackay, *The Little Theatre in the United States* (New York: Henry Holt and Company, Inc., 1917), pp. 1-23; Walter Eaton, introduction to *Washington Square Plays* (Garden City, N.Y.: Doubleday, Page, 1916), pp. v-xvi; Cheney, pp. 123-24, 152-54.

5. Hiram K. Moderwell, "The Art of Robert Edmond Jones," *Theatre Arts Magazine,* I (February 1917), 51-61; Alice Lewisohn Crowley, *The Neighborhood Playhouse, Leaves From a Theatre Scrapbook* (New York: Theatre Arts Book, 1959), pp. 36-38; Sheaffer, p. 205; Glaspell, p. 218.

6. Mackay, pp. 1-23; Dale Kramer, *Chicago Renaissance, The Literary Life in the Midwest, 1900-1930* (New York: Appleton-Century, 1966), pp. 159-62, 193-96, 310-12.

7. Gagey, pp. 30-31; John Henry Jennings, "A History of the New Theatre, New York, 1909-1911," unpublished Ph.D. dissertation, Department of Speech and Drama, Stanford University, 1952.

8. Albert Parry, *Garrets and Pretenders: A History of Bohemianism in America* (New York:

Dover Publications, Inc., 1960), p. 130; Ira Glackens, *William Glackens and the Ashcan Group* (New York: The Universal Library, 1957), pp. 140-44.

9. Crowley, p. 85.

10. Lawrence Langner, *The Magic Curtain* (New York: E. P. Dutton & Co., Inc., 1951), pp. 76, 90-105, 451-52; quoted from a program of the Washington Square Players, in clippings of the Washington Square Players, New York Public Library Theatre Collection, Lincoln Center, New York City, N.Y.

11. Lee Simonson, "The Painter and the Stage," *Theatre Arts Magazine,* I (December 1917), 3-12.

12. Glaspell, pp. 224-25.

13. Mary Heaton Vorse, "The Provincetown Players," *Time and the Town, A Provincetown Chronicle* (New York: Dial Press, 1942), pp. 116-26; Mary Heaton Vorse, *A Footnote to Folly: Reminiscences of Mary Heaton Vorse* (New York: Farrar & Rinehart, Inc., 1934), p. 129; Glaspell, p. 253.

14. Minute Book of The Provincetown Players, Inc., September, 4, 1916-November 8, 1923 in the New York Public Library Theatre Collection, Lincoln Center, New York City, N.Y.

15. Ibid.

16. William Zorach, *Art Is My Life* (New York: World Publishing Co., 1967), pp. 45-47; Helen Deutsch and Stella Hanau, *The Provincetown, A Story of the Theatre* (New York: Farrar & Rinehart, Inc., 1931), pp. 5-6, 18-19.

17. *Cocaine* is published in *The Provincetown Plays,* eds., George Cram Cook and Frank Shay (New York: D. Appleton & Company, 1921), pp. 73-94; John Reed, *Freedom, The Provincetown Plays,* 2nd series (New York: F. Shay, 1916), pp. 70-93; Norman A. Britten, *Edna St. Vincent Millay* (New York: Twayne Publishers, 1967), pp. 34-44; Deutsch and Hanau, pp. 29-30; Arthur Waterman, *Susan Glaspell* (New York: Twayne Publishers, 1966), pp. 68-71; Susan Glaspell, *Trifles* and *The People* in *Plays* (New York: Dodd, Mead & Company, Inc., 1931), pp. 3-59.

18. Sheaffer, pp. 192-200, 252, 275-78. *A Wife for a Life, Abortion,* and *Servitude* are printed in *The Lost Plays of Eugene O'Neill* (New York: The Citadel Press, 1963).

19. Eugene O'Neill, *Thirst, and Other One-Act Plays* (Boston: The Gorham Press, 1914). The plays have been reprinted in Eugene O'Neill, *Ten "Lost" Plays* (New York: Random House, Inc., 1964).

20. Doris Alexander, "Eugene O'Neill, 'The Hound of Heaven,' and the 'Hell Hole,' " *Modern Language Quarterly,* XX (December 1959), 307-14; Sheaffer, pp. 184-85.

21. Edna Kenton, "Provincetown and MacDougal Street," preface to George C. Cook, *Greek Coins, Poems* (New York: George H. Doran Company, 1925), p. 29.

PART THREE

Cultural Nationalism:
Toward a New American Culture

CHAPTER ELEVEN

The Cultural Nationalists

Because most participants wanted to forge a new painting and literature indigenously related to the American experience, an infectious spirit of cultural nationalism permeated the New York movement. The first Little Renaissance critic to articulate the concept of cultural nationalism was Herbert Croly, *The New Republic* editor. While a student at Harvard College, several professors had influenced his early thought in this direction, especially Josiah Royce, George Santayana, and Charles Eliot Norton. Royce had taught the receptive student to value a citizen's loyal identification with his local community and nation, while Santayana had awakened Croly to the conflict between materialism and idealism in culture and the moral regeneration of society through the arts. Croly had become further cognizant of America's cultural inferiority in Charles Eliot Norton's fine arts course. According to the urbane Norton, a nation's civilization was measured by its arts, and compared to the European past, particularly the Middle Ages, culture in the United States was second-rate, eclectic, and dominated by commercial standards.[1]

With these views in mind, Croly first began developing his concept of cultural nationalism in the *Architectural Record,* a journal that he edited between 1900 and 1906. Artistic standards, he suggested in several articles, were determined by popular demand rather than an intrinsic aesthetic taste rooted in political and social ideas. He accused architects of compromising their talent for material rewards in a country where there is little appreciation for art. Although America presently lacked a rich cultural tradition, Croly hoped that the country could create a climate conducive to artistic development. He criticized expatriation as a form of escapism and urged the artist to remain in America where he could forge a culture directly related to the nation's social, economic, and political life. "What the United States needs," he asserted, "is a nationalization of their intellectual life comparable to the nationalizing, now under way, of their industry and politics; and in the fulness of time American culture will be invigorated and informed by the same enterprising and co-operative spirit which had distinguished its industrial successes." According to Croly, American politics, economics, and culture were integrally related.[2]

Croly envisioned that the center of this nationalization would be located in New York City. With its "quickened and consolidated public and social life," this great metropolis had the potential to become another Athens. The city was already a thriving industrial center, declared Croly, but, despite its many art exhibitions and publishing houses, New York had still not "become a city in which the finer and more constructive social and aesthetic ideals . . . received any adequate expression." The city not only lacked architectural beauty and regulated urban planning but artists lived in separate bohemian areas isolated from the surrounding community. Croly nonetheless hoped Manhattan would someday become a cultural oasis. He seemed to be forecasting the Little Renaissance when he wrote that "New York is the most national of American cities, and since the cultural basis of a modern literature or art is not municipal, or provincial, but necessarily national, New York is the one American city in which something considerable may happen." [3]

Croly's ideas were reexpressed in his famous book *The Promise of American Life* (1909), an eloquent political tract of the Progressive period calling for the concentration of political and economic power in the federal government. The author's support of a national reconstructive policy was partly motivated by his desire to improve the arts. The inspiration for *The Promise of American Life* had stemmed from Judge Robert Grant's *Unleavened Bread* (1900), a novel concerning a young idealist architect whose high artistic standards are compromised by the demands of the marketplace. Croly admired the book because it succinctly portrayed the conflict between culture and materialism, particularly the business pressures on the artist. In *The Promise of American Life,* he repeated his earlier assertion that aesthetic standards were dominated by commercialism. Art, he suggested, should not be judged by its material worth but by how much it contributes to democracy and freedom of expression. Only a talented elite of dedicated artists and critics could lift America's artistic standards to higher ideals. Like other participants, Croly believed that art had the power to regenerate society, to "convert the community into a well-informed whole." The union of culture and politics would not only counteract the influence of materialism in the arts but also improve America's political tradition.[4]

Croly's program for a cultural renaissance was no doubt overly idealistic. The alliance between culture and politics was precarious, a relationship easily leading to art being used for propaganda and as a tool of the state. Croly's two objectives, the concentration of economic power and artistic freedom, were at odds. Even the author had pointed out how the architect succumbed to commercial pressure. Despite these weaknesses, Croly's ideas on cultural nationalism influenced other Little Renaissance writers, and eventually played an important role in shaping the editorial policy of *The New Republic*.

He and Willard Straight, a well-known banker and diplomat, founded this weekly liberal journal in 1914. The magazine's offices in an old yellow-brick brownstone in the Chelsea area became another important social center where writers and artists gathered. Here in miniature was Croly's ideal of a community of intellectuals, an educated elite, publishing a magazine which they hoped would influence public opinion. The journal's aim to promote political and cultural nationalism symbolized Croly's desire to integrate these two spheres in American life. With its headquarters in Manhattan, *The New Republic* could also help achieve Croly's aim of making New York the nation's cultural center.

In order to carry out his goals he enlisted a talented editorial staff led by Walter Lippmann. By 1914, Lippmann was over the Socialist phase of his early career and shared Croly's belief in pragmatic progressivism, national planning, and the interrelationship of culture and politics. In *A Preface to Politics* (1913), the author had suggested that "without a strong artistic tradition ... the politics of a nation sink into a barren routine." According to the journalist, the arts could serve as a "moral equivalent for evil, a medium by which barbarous lusts find civilized expression," and create an "atmosphere in which a humanly centered politics can flourish." Lippmann used the pages of *The New Republic* to reiterate the view that the purpose of art was to give human insights and moral leadership. Unlike the more idealist cultural nationalists on *The Seven Arts*, Lippmann based the alliance between culture and politics on pragmatic grounds—the direct application of the arts to statecraft.[5]

Lippmann and Croly, however, editorialized more on politics than culture in

THE
SEVEN
ARTS

YOUNG AMERICA
By Van Wyck Brooks

DECEMBER, 1916
25 Cents

Fig. 21. Left: Cover of *The Seven Arts* featuring Brooks's important article "Young America."

The New REPUBLIC

A Journal of Opinion

| VOLUME I | New York Saturday 7th November 1914 | NUMBER 1 |

THE New Republic is frankly an experiment. It is an attempt to find national audience for a journal of interpretation and opinion. Many people believe that such a journal is out of place in America; that if a periodical is to be popular, it must first of all be entertaining, or that if it is to be serious, it must be detached and select. Yet when the plan of The New Republic was being discussed it received spontaneous welcome from people in all parts of the country. They differed in theories and programmes; but they agreed that if The New Republic could bring sufficient enlightenment to the problems of the nation and sufficient sympathy to its complexities, it would serve all those who feel the challenge of our time. On the conviction that this is possible The New Republic is founded. Its success inevitably depends on public support, but if we are unable to achieve that success under the conditions essential to sound and disinterested thinking, we shall discontinue our experiment and make way for better men. Meanwhile, we set out with faith.

APART from the narrow margin whereby the Democrats retained control of the House of Representatives, the salient feature of the election is the apparently reactionary revulsion of popular opinion. Progressivism of all kinds has fared badly. The Progressive Party has been reduced to an insignificant remnant. The unprogressive members of the older parties are much more conspicuous on the face of the returns than are their progressive brethren. If we may judge by the fate of the proposed woman's suffrage amendments, progressive legislation has fared as ill as progressive candidates. The revulsion appears to be complete. No explanation can explain it away, but how is it to be explained?

In all probability it is more than anything else an exhibition of fatigue. Popular interest has been strained by a political agitation which has lasted too long and has made a too continuous demand upon its attention. It is tired of Congresses which do not adjourn, of questions which are always being discussed and never being settled, of supposed settlements which fail to produce the promised results, and of a ferment which yields such a small net return of good white bread. The voter whose interest is flagging reverts to his habits. He had been accustomed to vote as a member of one party when business was good, and sometimes to change over to the other party when business was bad. Business has been undeniably bad. His attention was not diverted from the business depression by the impulse of new and attractive political objects. On the contrary, progressive politics and economics had ceased to be either new or attractive. So the good voter cast his ballot as one or the other kind of a partisan, and the bi-partisan system has regained some of its old vitality. Neither should the substantial contribution which President Wilson has made to this result be overlooked. His scrupulous loyalty to his own party, and his determination to govern by means of a partisan machine and the use of partisan discipline, has resulted in the recrudescence of merely partisan Republicanism, and the increased political importance to the individual voter of a close connection with one of the two dominant parties.

THE severest blow which non-partisan progressivism received at the elections came from the apparently successful Senatorial candidacies of Sherman in Illinois, Gallinger in New Hampshire, and Penrose in Pennsylvania. These three gentlemen are all of them machine politicians with unsavory records, who represent everything most obnoxious to an American progressive. They were to a considerable extent opposed by the progressive elements in their own parties. Yet they were all nominated and elected by popular vote, and no adherent of popular government can question their title to their offices. The meaning of the lesson is unmistakable. Direct primaries and the direct popular election of Senators will not contribute much to the triumph of genuine political and social democracy so long as partisan allegiance remains the dominant fact in the voter's mind. Bi-partisanship will con-

Right: The first number of *The New Republic* magazine.

The New Republic; consequently, the responsibility for making the magazine a journal of the arts shifted mainly to Francis Hackett and Randolph Bourne. Hackett, the literary editor between 1914 and 1922, had earlier played a leading role in the Chicago Renaissance as editor and literary critic on the *Evening Post*'s lively *Friday Literary Review.* On *The New Republic* he continued to apply the sociological literary criticism he had practiced in Chicago. A supporter of social realism, he praised the poetry of Sandburg, Lindsay, and Masters, the fiction of Anderson, Lewis, and Cather, and the drama of the little theater movement. However, compared to the Continent, he found American literature second-rate and dominated by commercial standards. Criticizing most American novels as sentimental escapist trash, Hackett called on the country's novelists to realistically portray their environment. His literary criticism helped popularize writers who were unafraid to treat the seamy side of life.[6]

Before joining *The New Republic,* Bourne had already become aware of the need of a new American culture linked to national ideals and patterned on current European cultural movements. During the prewar years the Continent was seething with national movements in the arts and letters. In France he had met young students and writers who were motivated by the ideal of creating a national culture, and in Germany he admired the close association between the government and the arts and the country's civic architecture and town planning. After returning from Europe, Bourne sought a permanent position with a magazine. Ellery Sedgwick, editor of *The Atlantic Monthly,* and Charles A. Beard, his adviser at Columbia, prompted Croly to give the young writer a position as contributing editor on *The New Republic.* Croly, who quickly recognized he had a colleague in Bourne, wrote him how the magazine could change American culture: "I believe also that a certain amount of conscious patriotism in our critical standard is necessary in order to enable us to have the effect we should like to have upon the actual practice of the arts in this country. . . . That means, translated into practical terms that we have got to discover and try to develop the beginnings of sound work whenever they appear in this country." [7]

In his *New Republic* book reviews Bourne followed Croly's advice by promoting the work of the new American school of social realists. The critic believed that "sociological pertinency" was more important than "literary art" in evaluating a novel of social realism. For these reasons Bourne especially singled out Dreiser's novels for their honest picture of American life and open treatment of sex. Acknowledging the novelist's cumbersome prose and overly long sentimental plots, Bourne wrote that "one reads him because he never forgets that he is talking about life as it is lived, and because he takes it seriously." Bourne also found in Dreiser's German background a challenge to the Anglo-Saxon domination of American culture. "A true hypenate," he called him, "a product of that conglomerate Americanism that springs from other roots than the English tradition." In *The New Republic* he also penned important articles on progressive education, pragmatism, and feminism. Bourne later found a more sympathetic home among the cultural nationalists of *The Seven Arts,* but it was mainly in *The New Republic* that he wrote the pieces that underwrote the Little Renaissance rebellion in the arts, feminism, and education.[8]

Despite the fact that Bourne, Hackett, and other book reviewers rallied around the new American literary realism, the prewar *New Republic* never became unified around a self-conscious program of cultural nationalism. Politics rather than the arts dominated the magazine, especially during 1916 and 1917, when the nation was faced with the question of entering World War I. Croly wrote only one important piece on the theme of cultural nationalism, and this idea never became a major editorial concern.[9] Other contributors such as Alvin Johnson, George Soule, and Felix Frankfurter were also responsible for making *The New Republic* a voice of progressivism rather than a literary journal. Nor was the magazine a major outlet for modern poetry. Its pages were mostly a mixed assortment of political editorials, articles on current events and reform issues, and book and theater reviews. Lippmann realized that the journal had not unified art and politics as Croly had hoped. Hearing about the formation of *The Seven Arts* in 1916, he wrote Louis Untermeyer:

> I hope it'll [*The Seven Arts*] do what we haven't been able to do and haven't had spare [*sic*] to do in the *New Republic.* For stories and plays we haven't had room. Poetry we haven't been able to find or to choose well, and a group of younger critics of the arts simply hasn't materialized. What has struck us is the conventionality of the younger men on whom we counted ... their rather rubberstamp youthfulness, and the extraordinary lack of original perception.[10]

Croly's ambitions for American culture would become a more dominant theme in *The Seven Arts.*

The idea for *The Seven Arts* was first conceived by James Oppenheim during the summer of 1916. The project received a tremendous boost when he attained the financial backing of the wealthy socialite Mrs. A. K. Rankine. At the time she and Oppenheim were being treated by the Jungian analyst Dr. Beatrice Hinkle, who suggested to Rankine to finance the magazine as a therapeutic measure giving her an outside interest. Since she played a limited role in the magazine's editorial policy, Oppenheim became largely responsible for setting the mystical, visionary, and optimistic tone of *The Seven Arts*. Under the influence of Walt Whitman, Carl Jung, and current European cultural nationalism, he envisioned America developing a rich tradition in the arts. "I was shockingly idealistic," the editor later confessed:

> I believed that the lost soul among the nations, America, could be regenerated by art. . . . I even had a definite idea as to how America was to become more human. It was the dream so many have had: a magazine, *the* magazine which should evoke and mobilize all our native talent, both creative and critical, give it freedom of expression and so scatter broadcast the new Americanism which would naturally have the response of America.[11]

Full of enthusiasm for the project, Oppenheim obtained the editorial assistance of Waldo Frank to help formulate plans. In August, he sent the following note to Frank outlining his ideas:

> We must be careful not to make the *Seven Arts* sag with nay-saying. Brooks already is giving that aspect; so will Dewey to some extent: but both these men feel as we do—namely that consciousness on a national scale is being born. Our very magazine is a response to this renascence and so the brighter color of a new day must run through it. We bring good news, even if we have to cut our way through some swamps to bring it.

Appointed associate editor in charge of drama and fiction, Frank soon became instrumental in developing editorial policy, approving manuscripts, and soliciting contributions and subscribers. Like Bourne, Frank had become interested in cultural nationalism while living in Paris during 1912-13. A cultural movement had developed in France where young writers emphasized the establishment of a new art and literature related to national traditions and ideals. In Paris, he became acquainted with many writers associated with the literary journal *La Nouvelle Revue Française,* particularly André Gide, Romain Rolland, Jacques Copeau, and Gaston Gallimard. He later wrote *Our America* expressedly for Copeau and Gallimard and published a booklet describing Copeau's Théâtre du Vieux Colombier, a French national theater. Because of his experience abroad Frank eagerly joined Oppenheim's cultural nationalism crusade.[12]

Frank was also important in persuading Brooks to join the editorial staff. His reading of *America's Coming-of-Age* convinced him that Brooks was a writer who should join *The Seven Arts.* An avid cultural nationalist, Brooks had much in common with his two colleagues. As a young man he had been stirred by the fiery nationalism of Mazzini and "his idea of the function of nations as the workshops of humanity, each with a peculiar gift to contribute to the whole." Through his friendship with the painter J. B. Yeats and the writer Padraic Colum, Brooks became enthusiastic about the Irish literary renaissance and its goal of invoking "a national purpose and a literature . . . along the lines of its own racial genius." Brooks could easily identify with the struggle of the Irish writers to free their culture from English influences. "We had special reasons for our interest in this [the Irish Renaissance]," he declared, "for we felt we were on the verge of a not dissimilar movement of our own, the first phase of another revival that expressed an American coming-of-age, an escape from our colonial dependence on England." [13]

Brooks's travels to Europe early in his career also convinced him of America's cultural poverty. Compared to Europe, he wrote in *The Wine of the Puritans,* "Americans have no bonds with a remote antiquity, no traditions of the soil old enough as yet to have become instincts." Brooks dreamed of building an American culture modeled on ancient civilizations. *The Wine of the Puritans* ends with the hope that "a day will come when the names of Denver and Sioux City will have a traditional and antique dignity like Damascus and Perugia." [14]

Despite his admiration for European culture Brooks rejected a life of expatriation. A writer, he stated, should remain home to create a better cultural climate in America: "I was convinced . . . that a man without a country could do nothing of importance, that writers must draw sustenance from their own common flesh and blood." While in France, Frank also came to realize that the expatriate life had limitations despite the stimulating Parisian environment. He began to feel himself an escapist and a parasite living off another culture and found criticizing America from a distance self-defeating. Eventually, he felt the need to come home and to directly participate in the burgeoning Little Renaissance. Frank's and Brooks's experiences suggest that the participants never shared the enthusiasm for expatriation as the writers and artists of the 1920s.[15]

Another important contributor to *The Seven Arts* was Paul Rosenfeld, who was urged by Frank to join the magazine as a music critic. Frank had probably first encountered Rosenfeld at Yale University where they two had been students. After graduation in 1912, Rosenfeld had attended the Columbia University School of Journalism and had briefly served as a reporter on New York newspapers. A European trip in 1914 had increased his interest in modern painting and music, and upon returning to New York he made frequent visits to the city's concert halls to hear the new music played. When Rosenfeld came to *The Seven Arts* he was just beginning to form opinions on American culture similar to Frank, Bourne, and Brooks. Through his friendship with the staff he shortly became an avid exponent of cultural nationalism and wrote articles in the magazine popularizing modern American painting, music, and architecture.[16]

Oppenheim, Frank, Brooks, Rosenfeld, and Bourne formed an inner circle controlling editorial policy. Although Bourne was not on the editorial staff, he played an influential role especially during 1917 when he contributed many antiwar articles. The five cultural nationalists were an inseparable group sharing similar aspirations and ideas. All grew up either in or around New York City and were members of the same generation. In 1916, Brooks and Bourne were thirty; Oppenheim, thirty-four; Frank, twenty-seven; and Rosenfeld, twenty-six. Not only did this "league of youth" fraternalize at *The Seven Arts'* editorial office, located in a townhouse on Madison Avenue and Thirty-first Street, but they often visited one another socially. Bourne enjoyed going to Frank's apartment on East Thirtieth Street where the two would play Bach sonatas on the piano. He also became good friends with Brooks and Rosenfeld.

The Seven Arts expressed the basic ideas the social critics had developed in their earlier writings: cultural identity, the search for a usable past, organicism, and communitarianism. Editorials preached the message that art could regenerate the individual and society while another theme was the urging of a strong community life. Utopian and mystical in nature, the magazine envisioned a rich American arts and letters linked with other national cultures in

Fig. 22. *The Seven Arts* group. Above left: Van Wyck Brooks. Above right: Randolph Bourne. Courtesy, Butler Library, Columbia University, New York City. Below left: Waldo Frank. Courtesy, Van Pelt Library, University of Pennsylvania, Philadelphia. Below right: James Oppenheim.

an international world order. Both popular and high culture were viewed as equally important expressions. The magazine's pages were strewn with iconoclastic attacks on puritanism and the conflict in American values between commercialism and higher ideals. As a solution to this divisiveness, the editors aimed to unite the individual and the group, American literature and life, and the arts and social progress. Thus, unification was the key word in their program, and culture was the essential tool behind the process of unification.

The Seven Arts' manifesto, published in the first issue of November 1916, best expressed the staff's ideals. This statement was probably first written by Frank as part of a prospectus sent to various authors and interested parties. The credo has a ringing prophetic tone characteristic of the Little Renaissance:

> It is our faith and the faith of many, that we are living in the first days of a renascent period, a time which means for America the coming of that national self-consciousness which is the beginning of greatness. In all such epochs the arts cease to be private matters; they become not only the expression of the national life but a means to its enhancement.
>
> Our arts shown [*sic*] signs of this change. It is the aim of *The Seven Arts* to become a channel for the flow of these new tendencies: an expression of our American arts which shall be fundamentally an expression of our American life.
>
> We have no tradition to continue; we have no school of style to build up. What we ask of the writer is simply self-expression without regard to current magazine standards. We should prefer that portion of his work which is done through a joyous necessity of the writer himself. . . .
>
> In short, *The Seven Arts* is not a magazine for artists, but an expression of artists for the community.[17]

A strange contradiction existed between the two themes of cultural identity and cosmopolitanism. On one hand the magazine published articles praising European culture and describing various cultural movements led by young writers and artists in Ireland, Japan, India, and Spain. *The Seven Arts* group thought of themselves as part of an international community of national cultures led by young rebellious writers and artists. Despite these concerns, the magazine also called for a new art and literature independent of Europe. In one instance Frank could write glowingly of French literature, but in another article declare that

> these spirits of revolt—Andreyev, Wedekind, Maeterlinck, Romains—are not true for us. They have not reached up through labored fields that are our own. Absorption in them is a natural growth for their countrymen; for the American it is a dangerous trick.
> We have our own fields to plough; our own reality to explore and flush with vision. Let us do this first; humbly and doggedly as lowly toilers must.

What the staff wanted was a culture independent of Europe, but one modeled on the Continent's current national literary movements.[18]

By cultural identity the writers meant the establishment of an art and literature directly related to American life. Bourne believed that the only way to free American culture from British influence was "the cultivation of a new American nationalism," while Oppenheim called on artists to become self-conscious Americans. Brooks presented the best definition of what he and his colleagues meant by cultural identity. " 'National Culture,' " he declared, "... is only the perhaps too-conscious equivalent of this element in which everything admirably characteristic of a people sums itself up, which creates everywhere a kind of spiritual teamwork, which radiates outward and articulates the entire living fabric of a race." [19]

The Seven Arts writers were careful to point out that their desire for an indigenous American culture was not motivated by zealous patriotism. As a group they disliked imperialism and opposed the political nationalism of Europe that had led to World War I. They hoped, instead, that chauvinism could be channeled into cultural rather than military manifestations. Nor was their concept of cultural identity a narrow one, since the staff wanted to broaden the scope of American culture by recognizing the contributions of immigrant groups. Bourne's revealing article, "Trans-National America," pointed out that the immigrant added to the enrichment and diversification of American culture. Rejecting the idea of the "melting pot," he called for a polyglot federation of different ethnic cultures.[20]

Their interest in the concept of ethnicity and culture derived partly from the Judaic religious tradition. Oppenheim, Frank, and Rosenfeld were Jewish, and the racial-cultural concepts implied in the religion helped shape their beliefs. Oppenheim had worked from 1903 to 1905 as a social worker on the Lower East Side and later as a teacher at the Hebrew Technical School for girls. His novel *Doctor Rast* (1909) deals with a humanitarian Jewish physician living in the ghetto, while several of his poems are on Old Testament themes. *The Seven Arts* group viewed the Lower East Side as a closely knit community where race, nationality, and culture were integrally related. Brooks's observations on the Jewish quarter reflected the feelings of his colleagues:

> I . . . relish [ed] the slums, their colour and variety, the stir in the streets, the craftsmen plying their trades in little shops, and often I spent the whole of a Sunday at a café in East Houston Street, reading and writing at one of the marble-topped tables. I was surrounded there by the real mysteries of the ghetto and by Yiddish actors and newspapermen playing chess and drinking tea like figures from the Russian novels I was greedily absorbing.

In an important article entitled "The Jew and Trans-National America," Bourne praised Zionism as one of the "most inspiring conceptions of trans-nationalism," and stated that the Jewish immigrant could especially contribute to the goal of a rich American heterogenous culture. Zionism was never directly expressed in the pages of *The Seven Arts,* yet it served as a model for the type of cultural-racial nationalism the writers advocated.[21]

A major principle of *The Seven Arts* critics, especially Brooks, was that national culture should be organically related to American life. Brooks's organic theory of art and society derived from Emerson, Whitman, and Ruskin as well as his admiration for the aesthetic philosophy of the art critic Bernard Berenson.[22] Under their influence he came to believe that the artist was not a special person separate from society, but rather a creator who worked within his community and whose art should instinctively reflect his surrounding environment. In *America's Coming-of-Age* the author complained that the arts were separated from American life and that the nation was fragmented into two parts, materialists and idealists, "lowbrows" and "highbrows." In order to remedy this division Brooks supported a unification of American life through the establishment of a harmonious relationship between the artist and society. "It seems to me," wrote Brooks, "that an artist can produce great and lasting work only out of the materials which exist in him by instinct and which constitute racial fibre, the accretion of countless generations of ancestors, trained to one deep, local, indigenous attitude toward life." In *The Seven Arts* the social critic again pointed out that America had never established an organic native culture due to its materialism, gentility, and puritanism. As in his previous books, he called for an integrated culture in which "literature and society in America bore an organic relationship to one another." [23]

The organic unity of American culture was an important theme in Frank's *Our America.* His ideas in this book were largely a reexpression of the ideals of Brooks, Bourne, and Croly. To Frank, Croly was an inspirational thinker who had first pointed out the need of a new American culture tied to national ideals. With Croly's ideas in mind, Frank argued in his book for a rich community life in which the arts flourished. In *Our America* the author also followed Brooks by attacking the division in society between materialism and idealism. The individual and the community must be linked to a common purpose, and the artist must become absorbed in American life. Yet America had not achieved a sense of collective unity or an indigenous literary tradition. It "is still in the chaotic stage of individual effort: the individualism of the unintegrated herd as contradistinguished from that of the social unit. . . . Group life on the level of young America still fails." [24]

The Seven Arts staff searched for a usable past on which to build their vision of an organic culture. Oppenheim called this the discovery of a "noble lineage" or a "real tradition on which to nurture our new talent." Brooks coined the famous phrase the "usable past" in 1918, but well before that date he and his colleagues were interested in discovering the country's cultural history. To them, most of America's literary past was unusable. The romantic poems of Longfellow, Whittier, and Bryant seemed sentimental; Henry James's writing suffered from a lack of contact with American life, while Howells was accused of writing tea-cup novels. Among the literature of the Gilded Age, Twain's work drew most of their praise, especially *Huckleberry Finn,* which Frank called an American masterpiece.[25]

They discovered a more "usable past" among the writers of the first American literary renaissance during the 1830s and 1840s. Although they could point to the failings of Poe, Emerson, Hawthorne, Thoreau, and Whitman, these writers were the prewar generation's forebears. Bourne once called Emerson, Thoreau, and Whitman "great men" because they "express the American genius," while Brooks referred to Thoreau, Emerson, Poe, and Hawthorne as "possessions forever." [26] Thoreau's attacks on commercialism and his defiance of governmental authority appealed to the rebellious temperament of the social critics. They also readily identified with Emerson's call in "The American Scholar" for the development of a culture independent from Europe. As a result laudatory references to Emerson and Thoreau were scattered throughout *The Seven Arts.*

Whitman's writing was the most important American precedent for their ideas. In *Democratic Vistas* the poet had attacked the detrimental effects of commercialism on America's artistic growth and had called for a culture indigenously related to the nation's traditions, language, and people. To *The Seven Arts* staff Whitman represented a poet who had challenged literary restrictions by writing honestly about American life, sex, and the emotions. Brooks especially looked to Whitman as a prophet of cultural nationalism. "He assembled in himself and his writings the characteristics of America," he wrote, "with him originated the most contagious, the most liberating, the most unifying of native impulses." To Brooks, Whitman was also an early pathfinder who proposed an organic culture: "The real significance of Walt Whitman is that he, for the first time, gave us the sense of something organic in American life." [27]

Bourne, Frank, and Oppenheim were equally stimulated by Whitman's writing. "I have been reading Whitman the last few days," wrote Bourne. "If one could keep permanently that wonderful mood of serene democratic wisdom, that integration and understanding, I think everything one did would be beautiful and right." Frank and Oppenheim had also read Whitman's works early in their life and had been impressed by the poet's message of individual freedom and rebellion against literary convention. "We stemmed from Walt Whitman . . . as well as from Emerson," Oppenheim wrote about *The Seven Arts.* Frank seemed to agree. *The Seven Arts,* he declared, forged "a national programme after Whitman, by which America shall become a creative force in the modern world." Eulogistic references to the great bard seemed to appear in every issue and were especially prevalent in Oppenheim's editorials and poems. An important link between Whitman and *The Seven Arts* was Horace Traubel, the poet's secretary, who published in the magazine a memoir of his experiences with Whitman. References to the poet in *The Seven Arts* proved that the writers had found a usable past in Whitman's life and work.[28]

The Seven Arts contributed to the development of a new national culture by promoting the work of young talented American writers, particularly Sherwood

Anderson. Conscious of the prewar rebellion in the arts which surrounded them, the staff published modern poetry, including Carl Sandburg's poem "Grass" and Robert Frost's "The Bonfire." The journal also printed the verse of Jean and Louis Untermeyer, Amy Lowell, Vachel Lindsay, and Stephen Vincent Benét but, compared to *Others,* the poetry in *The Seven Arts* was not particularly outstanding. Much more noteworthy were the four powerful short stories by Anderson which were later included in *Winesburg, Ohio* (1919).[29] Frank, who had been drawn to Anderson's work by reading his novel *Windy McPherson's Son* (1916), was responsible for their appearance. Anderson symbolized the type of new writer the staff was searching for, an author who wrote honestly about American life. In either late 1916 or early 1917, Anderson traveled to New York where he became friendly with Frank, Brooks, and Rosenfeld, who stimulated him and helped him with his writing. Thus began a long important relationship between Anderson and *The Seven Arts* writers. During the following years they often met, corresponded frequently, and eagerly read one another's books.

By promoting the work of new writers and the idea of cultural nationalism *The Seven Arts* played a significant role in the Little Renaissance. In this regard it succeeded where *The New Republic* had failed yet the magazine had certain weaknesses because of its zealous editorial policy. At times a moral righteousness pervaded its pages. Oppenheim's rhapsodic editorials and poems suffered from didacticism and sentimentality, and in his hands the important message of the magazine was sometimes turned into rhetorical propaganda. The journal's most serious drawback was that its program was too impractical. The staff was almost blinded by the idea that art could regenerate society; in addition, their ideal of a world brotherhood of creative societies was rather quixotic. Still, the periodical's assets far outweighed its liabilities. As the summation of nine years of artistic ferment in New York, the iconoclastic and prophetic essays in *The Seven Arts* were in themselves a valuable part of the new prewar American culture the staff had been so eager to create.

NOTES

1. Charles Forcey, *The Crossroads of Liberalism: Croly, Weyl, Lippmann and the Progressive Era, 1900-1925* (New York: Oxford University Press, 1961), pp. 15-21, 202; David W. Levy, "The Life and Thought of Herbert Croly, 1869-1914," unpublished Ph.D. dissertation, Department of History, University of Wisconsin, 1967, pp. 37, 182-83, 205-6, 212-13, 298-331.

2. Herbert Croly, "American Artists and Their Public," *Architectural Record,* X (January 1901), 256-62; "Henry James and His Countrymen," *The Lamp (Book Buyer),* XXVIII (February 1904), 47-53. Quoted from Herbert Croly, "The New World and the New Art," *Architectural Record,* XII (June 1902), 153.

3. Herbert Croly, "New York as the American Metropolis," *Architectural Record,* XIII (March 1903), 198, 205.

4. Herbert Croly, "The Architect in Recent Fiction," *Architectural Record,* XVII (February 1905), 137-39; "Why I Wrote My Latest Book: My Aim in 'The Promise of American Life,' " *World's Work,* XX (May 1910), 13086. Quoted from Herbert David Croly, *The Promise of American Life* (New York: Capricorn Books, 1964, first published New York, 1909), p. 196.

5. Walter Lippmann, *A Preface to Politics* (Ann Arbor, Mich.: Ann Arbor Paperback, 1962, first published New York, 1913), pp. 86, 88-89, 232.

6. Bernard L. Duffey, *The Chicago Renaissance in American Letters, A Critical History* (East Lansing: Michigan State College Press, 1954), pp. 172-73; Dale Kramer, *Chicago Renaissance, The Life in the Midwest, 1900-1930* (New York: Appleton-Century, 1966), pp. 101-11; Francis Hackett, *American Rainbow, Early Reminiscences* (New York: Liveright Publishing, 1971), pp. 286-92.

7. Letter of Herbert Croly to Randolph Bourne, September 15, 1914, in the Bourne Collection, Columbia University, New York City, N.Y.

8. Randolph Bourne, "Sociologic Fiction," *New Republic,* XII (October 27, 1917), 359-60; "Desire as Hero," *New Republic,* V (November 20, 1915, part 2), 6; "The Art of Theodore Dreiser," *The Dial,* XLII (June 14, 1917), 509.

9. Herbert Croly, "Our Literary Poverty," *New Republic,* I (November 21, 1914), 10-11.

10. Letter of Walter Lippmann to Louis [Untermeyer], July 29, [1916], in the James Oppenheim Collection, New York Public Library, New York City, N.Y.

11. James Oppenheim, "The Story of the *Seven Arts,*" *American Mercury,* XX (June 1930), 156.

12. Letter of James Oppenheim to Waldo Frank, August 14, 1916, in the Waldo Frank Papers, University of Pennsylvania, Philadelphia, Pennsylvania; David Waldo Frank, *Our America* (New York: Boni and Liveright, 1919), pp. ix-xi; *The Art of the Vieux Colombier* (New York, 1918); "A Prophet in France," *The Seven Arts,* I (April 1917), 638-48. The latter article celebrates Jules Romains.

13. Van Wyck Brooks, *An Autobiography* (New York: E. P. Dutton & Co., Inc., 1965), pp. 327-28; *Scenes and Portraits, Memories of Childhood and Youth* (New York: E. P. Dutton & Co., Inc., 1954), pp. 172-73. See also Van Wyck Brooks, "Ireland, 1916," *The Dial,* LXI (November 30, 1916), 458-60; Padraic Colum, "Youngest Ireland," *The Seven Arts,* II (September 1917), 608-23.

14. Van Wyck Brooks, *The Wine of the Puritans* in *Van Wyck Brooks: The Early Years, A Selection From His Works: 1908-1921,* ed. Claire Sprague (New York: Harper Torchbooks, 1968), pp. 11, 59 (first published London, 1908).

15. *Scenes and Portraits,* p. 146; Waldo Frank, *In the American Jungle,* (New York: Farrar & Rinehart, Inc., 1937), p. 10.

16. Paul Rosenfeld [Peter Minuet], "The Masqueraders," *The Seven Arts,* I (December 1916),

179-85; Paul Rosenfeld, "The American Composer," *The Seven Arts,* I (November 1916), 89-94; Paul Rosenfeld [Peter Minuet], "291 Fifth Avenue," *The Seven Arts,* I (November 1916), 61-65.

17. *The Seven Arts,* I (November 1916), 52-53. The prospectus is in the Waldo Frank Papers, University of Pennsylvania.

18. John Dos Passos, "Young Spain," *The Seven Arts,* II (August 1917), 473-88; Seichi Naruse, "Young Japan," *The Seven Arts,* I (April 1917), 616-26; Lajpat Rai, "Young India," *The Seven Arts,* II (October 1917), 743-58; Padraic Colum, "Youngest Ireland," *The Seven Arts,* II (February 1917), 608-23. On Oppenheim's idea of an international community of youth see his poem, "The Young World," *The Dial,* LXIV (February 28, 1918), 175-80. Quoted from Waldo Frank, "Concerning a Little Theatre," *The Seven Arts,* I (December 1916), 164.

19. Randolph Bourne, "Our Cultural Humility," *Atlantic Monthly,* CXIV (October 1914), 506; Lloyd Morris, ed., *The Young Idea; An Anthology of Opinion Concerning the Spirit and Aims of Contemporary American Literature* (New York: Duffield, 1917), pp. 70-71; *America's Coming-of-Age,* in Brooks, *The Early Years,* ed. Claire Sprague, p. 132.

20. Randolph Bourne, "Trans-National America," *War and the Intellectuals,* ed. Carl Resek (New York: Harper Torchbooks, 1964), pp. 107-23.

21. Brooks, *An Autobiography,* p. 156; Randolph Bourne, "The Jew and Trans-National America," reprinted in *War and the Intellectuals,* ed. Carl Resek, p. 128.

22. William Wasserstrom, *The Time of the Dial* (Syracuse, N.Y.: Syracuse University Press, 1963), pp. 18-22, 26-36; Claire Sprague, "Introduction," *Brooks: The Early Years,* pp. xii-xxix; *An Autobiography,* p. 118.

23. "Toward a National Culture," *Brooks: The Early Years,* p. 185 (first published in *The Seven Arts,* March 1917).

24. *Our America,* p. 200. For Croly's influence see the dedication page in Waldo Frank, *The Re-discovery of America* (New York: Charles Scribner's Sons, 1929); "The Promise of Herbert Croly," *New Republic,* LXIII (July 16, 1930), 160-263; "Herbert Croly," *In the American Jungle,* pp. 75-81.

25. Oppenheim, *American Mercury,* XX (June 1930), 159; Van Wyck Brooks, "On Creating a Usable Past," *The Dial,* LXIV (April 11, 1918), 337-41; *Our America,* pp. 34-44.

26. Letter of Randolph Bourne to Alyse Gregory, January 5, 1914, in the Bourne Collection; *America's Coming-of-Age,* p. 98.

27. *America's Coming-of-Age,* pp. 135, 128.

28. Letter of Randolph Bourne to Alyse Gregory, June 14, 1913, in *Twice-a-Year,* nos. 5-6 (Fall-Winter 1940; Spring-Summer 1941), 87; James Oppenheim, *American Mercury,* XX (June 1930), 158; Frank, *The Re-discovery of America,* p. 318; Horace Traubel, "With Walt Whitman in Camden," *The Seven Arts,* II (September 1917), 627-37.

29. The stories were "Queer" (December 1916), "The Untold Lie" (January 1917), "Mother" (March 1917), "The Thinker" (September 1917). See also Waldo Frank, "Emerging Greatness," *The Seven Arts,* I (November 1916), 74. See also letters of Sherwood Anderson to Waldo Frank in Sherwood Anderson, *The Letters of Sherwood Anderson,* ed. H. M. Jones (Boston: Little, Brown and Company, 1953), pp. 3-6; Sherwood Anderson, *A Story Teller's Story* (New York: B. W. Huebsch, 1924), pp. 366-67, 392-93.

CHAPTER TWELVE

Mencken, Dreiser, and *The Smart Set*

In his writing in *The Smart Set* magazine, Mencken also called for the development of a new broader based American culture. Like *The Seven Arts* writers, he aimed to create a more liberal climate for the artist. Mencken looked to Europe, particularly Germany, as the type of culture he wanted America to have. He also combed the nation's literary history for a usable past and championed such contemporary American literary realists as Theodore Dreiser. Throughout the Little Renaissance his writing brilliantly dissected the American scene, its character, and language. Mencken, however, never believed in the prophetic self-conscious cultural nationalism of *The Seven Arts* group. A fatalist and individualist, Mencken found their idealism and collectivism anathema. In his famous 1920 essay "The National Letters," Mencken pessimistically wrote "that insurmountable natural obstacles stand in the way of the development of a distinctively American culture, grounded upon a truly egoistic nationalism." [1]

The social critic felt instead that any improvement in culture would come from an educated elite. A talented corps of literary critics, he believed, could help change aesthetic taste. Although these views were close to Croly's, he never shared the latter's collective nationalism, nor did he believe very strongly in the relationship between culture and politics. Mencken's opinions were also somewhat different than Brooks's. The latter wanted to mend the rift in American society between the "highbrow" genteel critics and the "lowbrow" masses. Mencken disliked the genteel "highbrows" as much as Brooks, but he desired to replace their leadership with a new intelligentsia. Mencken referred to

Fig. 23. Cover of *The Smart Set*. Reproduced by permission of The Huntington Library, San Marino, California.

the "lowbrows" as a permanent class of "boobs" who needed intellectual leadership. Brooks aimed to create a middlebrow tradition, while *The Smart Set* critic favored a high artistocratic culture.

One of Mencken's important *Smart Set* articles on the American character had as its subject the American language. Comparing the difference between the English and American languages, Mencken vastly preferred the latter. His Anglophobia influenced his opinion that "American" was much the better of the two tongues because of its rich vocabulary containing foreign words and flexible connotations. Our speech, he declared, had "broken down the old barriers between the nominative case and the objective, and brought about an occasional marriage between singular and plural, and declared war upon the superfluous consonant and the disguised vowel." Mencken concluded by calling for a linguistic study of the American language–"preeminent among the tongues of the earth for its eager hospitality to new words, and no less for its compactness, its naked directness, and its disdain of all academic obfuscations and restraints." [2]

The article was an important forerunner of his famous book *The American Language.* As early as 1908, he had begun reading the British press and taking notes on the different usages in the two languages. He completed the first draft of his study by the end of 1916 and later revised it for publication in 1918. The book's purpose reflected the Little Renaissance search for an indigenous cultural tradition. The study, wrote Mencken, digs "deeply into national idiosyncrasies and ways of mind. . . . What I have tried to do here is to make a first sketch of the living speech of These States." [3]

The first edition of *The American Language* was partly a restatement of the arguments in *The Smart Set* article but his presentation was more convincing and his examples more thorough, revealing that Mencken had become an expert on American syntax. With his discussion of the linguistic contributions of the Indian, the pioneer, and the immigrant, the author showed a grasp of the historical development of the nation's language from the Colonial period to the opening of the twentieth century. In the work the author continued his war against the genteel literary critics by criticizing their admiration for the refined prose and poetry style of English classicism. By contrast, he praised Twain, Howells, and Ring Lardner for using colloquial speech in their books. Like Whitman's *An American Primer,* Emerson's *The Poet,* and James Russell Lowell's *Biglow Papers,* Mencken's study served to liberate American culture from England by pointing to the intrinsic value of the nation's language for literary purposes.

Disliking affectation in either speech or writing, Mencken favored books accurately depicting American life. He called on the writer to be true to himself and his environment and not to compromise his standards by succumbing to sentimentality and commercialism. He felt that a novel should have a well-developed social background and contain a philosophical world view. Because of his fondness for Darwin's ideas, he admired naturalistic works depicting protagonists struggling against fate. Three of Mencken's favorite writers were the naturalists Stephen Crane, Jack London, and Frank Norris. In his *Smart Set* columns Mencken praised other contemporary realists such as Sherwood Anderson, Willa Cather, Sinclair Lewis, Upton Sinclair, and the work of the Chicago Renaissance writers.[4]

According to Mencken, most nineteenth-century American literature was worthless and sentimental, handicapped by moral inhibitions to deal realistically with life. The work of Cooper, Longfellow, Irving, and Hawthorne suffered from romantic escapism. Only Whitman and Poe among the pre-Civil War writers represented a usable tradition because of their defiance of conventionality. The critic had mixed feelings concerning the major writers of the Gilded Age. Like other participants, Mencken mistakingly classified William Dean Howells with the genteel tradition. Overlooking Howells insights into American life, Mencken declared that his writing suffered from a "sickly, *Ladies' Home Journal* sort of piquancy." He unfortunately agreed with Brooks and Croly that Henry James's writing lacked sustenance due to his expatriation. To him, Mark Twain was "the true father of our national literature, the first genuinely American artist of the blood royal." In *Huckleberry Finn,* Twain had immersed himself in the nation's life and written an American masterpiece.[5]

During the prewar period Mencken showered more praise on Theodore Dreiser than any other contemporary writer. The relationship between Dreiser and Mencken was one of the great literary friendships during the Little Renaissance. Dreiser's pen had been relatively quiet since *Sister Carrie* had been banned by Doubleday and Company in 1900, but suddenly, around 1908, his long overdue praise as an important contemporary novelist began. In 1907, *Sister Carrie* was republished by B. W. Dodge and Company, and the following year Grosset and Dunlap issued an inexpensive edition. The novel had largely escaped the notice of buyers and critics in 1900, but now it sold well and was hailed in reviews. In 1910, Dreiser resigned his position as editor of the commercial magazine *The Delineator* and began to concentrate on his writing. During the prewar period he published the novels *Jennie Gerhardt* (1911), *The Financier* (1912), *The Titan* (1914), and *The "Genius"* (1915). He further commenced work on his autobiography, published a volume of plays, and two travel books. Although *An American Tragedy* was not published until 1925, the Little Renaissance was Dreiser's richest period of creativity.

Like Sherwood Anderson, Dreiser was hailed by the social critics as a realist who wrote honestly about American life. His frank treatment of sexual relations contrasted sharply with the prudery of most nineteenth-century novels. Dreiser's work was backed by various groups in the Little Renaissance other than *The Smart Set* staff. *The Seven Arts'* editors rallied around Dreiser as a precursor of the new American writing. Although Bourne, Brooks, and Frank found the novelist's style and plots cumbersome, they praised his work for reflecting contemporary life. Dreiser was also lionized by the Greenwich Village crowd. In his small studio on West 10th Street, where he lived with the actress Kirah Markham, Dreiser held open house on Sunday evenings. Sometimes he would dine at Polly's restaurant or walk over to the Liberal Club to join other members. Young writers such as Dell enjoyed his company and tended to venerate him as the father of American realism. Dell had first met Dreiser in Chicago where the novelist had gone to do research on *The Titan.* The two renewed acquaintances again in the Village where Dell often visited his apartment and helped him edit *The "Genius."* Dell found Dreiser's novels overly pessimistic, but he gave his work friendly reviews in *The Masses.* The novelist's concern with the inequalities of American life mainly attracted the Greenwich Village radicals to his work.[6]

Mencken boosted Dreiser's writing more than any other critic. The two discovered they had much in common when they first met in New York in 1908. At that time Dreiser said "an understanding based on a mutual liking was established, and . . . I counted him among those whom I most prized —temperamentally as well as intellectually." They often met for lunch or dinner when Mencken was in New York expediting his editorial duties on *The Smart Set.* Dreiser came to have great confidence in his friend's ability as an editor. Throughout the era he sent him the manuscripts and galleys of his novels for his opinion and corrections. Mencken offered both encouragement and practical advice, pointing out both the good and bad points in his work. The critic usually found his novels overly long and advised him to make cuts. Once when Mencken wrote that *The Financier* was too wordy and suggested eliminating several pages, Dreiser replied: "I have to thank you for direct forceful statements which have brought about this final change. You always see a thing as a whole which is a God's blessing." [7]

Mencken was well aware of Dreiser's faults, especially his long intricate plots, clumsy style, and occasional sentimentality. He was also bothered by the formlessness of *The "Genius,"* yet he found *Jennie Gerhardt* the best book he had read in years: "The story comes upon me with great force, it touches my own experience of life in a hundred places; it preaches . . . a philosophy of life that seems to me to be sound; altogether I get a powerful effect of reality, stark and unashamed. It is drab and gloomy, but so is the struggle for existence." [8] As this comment suggests, both Dreiser and Mencken shared a Darwinian view of the world as a place of struggle and chance. Mencken published a long descriptive essay on Dreiser's work in *A Book of Prefaces*. His acute analysis included a discussion of the influences of Emile Zola, Thomas Hardy, and Herbert Spencer on the novelist's philosophy. As in his earlier articles he pointed to Dreiser's deficiencies, but praised his work for revealing the vast impersonal forces controlling human fate. Mencken's essay served as a fitting climax to the Dreiser boom of the Little Renaissance. Later, in 1923, he summed up Dreiser's significance for the prewar generation:

> It was probably Dreiser who chiefly gave form to the movement, despite the fact that for eleven long years he was silent. Not only was there a useful rallying-point in the idiotic suppression of *Sister Carrie;* there was also the encouraging fact of the man's massive immovability. Physically and mentally he loomed up like a sort of headland—a great crag of basalt that no conceivable assault seemed able to touch.[9]

The Mencken-Dreiser relationship also had an important bearing on the history of *The Smart Set* magazine. There are several stories of how Mencken obtained his position as the magazine's literary critic in 1908. One is that the assistant editor Norman Boyer, with whom Mencken had worked as a police reporter in Baltimore, recommended him for the job. Another version places the responsibility on Channing Pollock, a friend of Mencken's and the magazine's drama critic. The most popular account concerns Dreiser, who was friendly with *The Smart Set*'s editor Fred C. Splint. When Splint asked Dreiser if he knew of a good book reviewer and literary critic, the author recommended Mencken. At the time of joining *The Smart Set* Mencken was already an established writer. He had been manager of the Baltimore *Evening Herald* and since 1906 reporter-critic for the Baltimore *Sun*. He also had a volume of poetry and book-length studies of George Bernard Shaw and Friedrich Nietzsche to his credit. His new position on *The Smart Set* gave him a wider audience and the freedom to write anything he wanted. Between November 1908 and December 1923, he penned hundreds of lively pieces for the magazine. Highlighting his contributions were book reviews, iconoclastic essays, unsigned poetry, and several hundred "pertinent and impertinent" anecdotes under the pseudonym "Owen Hatteras." [10]

Even before Mencken joined *The Smart Set* the magazine had been noted for its saucy humor. The journal dated back to March 1900 when it was founded by Col. William D'Alton Mann, who had earlier published the successful periodical *Town Topics*. Mann had subtitled his monthly "A Magazine of Cleverness," which aimed to poke fun at the foibles of high society. *The Smart Set* was mainly tailored to the popular magazine market, and, compared to *The Masses*, its irreverent iconoclasm was more for amusement than social revolution. The monthly gave its readers an eclectic dose of reading material. Syrupy short stories were mixed in with serious fiction written by such authors as O'Henry, Zona Gale, James Branch Cabell, Damon Runyon, and Edith Wharton. There was always an uneasy alliance between its pretensions as a literary journal as well as a commercial magazine, a conflict which caused it to have an unsteady early career. By 1910 financial problems and reduced circulation plagued the monthly. Even the colorful writing of Mencken and its drama critic, George Jean Nathan, failed to boost sales. The following year Mann sold the journal to John Adams Thayer, a millionaire advertising executive who had once coowned *Everybody's Magazine*. Thayer, who was even more conservative than Mann, appointed Norman Boyer to succeed Splint as editor, but Boyer was not able to lift the magazine out of its doldrums. [11]

The appointment of Willard Huntington Wright as editor in 1913 was a major turning point in the magazine's history. A talented eclectic writer, Wright had been literary editor of the Los Angeles *Times* and on the editorial staff of *Town Topics*. In New York he became friendly with Mencken due to their similar philosophical and literary views, especially a reverence for German

Fig. 24. Left: H. L. Mencken.

Right: Drawing of Willard Huntington Wright

literature and the works of Nietzsche. Mencken, who was responsible for obtaining Wright a job on *The Smart Set* in 1912, later suggested to Thayer that Wright be appointed editor.

Although he edited the magazine for only one year, Wright was able to turn the monthly into a leading literary journal. A devotee of the new European writing, Wright hired Ezra Pound as foreign editor to obtain contributions abroad. The work of D. H. Lawrence, Joseph Conrad, Frank Wedekind, Arthur Schnitzler, and August Strindberg soon began to appear as well as poems by Sara Teasdale, Richard Le Gallienne, and William Butler Yeats. Under Wright *The Smart Set* no doubt became "Europeanized," but American writers were not neglected. Stories were published by Dell and Dreiser, and poems by Pound, Harriet Monroe, and Robinson Jeffers. Wright's eclectic taste unfortunately proved too daring for the conservative Thayer, who became worried as advertising and circulation declined. He constantly argued with Wright, once accusing him of printing too many lewd stories. As a result Wright resigned in early 1914, and became a columnist for the *New York Evening Mail* and an art critic for the *Forum* magazine. His work on *The Smart Set* and his books on Nietzsche, modern painting, and the *Encyclopaedia Brittanica* made Wright one of the most versatile participants.[12]

When Mencken and Nathan took over the helm of *The Smart Set* in autumn 1914 a new era in the rocky history of the magazine began. They aimed to make the monthly both an entertaining magazine and a distinguished literary journal, in which humorous drawings and articles would accompany serious writing. The two were responsible for content since a manuscript selected for publication needed both their approval. Nathan would send manuscripts to Baltimore for his colleague's opinion, and every third week Mencken came to New York for a few days to expedite his editorial duties. While in the city Mencken resided at the Hotel Algonquin and did most of his work while eating lunch at Luchow's or the Beaux Arts. A "Poet's Free Lunch" consisting of pretzels, smoked herring, olives, and cheese was also available to guests in the magazine's offices. Mencken's office hardly looked like a literary gentleman's. He plastered posters of Follies girls on the wall and on his desk were two large brass spittoons.[13]

The first three years of their editorship proved largely to be a disappointment. Compared to *The Smart Set* under Wright, the magazine published few serious writers. Despite their interest in good literature, Mencken and Nathan were too conscious of making the journal a commercial success and were rather reluctant to publish experimental poetry and stories. There were exceptions, of course, including short stories by James Joyce, Waldo Frank, and Sinclair Lewis, and plays by Dreiser and O'Neill. Mencken, however, wanted *The Smart Set* "to be lively without being nasty. On the one hand, no smut, and on the other, nothing uplifting. A magazine for civilized adults in their lighter moods. A sort of frivolous sister to the *Atlantic*." [14] The editors consequently gave their readers a dish of humorous drawings, witty anecdotes, and sentimental short stories. Only Mencken's writing and Nathan's drama criticism had bite.

Commercialism was not the only reason they failed to make the magazine a leading literary voice of the Little Renaissance. A political conservative, Mencken disliked the Socialist bohemian writers of Greenwich Village and consequently closed the magazine to some of the best prewar writers. He also had mixed feelings concerning modern poetry. He might admire the work of Pound or Masters, but generally he was ambivalent toward imagism and the free-verse experimental poets.[15] Thus Mencken's political conservatism and literary biases limited the scope of *The Smart Set*.

Dreiser was correct when he accused Mencken of turning the magazine into "a light, non-disturbing periodical of persiflage and badinage, which now and then is amusing but which not even the preachers of Keokuk will resent seriously. It is as innocent as the *Ladies' Home Journal*." Mencken told Dreiser that he had been forced to compromise his ideals in order to keep the magazine solvent. *The Smart Set*, he admitted, was not the place for serious literature: "The fat women, who read our grand family magazine like sweet stuff, and sweet stuff we shall give them." Unlike the average cheaply run prewar little magazine, *The Smart Set*'s literary content before 1918 suffered because of commercial considerations. Only after World War I did the magazine begin to print the country's best literature, including short stories by Fitzgerald, Anderson, and Willa Cather. After making *The Smart Set* a leading voice of the twenties Mencken and Nathan left the journal in 1923 to found the *American Mercury*.[16]

Even if the prewar *Smart Set* failed in some respects, Mencken's work as literary critic, linguist, and iconoclast remained extremely valuable. In *The Smart Set* he attacked outdated standards inhibiting freedom of expression and supported a new literature grounded on realism and naturalism, especially the work of Dreiser. Although never a self-conscious booster of cultural nationalism, he wrote extensively on the indigenous aspects of the American character and language. Hesitant about joining groups, Mencken individually tore down the shrines of the genteel tradition in an effort to create a new American culture.

NOTES

1. H. L. Mencken, "The National Letters," reprinted in *The American Scene, A Reader* (New York: Alfred A. Knopf, Inc., 1965), pp. 108-9 (first published in *Prejudices: Second Series,* New York, 1920). See also H. L. Mencken, "Diagnosis of Our Cultural Malaise," in *H. L. Mencken's Smart Set Criticism,* ed. William H. Nolte, pp. 2-8 (first published in *The Smart Set,* February 1919).

2. H. L. Mencken, "The American: His Language," *The Smart Set,* XL (August 1913), 95-96.

3. H. L. Mencken, *The American Language, A Preliminary Inquiry into the Development of English in the United States* (New York: Alfred A. Knopf, 1919), p. 11. See Betty Adler, *Henry Lewis Mencken, the Mencken Bibliography* (Baltimore, Md.: Johns Hopkins Press, 1961), p. 9; Isaac Goldberg, *The Man Mencken; A Biographical and Critical Survey* (New York: Simon and Schuster, Inc., 1925), pp. 213-14; Edgar Kemler, *The Irreverent Mr. Mencken* (Boston: Little, Brown and Company, 1950), pp. 34-37, 106; Carl Bode, *Mencken* (Carbondale: Southern Illinois University Press, 1969), p. 120.

4. See various articles in *Mencken's Smart Set Criticism,* pp. 272-85; H. L. Mencken, "The Literary Capital of the World," *Nation* (London), (April 17, 1920).

5. H. L. Mencken, *A Book of Prefaces* (New York: Garden City Publishing Co., 1927, first published New York, 1917), pp. 156, 210, 213-16; "The Dean," *Prejudices: First Series* (New York: Alfred A. Knopf, Inc., 1919), pp. 52-58; quoted from "Our One Authentic Genius," *Mencken's Smart Set Criticism,* p. 179.

6. Randolph Bourne, "Desire as Hero," *New Republic,* V (November 20, 1915, part 2), 5-6; "Theodore Dreiser," *New Republic,* II (April 17, 1915, part 2), 7-8; Van Wyck Brooks, "Toward a National Culture," in *Van Wyck Brooks: The Early Years, A Selection from His Works, 1908-1921,* ed. Claire Sprague (New York: Harper Torchbook, 1968), pp. 186-87 (first published in *The Seven Arts,* March 1917); Waldo Frank, *Time Exposures by Search-Light: Being Portraits of Twenty Men and Women Famous in Our Day* (New York: Boni and Liveright, 1926), pp. 159, 164; Floyd Dell, "Mr. Dreiser and the Dodo," *The Masses,* V (February 1915), 17; "Talks with Live Authors, Theodore Dreiser," *The Masses,* VIII (August 1916), 36.

7. Theodore Dreiser, "Henry L. Mencken and Myself," in Isaac Goldberg, *The Man Mencken,* p. 378; letter of Dreiser to Mencken, October 8, 1912, in *Letters of Theodore Dreiser, A Selection,* vol. 1, ed. Robert H. Elias (Philadelphia: University of Pennsylvania Press, 1959), p. 148.

8. Letter of Mencken to Dreiser, April 23, 1911, in *Letters of H. L. Mencken,* ed. Guy J. Forgue (New York: Alfred A. Knopf, Inc., 1961), p. 12.

9. H. L. Mencken, "Theodore Dreiser," *A Book of Prefaces,* pp. 67-148; quoted from "Fifteen Years," *H. L. Mencken's Smart Set Criticism,* p. 328 (first published in *The Smart Set,* December 1923).

10. Bode, *Mencken,* pp. 60-61; Nolte, introduction to *Mencken's Smart Set Criticism,* pp. xii-xv;

Carl R. Dolmetsch, *The Smart Set, History and Anthology* (New York: The Dial Press, Inc., 1966), p. 24.

11. Dolmetsch, passim; Frank Luther Mott, *A History of American Magazines,* vol. 5: *Sketches of Twenty-One Magazines, 1905-1930* (Cambridge, Mass.: Belknap Press, 1968), pp. 246-51.

12. Bode, pp. 65-67; Mott, pp. 257-58; Dolmetsch, pp. 32-42; Nolte, introduction to *Mencken's Smart Set Criticism,* pp. xv-xvi; Burton Rascoe, " 'Smart Set' History," *The Smart Set Anthology,* eds., Burton Rascoe and Graff Conklin (New York: Reynal & Hitchcock, 1934), p. xxii.

13. Bode, pp. 67-73; Goldberg, pp. 187-96; Dolmetsch, pp. 44-45, 67; Sara Mayfield, *The Constant Circle, H. L. Mencken and His Friends* (New York: Delacorte Press, 1968), p. 13.

14. Letter of H. L. Mencken to Ellery Sedgwick, August 25, 1914, in *Letters of H. L. Mencken,* p. 49.

15. H. L. Mencken, *A Personal Word* (New York: privately printed, 1920), p. 8.

16. Letter of Dreiser to Mencken, April 20, 1915, in *Letters of Theodore Dreiser,* pp. 187-89; letter of Mencken to Untermeyer, April 19, 1916, in *Letters of H. L. Mencken,* p. 79.

CHAPTER THIRTEEN

The New York Scene

During the Little Renaissance a large number of writers and artists were turning to the American scene as subject matter for their writing and painting. In so doing they were creating a new national culture tailored to the literary and social critics' ideals. Concerned with portraying their immediate surroundings, both realists and modernists used New York City and its inhabitants as subjects for novels, poems, essays, and paintings, but they generally tended to interpret the metropolis in a different manner. The Eight artists and the Stieglitz group might disagree over aesthetic principles but they both felt that an artist should interpret his environment. Despite their differences Robert Henri and Alfred Stieglitz were avid cultural nationalists, arguing for the birth of an American art and sharing the faith that art could regenerate society.

New York fascinated the artist and writer as a symbol of American technology and cosmopolitanism. With its bustling activity and skyscrapers, the metropolis epitomized industrial progress and early twentieth century mechanical civilization. Reed, for example, celebrated the New York skyline in several poems, and interpreted Manhattan as a world center where one found "All professions, races, temperaments, philosophies / All history, all possibilities, all romance." [1] The modern poets and painters especially viewed the dynamism of New York as representing the entire spirit of modernism. The Little Renaissance realists were more entranced by the city's variety of life and cosmopolitan atmosphere. New York's avenues, squares, parks, restaurants, and transportational facilities offered infinite possibilities as subject matter for their writing and painting.

Realist writers and painters were particularly fascinated by Jewish immigrant life on the Lower East Side as well as poor people in general. They tended to romanticize the immigrants' poverty, feeling that their humble existence brought them close to the raw facts of life. This was the outlook of Reed and Alfred Kreymborg, who both described the life of the poor in early magazine and newspaper articles. Although Hutchins Hapgood's *The Spirit of the Ghetto* (1902), a pioneer study of New York's Jewish quarter, predated the Little Renaissance, the author's romantic description of immigrant life typified the writers' sentimental outlook. Hapgood's *Types from City Streets* (1910) also depicted New York's low life, including Bowery bums, bohemians, and prostitutes. An established journalist, Hapgood was friendly with many of the artists and writers and his participation in the Provincetown Players also linked him with the prewar generation.[2]

By contrast, Waldo Frank's interpretation of New York represented the modernists' viewpoint. The metropolis' fast pace and towering skyscrapers expressed two conflicting values to Frank: energetic materialism and mystical promise. In *Our America,* he devoted an entire chapter to discussing the city's dual nature, especially the difference between its inhabitants and architecture. The business-minded New Yorker lacked a spiritual inner life, he wrote, but, on the other hand, Manhattan's buildings expressed American dynamism: "New York is a resplendent city. Its high white towers are arrows of will: its streets are the plowings of passionate desire. A lofty, arrogant, lustful city, beaten through by an iron rhythm. . . . America is the extraverted land. New York, its climax." [3] Frank's interpretation no doubt derived from the concept of mythic America propounded by Whitman.

Because New York was a city of contrasts other writers such as Dreiser shared Frank's ambivalent attitude toward their environment. For Dreiser, the city epitomized a vast Darwinian struggle for existence. Awed by its magnitude and vigor, the novelist viewed the metropolis as a spectacle of life in which cruel impersonal forces created a wide gulf between rich and poor. In a number of early sketches of New York he described the city as a contrast "between the dull and the shrewd, the strong and the weak, the rich and the poor, the wise and the ignorant. . . . The glory of the city is its variety," he declared. "The dream of it lies in its extremes." His portraits of tramps, peddlers, tenement dwellers, and newly arrived immigrants revealed his fascination with Manhattan's heterogenous population. Like Hapgood and the other realists, Dreiser tended to romanticize poor people as fascinating individuals close to the reality of life.[4]

The novelist's descriptions of New York's harbors, rivers, and railroad junctions resemble the pictorial subject matter of an Eight painting. "If I were a painter one of the first things I would paint would be one or another of the great railroad yards that abound in every city . . . ," he wrote. "There would be pictures of it in sunshine and cloud, in rain and snow, in light and dark. . . ." Both Dreiser and The Eight observed the beauty and squalor of urban life in an attempt to realistically portray their surroundings. Indeed, direct contact with the realist painters stimulated Dreiser. He once lauded Henri and his group in an early magazine piece and wrote a short praiseworthy description of George Bellows's *Cliff Dwellers* (Fig. 25).[5]

Fig. 25. George Wesley Bellows, *Cliff Dwellers* (1913). Los Angeles County Museum of Art, Los Angeles County funds.

While living in Greenwich Village Dreiser visited the studios of Everett Shinn and John Sloan in search of background material for *The "Genius,"* a novel concerning Eugene Wilta, a young talented painter. Although the artistic side of Wilta represents a composite picture of an Eight artist, it was Shinn among the group who became the leading model for the fictional character. In the novel the author presents an almost verbatim description of Shinn's studio and depicts Wilta as a realist who paints the city because it is a vast spectacle. Wilta paints working girls returning home after work, which is the subject of Shinn's *Rush Hour* (1908). He also sketches Greeley Square in the rain and an elevated train above the Bowery—subjects painted by Sloan. (See Fig. 26.) *The "Genius"* cogently illustrates the close relationship between Dreiser and The Eight.[6]

Fig. 26. John Sloan, *Six O'clock Winter* (1912). The Phillips Collection, Washington, D.C.

If Dreiser helped establish a new native school of literary realism, The Eight painters led by Robert Henri helped create a new national painting depicting the New York scene. Progressive critics hailed Henri and his group for breaking from the stilted conventions of nineteenth-century painting and turning to urban America for inspiration. Their combination of urban realism and cultural nationalism was derived from Henri's aesthetic philosophy. As an art teacher he told his students to paint average Americans and the natural environment around them. Gypsys, Indians, and farmers were often the subjects of his paintings as well as the busy thoroughfares of New York. A disciple of Emerson and Whitman, Henri shared the same spirit of cultural nationalism as *The Seven Arts* group. Like the magazine's staff, he believed that a rich culture was conducive to social reform and a measurement of a nation's progress:

In America, or in any country, greatness in art . . . can only come by the art spirit entering into the very life of the people, not as a thing apart, but as the greatest essential of life to each one. It is to make every life productive of life—a spiritual influence. It is to enter government and the whole material existence as the essential influence, and it alone will keep government straight, end wars and strife; do away with material greed.[7]

To Henri, an indigenous art developed out of two important factors: a knowledge of American values and artistic freedom. A national culture, he declared, could not be formed through blatant patriotism or artificial means: "It is not possible to create an American art from the outside in . . . [or] start out with a self-conscious purpose of springing a ready-made national art on the public." Like Brooks, he believed that an organic culture derived instead from the intuitive response of the artist to. his immediate environment. These developments were valueless without freedom of expression, which alone allows the artist "to express the quality of his country" and "speak the language of his native land." [8]

As The Eight's most acute observer of urban life, John Sloan's work best reflected Henri's ideals. To him, Manhattan was a "cosmopolitan palette in which all colors mingle and then appear sharply by turns." [9] From his attic studio in Chelsea, Sloan watched New Yorkers going about their daily tasks. Women doing domestic chores or going home after work captured his imagination as much as fashionable society on Fifth Avenue. His early work chronicled New York's favorite places of rendezvous, including the Haymarket,

Lafayette Hotel, Renganeschi's Italian restaurant, and McSorley's Bar. The city's transportational system was the subject of *Wake of the Ferry* (1907) and *Six O'clock, Winter* (1912), a painting of the Third Avenue El. Whether a dust storm or a sunset on Twenty-third Street, Sloan was fascinated by the city's different moods. He fulfilled Henri's aims by creating works that instinctively revealed everyday life and contributed to the growth of a new American scene painting.

A disciple of Henri, George Bellows was another urban painter interested in portraying the multifarious aspects of New York. He painted colorful panoramas of the Hudson River and the city's crowded tenements as in his famous *Cliff Dwellers*. His *Steamy Streets* (1908) and *New York* (1911) caught the bustling activity, heavy traffic, and large crowds in Manhattan. New York's immigrants and dock workers were also among his favorite subjects. Closely associated with the ideals of The Eight, Bellows found inspiration in the city's streets and in so doing helped forge Henri's goal of attaining an art reflecting American life.

Although Stieglitz favored semiabstract painting more than realism, he was as much a prophet of cultural nationalism as Henri. The aesthetic principles of the 291 group were rooted in European modernism, but they still thought of themselves as a community of artists creating a new American culture. Like Henri, Stieglitz believed that art could regenerate society by bringing a sense of order and harmony to civilization. In his own work Stieglitz photographed Manhattan in both realistic and symbolic terms. Like The Eight painters, he caught the atmosphere of the city's waterfront, railroad yards, and ferries. His famous photograph, *The Steerage* (1907), depicting immigrants huddled in a ship, revealed his interest in portraying immigrant life. Other studies interpreted New York's skyscrapers as symbols of technological power.[10]

One reason behind Stieglitz's interest in modern architecture was that New York underwent rapid construction at this time. Tall skyscrapers including the forty-seven-story Singer Building (1908) and the sixty-story Woolworth Building (1913) came to rule over the skyline. To modern artists these buildings expressed the dynamic forces of America's industrial civilization. This was also true of the city's new bridges, especially Brooklyn Bridge (1883), a beautifully designed cable suspension structure. European modern artists such as Albert Gleizes and Francis Picabia saw in these structures values they were expressing in their own work. Inspired by the city's tempo and architecture, Gleizes walked the city's streets in search of subject matter. The skyscrapers, he declared are works of art. They are creations in iron and stone which equal the most admired Old World creations. And the great bridges here—they are as admirable as the most celebrated cathedrals. The genius who built the Brooklyn Bridge is to be classed alongside the genius who built Notre Dame de Paris. The same spirit underlies all supreme achievements. It is a very mistaken impression that one must go to Europe to see beautiful things.

Francis Picabia had the same reaction to Manhattan. "New York is the cubist, the futurist city," he wrote. "It expresses in its architecture the modern thought." [11]

John Marin, the foremost city painter among the Stieglitz group, was inspired to paint New York for similar reasons. He viewed the city as a place of turbulent movement and conflicting contrasts, an electric battleground of forces each fighting for supremacy. Marin's watercolors, paintings, and etchings of Brooklyn Bridge, the Woolworth Building, and Fifth Avenue are quite different than the realism of The Eight, for here the city's bridges and edifices are no longer solid structures but are broken up into surging lines and fragmented planes. (See Fig. 14.) Under Marin's hand New York has become a symbol of moving energy and power.

The city's rhythmic speed and tempo also stimulated Max Weber to paint the New York scene. In such works as *New York* (Fig. 27), completed in 1912, and *The City* (1910-18), Weber painted huge blocks of skyscrapers that occupy almost the entire canvas. In his cubist-futurist painting *Rush Hour, New York* (1915), he portrayed the city's turbulent pace through a play of lines and diagonals and a profusion of cones, semicircles, and discs creating the effect of unending movement. Another work, *New York at Night,* was a maze of intersecting shafts of colored lights and geometric shapes. Like other modernists, Weber was entranced by Brooklyn Bridge:

This morning early I was on the old Bridge of this New York. Midst din, crash, outwearing, outliving of its iron and steel muscles and sinews, I stood and gazed at the millions of cubes upon billions of cubes pile upon pile, higher and higher, still piled and still higher with countless window eyes, befogged, chimney throats clogged by steam and smoke—all this framed and hailed together in mighty mass against rolling clouds—tied to space above and about by the infinitely numbered iron wire lines of the

Fig. 27. Max Weber, *New York* (1912). Courtesy, Forum Gallery, New York City.

bridge, spreading interlacedly in every angle. Lulled into calm and meditation (I gazed) by the rhythmic music of vision (sight). I gazed and thought of this pile throbbing, boiling, seething, as a pile after destruction, and this noise and dynamic force created in me a peace the opposite of itself. Two worlds I had before me the inner and the outer. I never felt such. I lived in both! [12]

Equally drawn to painting New York's modern architecture and immigrant life was Joseph Stella. Born in Italy in 1877, Stella had emigrated to New York in 1896, where he had become a newspaper and magazine illustrator. At first Stella combed the city's streets in order to draw what he called New York's "striking characters" and "curious types." His well-executed realistic drawings of factory workers and immigrants were printed in newspapers and journals. Stella gradually turned from realism to modernism as a result of his travels in Europe where he came under the influence of futurism. Returning to New York in 1912, Stella viewed the city's modern architecture with fresh eyes. He was now thrilled, he wrote

to find America so rich with so many new motives to be translated into a new art. Steel and electricity had created a new world. A new drama had surged from its unmerciful violation of darkness at night, by the violent blaze of electricity and a new polyphony was ringing all around with the scintillating, highly-colored lights. The steel had leaped to hyperbolic altitudes and expanded to vast latitudes with the skyscrapers and with bridges made for the conjunction of the worlds. A new architecture was created, a new perspective. [13]

Like Weber, Stella began to furiously paint New York's factories, bridges, and skyscrapers. His famous painting *Battle of Lights, Coney Island* (1913-14) captured the hectic atmosphere of the amusement park with its surging crowd and revolving machines. About 1916 he moved to Brooklyn where he enjoyed gazing at the famous bridge. He called it a

weird metallic Apparition under a metallic sky, out of proportion with the winged lightness of its arch, traced for the conjunction of WORLDS, supported by the massive dark towers dominating the surrounding tumult

Fig. 28. Joseph Stella, *Brooklyn Bridge* (1917-19). Yale University Art Gallery, Collection of Société Anonyme.

of the surging skyscrapers with their gothic majesty sealed in the purity of their arches, the cables, like divine messages from above, transmitted to the vibrating coils, cutting and dividing into innumerable musical spaces the nude immensity of the sky.[14]

Between 1917 and 1919, Stella finished his first Brooklyn Bridge painting, a kaleidoscope of jewellike sparkling colors which transformed the structure into a mystical symbol of modern America. (See Fig. 28.)

Modern artists like Stella, Weber, and Marin thus joined the realist painters in celebrating the New York scene. Despite their different interpretations of New York, the modernists and realists used diverse styles to develop a national painting reflecting the American environment. Stieglitz and Henri were avid cultural nationalists, who shared Croly's and *The Seven Arts* writers' aspirations for a new culture. Cultural nationalism gave the participants a rallying point around which to challenge the older genteel tradition, and the attraction of local subject matter motivated the artists and writers to forge the new American culture they had envisioned.

NOTES

1. John Reed, "America, 1918," *New Masses*, XVI (October 15, 1935), 20. See also John Reed, "A Hymn to Manhattan" and "The Foundations of a Skyscraper," in *Tamburlaine, and Other Verses* (Riverside, Conn.: Hillacre, 1917), pp. 16-17.

2. Kreymborg wrote a series of studies on tramps for the New York *Sunday Morning Telegraph* entitled "The Joys of Being a Mongrel"—see Alfred Kreymborg, *Troubadour, An American Autobiography* (New York: American Century Series, 1957), p. 166. John Reed, "Immigrants," *Collier's* (May 19, 1911). Hutchins Hapgood, *The Spirit of the Ghetto, Studies of the Jewish Quarter of New York* (New York: Schocken Books, 1965, first published New York, 1902); *Types from City Streets* (New York: Funk & Wagnalls, 1910).

3. Waldo Frank, "New York," *Our America* (New York: Boni and Liveright, 1919), p. 171.

4. Theodore Dreiser, *The Color of a Great City* (New York: Boni and Liveright, 1923), pp. 1-2, 154. Most of these essays were written before 1918.

5. Ibid, p. 68. See also Joseph J. Kwiat, "Dreiser's The 'Genius' and Everett Shinn, The Ashcan Painter," *PMLA*, LXVII (March 1952), 15-31; Cyrille Arnavon, "Theodore Dreiser and Painting," *American Literature*, XVII (May 1945), 125-26; Theodore Dreiser, "A Note on the *Cliff Dwellers*, A Painting by George Bellows," *Vanity Fair*, XXV (December 1925), 55, 118.

6. Theodore Dreiser, *The "Genius"* (New York: New American Library, 1967, first published New York, 1915), especially pp. 103, 105, 107.

7. Robert Henri, *The Art Spirit* (New York: Keystone Books, 1960, first published New York, 1923), pp. 188-89.

8. Robert Henri, "Progress in Our National Art Must Spring from the Development of Individuality of Ideas and Freedom of Expression: A Suggestion for a New Art School," *The Craftsman,* XV (January 1909), 388. See also Robert Henri, "What About Art in America?," *Arts and Decoration,* XXIV (November 1925), 75.

9. John Sloan, "Souls of Our Cities Seen in Color," p. 7, unpublished MS. in the John Sloan Trust, Wilmington, Delaware.

10. A good portfolio of Stieglitz's New York photographs can be found in *Camera Work,* no. 36 (1911).

11. "The European Art Invasion," *The Literary Digest,* LI (November 27, 1915), 1224-25; Francis Picabia, "How New York Looks to Me," from a newspaper clipping in Mabel Luhan's scrapbook called "Scrapbook on the Armory Show" in the Mabel Luhan Collection, Beinecke Library, Yale University, New Haven, Connecticut.

12. Max Weber, "On the Brooklyn Bridge," unpublished MS. dated 1912 in Miscellaneous Correspondence, vol. 3, part 2, p. 136, in the Weber Oral History Collection, Columbia University.

13. Joseph Stella, "Discovery of America: Autobiographical Notes," *Art News* (November 1960), 41, 64-65. On Stella's life and artistic development see Marie Lenfest, "Joseph Stella—Immigrant Futurist," unpublished Master's thesis, Columbia University, 1959; Irma Jaffee, *Joseph Stella* (Cambridge: Harvard University Press, 1969).

14. Joseph Stella, "The Brooklyn Bridge (A Page of My Life)," *Transition,* nos. 16-17 (June 1929), 87.

PART FOUR

World War I and After:
The Decline and Aftermath of the
Little Renaissance

CHAPTER FOURTEEN

"A Sudden, Short Stop"

"One has a sense of having come to a sudden, short stop at the end of an intellectual era," declared Bourne in the October 1917 issue of *The Seven Arts*.[1] As the perceptive critic suggests, America's intervention in World War I brought the Little Renaissance to a close. Up to 1916 the question of America's participation was not a divisive issue among the participants. Many writers were Anglophobes both in literature and politics and had little enthusiasm for the English cause. As artists they were particularly sensitive to the atrocities of war and looked upon the European conflict with horror. They felt that America had the mission to uphold culture while the Continent was in turmoil and feared that involvement would crush the renaissance at home.

Bourne was in Germany when the conflict erupted during August 1914 and was immediately incensed by what he saw. The Germans, he observed, were now "swayed by one impulse, one desire–to war!" German nationalism had helped create a rich *Kultur* but now it had turned into militarism. Finding the atmosphere in Berlin suffocating, Bourne fled to Sweden and eventually returned home. Disillusioned with Europe, he now viewed America as the last refuge of the arts. He wrote his friend Alyse Gregory that

> the wheels of the clock have so completely stopped in Europe, and this civilization that I have been admiring so much seems so palpably about to be torn to shreds that I do not even want to think about Europe until the war is over and life is running again. I wish now I could find some way to see America as extensively as I have been seeing Europe, and feel its currents as sympathetically as I have been trying to feel those abroad.[2]

As a result of the war some European artists fled to America's shores; others such as the French writer Romain Rolland remained in Europe and looked to America as the last bastion of cultural freedom. He asserted that "on our old Continent, civilization is menaced. It becomes America's solemn duty to uphold the wavering torch." The writer called on American artists to "make of your culture a symphony that shall in a true way express your brotherhood of individuals, of races, of cultures banded together." This sense of responsibility had the effect of stimulating New York's cultural renaissance. According to Dell, events in Europe made *The Masses* a better magazine. It "became, against the war background, a thing of more vivid beauty. Pictures and poetry poured in—as if this were the last spoils of civilization left in America." [3]

By contrast, once America entered the war a dark shadow was cast over the movement. A somber mood displaced the carefree tone of the prewar years and writers began to lose their youthful optimistic idealism. Since some writers supported Wilson's action, dissension broke out among the participants, precipitating bitter quarrels among former cohorts. "The war had scattered and divided us," Dell recalled, "friend was set against old friend; and even if that had not been unhappily true, the war would inevitably have brought to an end that glorious intellectual playtime in which art and ideas, free self-expression and the passion of propaganda were for one moment happily mated." [4] The social critics had sometimes debated Socialist politics and the aesthetics of modern art but these quarrels were minor compared to the war question. There was enough of a vocal minority supporting Wilson's decision to cause a rift among the intellectuals.

Some writers and artists were outspoken prowar advocates. One was the poet Alan Seeger, a Harvard classmate of Reed, and a friend of several Little Renaissance writers. Inspired by a romantic attitude toward war, Seeger enlisted in the French Foreign Legion and was killed in battle at the age of twenty-eight. Before his death, Seeger wrote some dramatic war poems and a moving diary of his experiences as a soldier. Other participants aided the war effort at home. Gertrude Vanderbilt Whitney staged several art shows for the benefit of war relief organizations, and Greenwich Village writers and artists produced a MacDougal Alley Fiesta to promote the sale of Liberty Bonds. [5]

The only major Little Renaissance magazine editorially supporting Wilson's decision was *The New Republic*. At first the journal defended neutrality, but gradually during 1916 the editors began to back intervention. This policy change was not warmly greeted by all contributors. Croly and Lippmann supported Wilson's action but Bourne, Stearns, and Hackett repudiated the new prowar position. Hackett's relationship with the editors consequently cooled, while Stearns's and Bourne's contributions trickled to a few pieces. The radical participants vehemently criticized the fickle liberalism of the prowar *New Republic* editors. *The Masses* denounced the magazine for changing its position, while Bourne used the pages of *The Seven Arts* to attack his former colleagues. Such bitter feuding caused the harmonious relationship between participants to break down.[6]

America's intervention also crippled the financial resources sustaining the Little Renaissance. Since the war led to economic constriction Americans avoided purchasing unnecessary magazines, books, and paintings. Little magazines on a limited budget began to lose money. Stieglitz suspended publication of *Camera Work* in 1917 because he received only fourteen subscription renewals. He also decided to close Gallery 291 the same year. The little theater movement was hit hard when the Washington Square Players broke up because many members were drafted. By the end of 1917 many important Little Renaissance institutions had been forced to disband.

Antiwar advocates also found magazines closed to them because of their views. When England became our ally the writers' Anglophobia appeared traitorous; consequently, genteel critics accused them of "Germanizing" American literature. Dreiser was especially singled out because of his German descent, and Mencken's admiration for Nietzsche and German culture was branded unpatriotic. A supporter of neutrality, Mencken viewed the war as a state of extreme madness. During 1917 the critic refrained from commenting on the conflict in *The Smart Set,* a policy that enabled the magazine to escape indictment and survive the war years. Because of his reputation as a pro-German sympathizer Mencken found it difficult to publish his work. He had gone to Germany in late 1916 to report on the war for the Baltimore *Sun,* but a book about his experiences never found a publisher. *A Book of Prefaces* (1917) was coldly received by genteel critics, particularly Stuart Sherman, who attacked Mencken for his Teutonic prejudices. During this time Mencken received threats, his mail was opened, and he believed that he was being spied on. Because of the war the literary battle between the genteel and social critics was extended into a political foray.[7]

A more serious incident involved Willard Huntington Wright, literary editor of the pro-German *New York Evening Mail* in 1917. Wright's secretary was hired by the Creel Press Bureau to spy on him and to make carbon copies of his correspondence. Discovering her actions, Wright played a practical joke by dictating a fictitious letter to a friend outlining subversive plots against the United States. As she started making copies of the letter, Wright asked her what she was doing. Suddenly she became afraid and ran downstairs with the letter in order to call the police. Wright ran after her and discovered his secretary in a nearby phone booth, where he grabbed the telephone out of her hands. Soon the police arrived and released him, but because he had cast suspicion upon himself Wright was fired from his job. He suffered a serious breakdown of his health and never regained his stature as a perceptive literary and art critic. After the war Wright turned to writing Philo Vance detective novels under the pseudonymn "S. S. Van Dine." [8]

Another writer under suspicion by the government was Randolph Bourne. A staunch pacifist since his experience in Germany, Bourne continued to oppose intervention on moral grounds. He joined the antiwar Committee for Democratic Control and spoke out against the conflict in his work. Because of these activities Bourne felt that the Department of Justice was investigating his actions and that his letters were being censored. While vacationing in Martha's Vineyard in 1918, he and his girl friend, Esther Cornell, were questioned on the beach by a Navy officer who accused them of giving signals to a passing boat. The two were sent to Boston, questioned, and set free. Bourne also found it difficult to publish his writing at this time. In March 1917 he joined the staff of *The Dial* as contributing editor, but after publishing a vehement antiwar article the editors limited his contributions mainly to book reviews.[9]

Only in *The Seven Arts* did Bourne find a journal where he could freely voice his dissent. John Dewey's prowar articles in *The New Republic* had drawn Bourne's anger, particularly the philosopher's view that America's intervention was an opportunity to control the events in Europe toward a benevolent solution. In several *Seven Arts* articles the social critic bitterly denounced Dewey's use of pragmatism to justify involvement. By giving up its neutrality, declared Bourne, the country had lost the opportunity to determine the future peace. He felt pragmatism was an inadequate philosophy in a wartime situation. "What I come to," he wrote dejectingly, "is a sense of suddenly being left in the lurch, of suddenly finding that a philosophy upon which I had relied to carry us through no longer works." As the war dragged on during 1918, Bourne became completely disillusioned with Dewey's expediency. Brooks and Frank also joined him in denouncing pragmatism as a bankrupt philosophy lacking higher ideals.[10]

There was another important reason why Bourne and *The Seven Arts* staff spoke out against intervention. The instinct for militarism, wrote Bourne, was antithetical to artistic freedom and creativity. "The war," he asserted, "will leave the country spiritually impoverished, because of the draining away of sentiment into the channels of war." Feeling that the conflict would dissipate the renaissance, the author advised his readers to choose either "the war—or American promise. . . . One cannot be interested in both. For the effect of the war will be to impoverish American promise." [11] Like Bourne, Frank and Oppenheim feared that the conflict would put an end to the New York artistic ferment. Although Oppenheim rarely editorialized against the war, he once wrote a vitriolic play attacking Wilson and solicited antiwar articles. *The Seven Arts* became so noted for its opposition that Justice Department agents were sent to the editorial offices to investigate the journal.

The publication of political articles in *The Seven Arts* disturbed certain staff members. Although a neutralist, Brooks nonetheless believed that the journal should remain exclusively dedicated to the arts. "It was an error of judgment to jeopardize the magazine by making a special point of attacking the war," he recalled. "It was evident that if we did so our subsidy would be withdrawn, and I saw it as a magazine of *letters and art*. To make a political issue the principal issue seemed to me a mistake, and I regretted it and still regret it." Robert Frost, who was on the magazine's board, agreed with Brooks. Aware of the problem, he composed the following jingle for Louis Untermeyer:

> In the Dawn of Creation that morning
> I remember I gave you fair warning
> The Arts are but Six!
> You add Politics
> And the Seven will die a-Bourneing.[12]

Antiwar comments in *The Seven Arts* eventually caused Annette Rankine to withdraw financial support, an action that crippled the journal and led to its demise. She was considerably pressured into this decision by her family, wealthy owners of a food concern. In a letter to Oppenheim, she asserted: "I do not agree with the War policy of the magazine, and do not approve of the war articles which have appeared in the last few issues. . . . I wish to state further that I am desirerous [sic] of with drawing [sic] my support, and severing my connection with the Company as soon as possible." A few weeks after her action Rankine committed suicide. An editorial in the last issue of The Seven Arts announced that the magazine had lost its financial support and denounced the wartime hysteria: "Such is the awakening of tribal consciousness in the madness of war, that no longer is there that generous allowance for free expression, for diversity of opinion." [13]

The magazine might have continued publication if it was not for an editorial squabble. The editors first attempted to raise $25,000 to keep the journal alive but they were unsuccessful. Scofield Thayer, a wealthy staff member of The Dial, finally offered to purchase The Seven Arts on the stipulation that Oppenheim resign as editor-in-chief and share editorial responsibilities with a board. Oppenheim balked at Thayer's suggestion upon learning that Frank was behind the scheme. In an angry letter he accused Frank of trying "to make use of the crisis in which the magazine found itself, for your advancement." As far as he was concerned, the editor declared, "The Seven Arts is at an end, is gone, and that practically it can make no difference as to who has authority and who hasn't." Frank wrote back accusing Oppenheim of authoritarianism and of treating him as an underling. As for Oppenheim's assertion that he was trying to advance himself, Frank replied: "I felt merely that my position must be made to correspond in responsibility with what I had made that position actually to be." Thus The Seven Arts was never revived because of mutual distrust. By autumn 1917 the once closely knit coterie of writers had lost their sense of common purpose.[14]

The current atmosphere of intolerance against dissent also led to the closing of other antiwar journals. The 1917 Espionage and Sedition Acts gave the federal government power to curtail the publication and dissemination of any material attacking or preventing military and conscription policies. Antiwar magazines were subsequently banned from the mails, and dissenters and pacifists arrested. Since many Socialists opposed Wilson's action, antiradicalism accompanied the wartime hysteria. Because of its antiwar position The Masses was banned from the mails and newstands in 1917, and several of its editors and contributors were indicted under the Espionage Act.

The contributors to The Masses were themselves divided over the question of

America's involvement. A majority led by Eastman, Dell, Reed, and Young opposed the President's decision on both moral and political grounds. Although most Socialist party members opposed intervention, the party itself was split over the issue. The division was evident on *The Masses* where certain moderate Socialists backed Wilson. Sloan felt that the magazine's antiwar position undermined the purpose of publishing art and literature, while Bellows executed many war posters. Dissension became evident in May 1917 when the right-wing Socialist William English Walling resigned from *The Masses,* feeling that the magazine had become pro-German. In an irate letter of resignation to Eastman he declared that "you and Reed take exactly the same view of the duty of Americans at this juncture as the Kaiser, Bethmann-Hollweg and Zimmerman. Of course, I desire to disconnect myself from you. Heaven knows what perverse emotion or pseudo-reasoning have brought you to support Militarism in this grave crisis!" Eastman replied that he equally disliked the German war machine but that it was best America remain neutral.[15]

The Masses attack against the war had been gaining momentum for several years. The September 1914 issue blatantly proclaimed the editors' view that the European war was a capitalist affair. "This is not our war," Reed asserted, "it is a clash of traders," while Eastman called it a futile commercial "gambler's war." Art Young's drawings also interpreted the war as a venture for commercial profit. Seeing the turmoil firsthand increased the opposition of Reed and Eastman, who traveled to Europe during 1915. Reed found the war atrociously dull and disliked the bellicose superpatriotic atmosphere that had overrun the Continent. "I hate soldiers," he stated. "I hate to see a man with a bayonet fixed on his rifle, who can order me off the street." Eastman called the dismal trench warfare in Europe a tedious exercise in futility. "We want to see the German invasion repulsed–we want to see the Kaiser's expectations smashed," he declared. "But, whether they are smashed or not, we do not want to see the United States at war." During 1916 *The Masses* began to crusade even more vehemently against the war. In an issue attacking the country's military preparations, Eastman spoke out against drafting men into the National Guard, while Reed criticized Theodore Roosevelt's support of England. By the end of 1916 *The Masses* was irrevocably dedicated to keeping America out of the war.[16]

Wilson's decision to intervene in April 1917 came as a shock to the editorial staff. Hoping that the President would keep the country out of war, Reed had voted for him in 1916 but now the editors lashed out at Wilson. The President has betrayed the nation, stated Reed; it is now "Woodrow Wilson's and Wall Street's war." Eastman warned his readers to "resist the war-fever and the patriotic delirium, the sentimental hatred, the solemn hypocrisies of idealists. . . ." Opposition to conscription became a major issue in *The Masses*. "I do not recognize the right of a government to draft me to war whose purposes I do not believe in," stated Eastman. Reed commented before the House Judiciary Committee, holding hearings on the Espionage Act, that he would rather be shot as a traitor than serve in the war. Feeling that the war was a capitalist crusade and morally wrong, Dell also took a pacifist position by writing "conscientious objector" on his draft card.[17]

The Masses soon began to feel the effects of its opposition to intervention. Antiwar editorials, articles, and drawings now came to dominate the monthly, and its literary and artistic contributions lacked the luster of earlier years. In March 1916, Ward and Gow refused to distribute the magazine because of its alleged unpatriotic and irreligious contents, and it was barred from several libraries, bookstores, and newsstands. *The Masses* staff also came under attack. The prowar *Metropolitan Magazine* suddenly fired Young and Reed as correspondents, while the latter was constantly followed by detectives. In October 1917, Postmaster General T. G. Patten issued an order canceling its mailing privileges. As a little magazine subsisting on limited finances the government's decree hit the journal hard. Eastman immediately wrote President Wilson complaining of the government's action and asking him to clarify the unmailable content in the magazine. "I ask you," he wrote, "whether it is with your authority that an appointee of yours endeavors to destroy the life of the three growing Socialist magazines in the country, as a war measure in a war for democracy." [18] Wilson replied that he disapproved of the journal's antiwar comments and that certain restrictions on freedom of expression were necessary in wartime.

Seven members of *The Masses* were indicted under the Espionage Act: Eastman, Dell, Reed, Young, Henry J. Glintenkamp, Josephine Bell, and Merrill Rogers, the magazine's business manager. Charged with promoting conspiracy, insubordination, and mutiny in the military and naval forces and obstructing recruitment, the defendants were liable to a penalty of twenty years in jail and a fine of $10,000. Eastman was specifically charged with writing an article supporting pacifism, and Dell for defending the rights of English conscientious objectors. Reed was subpoenaed for his article describing soldiers who had suffered mental disorders due to the war. The government indicted Young for his cartoon, "Having Their Fling," suggesting that government, business, religion, and the press had conspired to cause the war.

The first trial in April 1918 was held in an atmosphere of antiradical hysteria. Because so many Socialists opposed the war, most radicals were branded by the public as traitors. Due to the Bolshevik Revolution and a fear of communism at home, the country was just then entering a period of intolerance known as the Red Scare. During the trial the prosecution, led by Assistant District Attorney Earl Barnes, accused the defendants not only of obstructing the war effort but of being Communist sympathizers. Ironically, as a result of the Russian Revolution, Eastman and Dell now had fewer qualms against the war and felt that Germany had become an enemy of Russian socialism. A few months before the trial Dell had willingly submitted to the draft but had been discharged because of his indictment.

At times the atmosphere in the courtroom verged from tragedy to comedy. "It was fantastic, grotesque, in the mood of a dream or of a tragic farce," reported Dell. "It was like a scene from 'Alice in Wonderland,' rewritten by Dostoievsky." During the proceedings the sounds of a band playing military marches outside in a nearby park entered the courtroom. Despite the noise Young had a difficult time staying awake, and in order to keep from sleeping drew a picture of himself dozing at the trial. When called to the stand to testify why he had used the figure of the devil leading a band in his antiwar cartoon, Young replied that "General Sherman described war as Hell, thus it seemed to me appropriate that the Devil should lead the band." A more serious moment occurred when Morris Hillquit and Dudley Field Malone pleaded the defendants' case on their right to freedom of speech. Their arguments were persuasive enough to convince two of the twelve jurors to vote for acquittal and the trial ended in a hung jury.[19]

The second trial took place five months later in which the defendants were allowed to address the jury. Reed, who had been in Russia during the first trial, described how he had hated war ever since he covered the conflict as a reporter. The only war that interested him was the war against capitalism. Eastman insisted that there was no conspiracy on the part of the staff to obstruct conscription, and that many of the antiwar articles were written before

America's intervention. Eastman then spoke of his right to freedom of speech, an argument that must have been convincing since the jury voted eight to four for acquittal.[20] As a result of a second deadlock the government dropped the case. Suppression had nonetheless damaged the financial security of *The Masses,* and the November-December 1917 issue turned out to be the last. With the demise of *The Masses* and *The Seven Arts* two of the era's major voices had disappeared.

By the end of 1917 the Little Renaissance was in a state of collapse. Everywhere there was a sense of frustration, failure, and pessimism. During spring 1917, Reed wrote despondently: "I am twenty-nine years old, and I know that this is the end of a part of my life, the end of youth. Sometimes it seems to me the end of the world's youth too; certainly the Great War has done something to us all." While walking down Fifth Avenue, Lippmann remarked to a friend that "the world we have known is finished. It will never be the same again." Because of the changed atmosphere many participants would have a difficult time adjusting to the climate of postwar America.[21]

NOTES

1. Randolph Bourne, "Twilight of the Idols," reprinted in Randolph S. Bourne, *War and the Intellectuals, Collected Essays, 1915-1919,* ed. Carl Resek (New York: Harper Torchbooks, 1964), p. 59 (first published *The Seven Arts,* II (October 1917), 688-702).

2. Randolph Bourne, "Berlin in War Time," *Travel,* XXIV (November 1914), 58-59; letter of Randolph Bourne to Alyse Gregory, August 25, 1914, in the Bourne Collection, Columbia University. See also Randolph Bourne, "A Glance at German 'Kultur,' " *Lippincott's Monthly,* XCV (February 1915), 22-27.

3. Romain Rolland, "America and the Arts," *The Seven Arts,* I (November 1916), 47; Floyd Dell, *Homecoming* (New York: Farrar & Rinehart, Inc., 1933), p. 292.

4. Floyd Dell, *Love in Greenwich Village* (New York: George H. Doran Company, 1956), p. 27.

5. Alan Seeger, "As a Soldier Thinks of War," *The New Republic,* III (May 22, 1915), 66-68; Harrison Reeves, "The Tragedy of Alan Seeger," *The New Republic,* X (March 10, 1917), 162-63; Alan Seeger, *Poems* (New York: Charles Scribner's Sons, 1917); "Gertrude Vanderbilt Whitney," p. 8, unpublished collection of material pertaining to Whitney in the library of the Whitney Museum of American Art, New York City; Albert Parry, *Garrets and Pretenders: A History of Bohemianism in America* (New York: Dover Publications, Inc., 1960), p. 292.

6. Charles Forcey, *The Crossroads of Liberalism, Croly, Weyl, Lippmann and the Progressive Era,*

1900-1925 (New York: Oxford University Press, 1961), pp. 221-72, 279-80; Harold E. Stearns, *The Street I Know* (New York: Lee Furman, 1935), pp. 144, 162.

7. Robert H. Elias, *Theodore Dreiser: Apostle of Nature* (New York: Alfred A. Knopf, Inc., 1949), p. 184; William Manchester, *Disturber of the Peace, The Life of H. L. Mencken* (New York: Harper, 1951), pp. 89, 99, 105; Carl Bode, *Mencken* (Carbondale: Southern Illinois University Press, 1969), pp. 112-16, 129; Isaac Goldberg, *The Man Mencken: A Biographical and Critical Survey* (New York: Simon and Schuster, 1925), pp. 208-9; Carl Dolmetsch, *The Smart Set, History and Anthology* (New York: The Dial Press, Inc., 1966), pp. 52-53; Edgar Kemler, *The Irreverent Mr. Mencken* (Boston: Little, Brown and Company, 1950), pp. 93-95.

8. Manchester, p. 110; Dolmetsch, p. 41.

9. Randolph Bourne's article was a vehement attack on Dewey's use of pragmatism to support the war–see "Conscience and Intelligence in War," *The Dial*, LXIII (September 13, 1917), 193-95. The editors wanted to keep Dewey as a contributor and thus silenced Bourne's antiwar protest–see Nicholas Joost, "Culture Versus Power: Randolph Bourne, John Dewey and *The Dial*," *Midwest Quarterly*, IX (April 1968), 247-48, 252-53.

10. Randolph Bourne, "Twilight of Idols," *War and the Intellectuals*, p. 55; Van Wyck Brooks, "Our Awakeners," *The Seven Arts*, II (June 1917), 235-48; Waldo Frank, *Our America* (New York: Boni and Liveright, 1919), pp. 26-29, 199.

11. Randolph Bourne, "A War Diary," *War and the Intellectuals*, pp. 45-46.

12. Letter of Van Wyck Brooks to Ilse Dusoir, March 13, 1940, reprinted in Ilse Dusoir, "The History of the *Seven Arts*," unpublished Master's thesis, New York University, 1940, p. 99; letter of Frost to Untermeyer, November 3, 1917, in *Letters of Robert Frost to Louis Untermeyer* (New York: Holt, Rinehart, and Winston, Inc., 1963), p. 60.

13. Letter of Rankine to Oppenheim, August 22, 1917, in the Oppenheim Collection, New York Public Library; "To the Friends of the *Seven Arts*," *The Seven Arts*, II (October 1917).

14. Letter of Oppenheim to Frank, September 28, 1917; letter of Frank to Oppenheim, October 21, 1917, Waldo Frank Papers, Van Pelt Library, University of Pennsylvania.

15. John Sloan, "1950 Notes," pp. 36-37, unpublished MS. in the John Sloan Trust, Delaware Art Center; Charles H. Morgan, *George Bellows, Painter of America* (New York: Reynal & Company, Inc., 1965), p. 208; "A Separation," *The Masses*, X (May 1917), 14.

16. John Reed, "The Trader's War," *The Masses*, V (September 1914), 16-17; Max Eastman, "War for War's Sake," *The Masses*, V (September 1914), 5; Art Young, *The Masses*, V (September 1914), 3; John Reed, "The Worst Thing in Europe," *The Masses*, VI (March 1915), 18; "Editorial," *The Masses*, VI (August 1915), 11. The preparedness number is *The Masses*, VIII (July 1916).

17. John Reed, "Woodrow Wilson," *The Masses*, IX (June 1917), 22; Max Eastman, "Advertising Democracy," *The Masses*, IX (June 1917), 6; Max Eastman, "Conscription for What," *The Masses*, IX (July 1917), 18; Dell, *Homecoming*, pp. 310-11.

18. "To Woodrow Wilson," *The Masses*, X (November-December 1917), 24.

19. Floyd Dell, "The Story of the Trial," *The Liberator*, I (June 1918), 7; *Art Young, His Life and Times*, ed. John N. Beffel (New York: Sheridan House, 1939), pp. 335-36.

20. Max Eastman, *Max Eastman's Address to the Jury in the Second Masses Trial in Defense of the*

Socialist Position and the Right of Free Speech (New York: Liberator Publishing Company, 1918), passim.

21. John Reed, "Almost Thirty," *The New Republic Anthology,* ed. Graff Conklin (New York: Dodge Publishing Company, 1936), 57; Carl Binger, "A Child of the Enlightenment," *Walter Lippmann and His Times,* eds. Marquis Childs and James Reston (New York: Harcourt, Brace and Company, Inc., 1959), p. 36.

CHAPTER FIFTEEN

The Influential and the Disillusioned

Certain Little Renaissance values and movements appeared antiquated after World War I had ended but others fitted in well with the postwar mood. The ideas of cultural nationalism and social regeneration through art were antithetical to the overall spirit of the twenties. The so-called lost generation opted instead for nihilism and expatriation. A book characteristic of the new mood, Harold Stearns's *America and the Young Intellectuals* (1921), criticized the participants' idealistic optimism. There was little for young men to do in 1921 except flee to Europe, suggested a disillusioned Stearns. The young people of the 1920s, he wrote, "turn with disgust from such self-conscious and helpless groups as . . . the League of Youth." Although Stearns had been affiliated with the early *New Republic,* he found the values of his cohorts now dated and irrelevant.[1]

This is not to say that none of the prewar ideas and movements influenced the next decade. The attack against commercialism and puritanism, which had begun during the Little Renaissance, was continued with renewed vigor in the postwar period. The next generation might reject the idealism of their predecessors, but their social criticism seemed pertinent since novel after novel was published criticizing the country's business ethic and small-town life. Stearns's caustic anthology, *Civilization in the United States* (1922), contained criticisms of society and the arts by Brooks and Mencken. Brooks's two books, *The Ordeal of Mark Twain* (1920) and *The Pilgrimage of Henry James* (1925), castigated America as an inhospitable climate for the artist. The iconoclast who made the most successful adaptation to the 1920s was Mencken. This was

227

mainly because he was less idealistic than the other social critics, and his deterministic philosophy fit in well with the later period. Mencken's puritan-baiting in *The Smart Set* and *American Mercury* became fashionable as the 1920s progressed.

The Little Renaissance modern poetry and theater movements had a great influence on the 1920s. Less political than other prewar groups, the modernists had little trouble adapting to a postwar climate stressing art for art's sake and experimentalism. The *Others* poets, William Carlos Williams, Wallace Stevens, and Marianne Moore, reached maturity during the 1920s and wrote some of their best verse. After World War I the Broadway stage absorbed the prewar theater movement by opening its doors to new playwrights, directors, and stage designers. Such fine plays as *Anna Christie* (1920), *The Emperor Jones* (1920), and *The Hairy Ape* (1921) made O'Neill the country's leading dramatist. Out of the Washington Square Players came the Theatre Guild, established in 1919 by among others Lawrence Langner, Helen Westley, Lee Simonson, and Philip Moeller. Since the Guild produced many of the best plays in the postwar American theater, the Washington Square Players helped lay the groundwork for further developments on the nation's stage.

The modern art movement also flourished after World War I. Stieglitz exhibited the work of the 291 group at the Intimate and American Place Galleries, where he continued to uphold his earlier artistic principles. The art of Hartley, Dove, Marin, and O'Keeffe remained in the forefront of modern painting. In 1930, the Whitney Museum of American Art was founded to promote American painting by holding exhibitions of the country's best artists. The museum's purpose not only echoed the ideals of the prewar cultural nationalists but also its origin dated back to Gertrude Vanderbilt Whitney's tiny studio on Eighth Street. After World War II New York became the world's leading center of modern art, a development that had begun with Gallery 291 and the Armory Show.

The new publishing houses, which originated during the prewar era, also contributed to the literary renaissance of the 1920s. Before the war these small firms were relatively unknown to the public; nonetheless, they had helped play an important role in publishing the Little Renaissance authors. Like the little magazines, they had been formed mainly because the older established publishing firms generally refused to handle experimental writing. By publishing the best examples of new American and European literature they revolutionized the book trade as conservative firms began following their precedents.

The most important new publishing house was Alfred A. Knopf, established in 1915. Knopf had first become interested in serious literature as an undergraduate at Columbia University, where he worked with Bourne as advertising and business manager on the *Columbia Monthly*. After graduation in 1912, he traveled to Europe where he met several writers and publishers who convinced him that the new European literature needed an outlet in the United States. After returning home he obtained a job as a salesman with Mitchell Kennerley, whose interest in quality book design and typography impressed the young Knopf. Kennerley's own publishing record during the Little Renaissance was outstanding and included Lippmann's major works and Eastman's poetry.[2]

Using Kennerley as a model, Knopf decided to form his own firm in 1915. With the help of an assistant and his wife, he began issuing classics and contemporary European works under the Borzoi label. His first publication was a volume of four plays by the French dramatist Emile Augier. Bound in a sturdy orange and blue cover and printed in fine Cheltenham type, the volume epitomized the publisher's interest in issuing attractively designed quality books. Most novels Knopf issued between 1915 and 1917 were by foreign writers, but he gradually began gathering a list of new American authors, including Mencken, Willa Cather, Carl Van Vechten, and Joseph Hergesheimer. By the end of the twenties Knopf was one of the country's foremost quality publishers.

The firm of B. W. Huebsch can also be traced back to the Little Renaissance. Huebsch was friendly with *The Seven Arts* crowd and a member of the Provincetown Players. He contributed to the prewar literary ferment by publishing *America's Coming-of-Age*, Brooks's and Bourne's *Seven Arts* essays, and Wright's critical works. Noted for his uncanny sense for good literature, he acquired the American rights to D. H. Lawrence's *The Rainbow* and Joyce's *Portrait of the Artist as a Young Man*, and later published Anderson's *Winesburg, Ohio* and *Poor White*. Before his firm merged with the Viking Press in 1925, Huebsch's books had helped create a new American literature.[3]

Albert Boni, who had been prominent in the prewar Village, and Horace Liveright, a former stockbroker, decided to form their own publishing firm in 1917. Boni and Liveright aimed "to publish only new books with a permanent value—books which will be as vital in twenty-five years as they are today. Our standard of accepting a manuscript will be based wholly on its merit, and we will issue no transient or merely popular work. . . . We know we will never get rich—but that is not primarily our ambition." The new European and American literature became their speciality, but in 1917 they also began to issue inexpensive reprints of standard works under the Modern Library title, a series that revolutionized the book trade. Boni and Liveright continued to publish an outstanding list of authors after World War I. They issued Reed's *Ten Days That Shook the World,* Frank's *Our America,* and O'Neill's *The Moon of the Caribbees, and Six Other Plays of the Sea.* The company also brought out the postwar work of Kreymborg and Eastman as well as that of Dreiser, Pound, Cummings, Anderson, and Hart Crane. Due to a quarrel, Albert Boni left the firm in 1923 and with his brother Charles formed a new company that pioneered in paperback books. Thus the three houses of Boni and Liveright, Huebsch, and Knopf had grown from small firms publishing the new prewar writing to major companies involved in the postwar literary renaissance.[4]

Unlike the publishers, the prewar Greenwich Village rebels found the climate of the 1920s unconducive to their ideas. One reason for this was that after 1917 the Village changed from an area of serious artistic purpose and social protest to one of commercial pseudo-bohemianism. By 1920 the Village had become a place of high rents, night clubs, speakeasies, and tourist attractions. No doubt there were dedicated artists in the postwar Village but they had little interest in the feminism, socialism, and educational reform movements of the older inhabitants. Malcolm Cowley, who spoke for the lost generation, noted the difference between the two groups: " 'They' had been rebels: they wanted to change the world, be leaders in the fight for justice and art, help to create a society in which individuals could express themselves. 'We' were convinced at the time that society could never be changed by an effort of the will." [5]

After 1917 the prewar Villagers began to leave the area, their famous landmarks disappearing with them. One could still find the Provincetown Players but the offices of *The Masses* and the headquarters of the Liberal Club were now closed. Polly Holliday's restaurant went out of business, the owner spending her last years in a mental institution. Mabel Luhan gave up her soirees around 1916 and moved to the nearby suburb of Croton-on-Hudson. "Fifth Avenue ceased to exist for me," she wrote, "and the anarchists and other radicals had disappeared out of my life along with Leagues, Movements,

Committees and Causes." [6] In Croton and later in Taos, New Mexico, Luhan continued to lead an adventurous life among artists, but she never really recaptured her days among the "movers and shakers."

Other participants were desirous of getting away from the city and living close to nature; indeed, Croton became a type of Greenwich Village bohemia in the suburbs. Dell moved here in 1919 as well as Eastman and Boardman Robinson. During the 1920s Young settled on a farm in Bethel, Connecticut, and Brooks bought a house in Westport. Some expatriates, including Stearns, left for Paris, while Cook ended his days in Greece. Although Sloan continued to reside in the Village, he spent his summers in Gloucester, Massachusetts, and then later in Santa Fe, New Mexico. A few writers, like Frank and Rosenfeld, remained in the city but most chose to commute to New York, revealing that the participants were a generation whose values were partly rooted in an older rural America.

Dell epitomized the prewar Villager who found the atmosphere in the postwar Village commercialized. "The Greenwich Village that was, is no more," he lamented. In *Love in Greenwich Village* (1926), he nostalgically described the prewar community in glowing terms and attacked the new Village as "a side-show for tourists, a peep-show for vulgarians, a commercial exhibit of tawdry Bohemianism." Dell was shocked to discover that he and his colleagues' views were looked on as outdated by the new Villagers:

> I found that I was regarded by these younger people as one of the pillars of a hated Village orthodoxy. *The Masses,* and subsequently *The Liberator,* though regarded by the rest of America as daringly modern in its pictures and poetry, was thought of by the younger Villagers as tame, old-fogy, stupidly conservative. I had been told that young writers sat about in basement cafes and cursed me.[7]

Perhaps they had good reason to do so for Dell had grown conservative in his feminist and literary views during the 1920s. His psychoanalysis and marriage in 1919 made him less a defender of sexual freedom, and in his writings he began advocating matrimony and stable sexual relationships. Finding that most new writers failed to express idealism in their work, he condemned much of the experimental literature of the 1920s, especially the work of Anderson, Pound, and Eliot. Although Dell himself wrote important novels at this time, including

Moon-Calf (1920) and *The Briary Bush* (1921), their themes of individual freedom and the rebellion of youth were rooted more in the values of the Little Renaissance than the Jazz Age.[8]

The socialism of Dell and his cohorts on *The Masses* also set them apart from the apolitical lost generation. Many important *Masses* writers remained radicals after 1917 mainly because they found a new faith in the Bolshevik Revolution. The question of applying the lessons of the revolution to the United States, however, created dissension among the former staff and other participants. The right-wing Socialists generally rejected communism, while the more left-wing radicals such as Reed, Dell, and Eastman avidly supported the Russian experiment. Quarrels suddenly flared up over the meaning of the revolution and its applicability to the United States.[9] The prewar era had tolerated all shades of radicalism but now one had either to declare himself a Communist sympathizer or be accused of bourgeois sentimentality. A magazine like *The Masses,* which had opened its pages to all types of Socialist opinion, was no longer possible in the postwar climate of interparty rivalry.

The old *Masses* stalwarts, Dell and Reed, viewed the revolution as an inspiring event epitomizing dramatic social change. "How can one be an artist in a time when the morning paper may tell of another Bolshevik revolution somewhere?" Dell asked. Reed, who had been sent by *The Masses* to cover the uprising, was more personally involved with the event. Disillusioned by the shock of World War I, Reed suddenly found a new faith. "Something is taking shape—something grand, and simple, and human," he sensed. Kerensky's government, however, left him cold, and he sided with Lenin. On November 13 he excitedly cabled the *New York Call:* "This is the revolution, the class struggle, with the proletariat, the workmen, the soldiers and the peasants lined up against the bourgeoisie. Last February was only the preliminary revolution. At the present moment the proletariat are triumphant." [10]

Reed used the pages of *The Liberator* to speak out on behalf of Soviet communism. Published between March 1918 and October 1924, *The Liberator* aimed to continue *The Masses* tradition, and, like its predecessor, was edited by Eastman. Reed and Dell were on the staff and drawings by Young, Robinson, and Minor decorated its pages. Perceptive social criticism highlighted the doctrinaire *Liberator,* but the quality of its art and literature never matched the prewar journal. Reed's brilliant articles on the Russian Revolution in the *Liberator* formed the basis of his classic *Ten Days That Shook the World* (1919). As this book suggests, events in Russia made him a much more serious radical, and he began to turn away from his earlier utopian views, which now seemed to him as overly idealistic. Returning home in April 1918, Reed became a propagandist for the Soviet Union by writing pro-Bolshevik articles in many radical publications, including the *New York Communist,* which he edited in early 1919. He also made speeches throughout the country, and along with other left-wing Socialists helped form the Communist Labor Party.

Reed's infatuation with communism was short-lived. In 1919, he returned to the Soviet Union to attend a world congress as a delegate of the Communist Labor Party. While there he quarreled with the government hierarchy over the issue of trade unions, urging the Soviets to work through the I.W.W. rather than the A.F.L. Encountering stiff opposition to his views, he became aware of the authoritarian nature of decision-making in the Communist system. Although Reed was too much of a dedicated radical to become completely disillusioned with communism, he told Eastman before he died that the class struggle interferes with one's writing. If he had lived Reed would have had to face the conflict between artistic freedom and the regimentation of the Soviet system. As it was he died of typhus at the age of thirty-three in the Soviet Union on October 17, 1919. The once rebel of Greenwich Village was buried in the Kremlin and later deified as a Communist martyr, poet, and historian.[11]

Dell and Eastman lived long enough to discover that the values they placed in individualism conflicted with the collectivism implied in the Soviet system. Although never a card-carrying Communist, Dell became increasingly disenchanted with communism beginning in the late 1920s and refused to bend to the party line by writing Socialist propaganda novels. He eventually came to disagree with the hard-boiled radical writers of the late 1920s and 1930s, particularly *The New Masses* crowd.

This new radical literary magazine had been formed in 1926 by Michael Gold and Joseph Freeman, both of whom had worked on *The Liberator.* Freeman had idolized *The Masses* writers as a young man and looked back on the prewar publication as his high school education. *The New Masses* attempted to carry on the *Masses* name by mixing socialism, art, and literature in its pages and several prewar writers and artists contributed to the journal. Outside of these similarities, the dogmatic *New Masses* had little in common with the earlier publication. As a voice of the radical 1930s, *The New Masses* lacked the humor and undogmatic tone of the prewar journal. Although it is fashionable to trace a tradition of literary radicalism beginning with *The Masses* and extending to *The Liberator, The New Masses,* and its successor *Masses and Mainstream,* the latter three magazines were much more dominated by doctrinaire politics.[12]

Dell's resignation as contributing editor of *The New Masses* during spring 1929 illustrates the difference between the two radical generations. The ex-Village rebel broke with the editorial staff over their policy of almost exclusively publishing proletarian writing. Feeling that the editors were restricting artistic freedom, Dell severed his relationship with the magazine. As a result he promptly became a favorite target for the new literary radicals. Michael Gold, the magazine's editor, called him a Greenwich Village pseudo-radical who writes novels for the bourgeoisie. The Marxist literary critic V. F. Calverton also accused him of compromising his political beliefs to "sex playboying." Since Dell's politics were rooted in the Little Renaissance, he found the conformity demanded by the new breed antithetical to his views.[13]

Eastman also became disenchanted with communism after he discovered the totalitarian nature of the Soviet system. He had first been attracted to Communism partly because of the scientific planning of the Soviet state and what he called the daring experimentalism of Lenin. Although never a card-carrying member, he had supported the Communist Labor Party when it was first formed. Residence in the Soviet Union during 1922-23 generally affirmed his favorable opinion of communism. As the twenties progressed, however, he began to have second thoughts. Stalin's quarrel with Trotsky changed his thinking and in several books he attacked the Soviet premier. In *Artists in Uniform* (1934), he criticized the sterility of proletarian art and lack of artistic freedom in the Soviet Union. Stalin's continued purges and the Nazi-Soviet Pact only confirmed his suspicions. Because of these views Eastman was castigated by hard-line Stalinists for his Trotskyite skepticism, and he became an isolated figure in Communist circles.[14]

By 1940 he was ready to abandon his radical convictions for a newfound faith in the capitalist system. He joined the tirade of vehement anticommunism during the 1950s by working for the conservative *Reader's Digest* and writing articles for the *National Review.* Gold, dismayed over Eastman's about-face, wondered "how such a figure could have turned into the zombie now associate editor on the fascistic *Reader's Digest.*"[15] Such a change is not difficult to explain, for Eastman had always been a defender of individual freedom in culture and politics. He could easily fear the collectivism of both the Soviet system and the increased bureaucratic powers of the federal government since the New Deal. Like many American literary radicals, Eastman and Dell (who became a liberal Democrat), eventually turned conservative. Time was a factor but much more important were their libertarian beliefs that had been formed long ago during the Little Renaissance.

The war and its aftermath also contributed to the breakup of *The New Republic* group. Lippmann left the magazine in 1920 and Hackett resigned two years later to reside in Ireland and Denmark, where he turned to writing historical novels. One by one *The New Republic* staff renounced their faith in political-cultural nationalism and progressive reform. Stearns turned to attacking the prewar liberalism of his colleagues while Weyl confessed his loss of faith in humanity and weariness with idealistic reform.[16] The war caused Lippmann to experience a crisis in values and to reaffirm the importance of traditional ethics. As an editorialist with the *New York World* and then later with the New York *Herald Tribune,* he urged the principles of world peace and moral responsibility. The problem of communications, the government, and an informed citizenry became the subject of *Public Opinion* (1922), while Lippmann sought to define a system of rational values in *A Preface to Morals* (1929). During the 1930s the ex-Socialist refuted both communism and the state-planning of the New Deal. Although he still spoke out for individual freedom and pragmatic flexibility in decision-making, his role as a Little Renaissance crusader was far in the past.

His old friend Herbert Croly never seemed to recover from the war. The Versailles Treaty had not established his long-sought aim of international peace and social reconstruction but had instead increased bitter feuding among nations. America's cultural renaissance still remained an unfulfilled dream to Croly. Disillusioned with nationalism, he began promoting loyalty to local communities rather than the state. He moved to the left in his political views and searched vainly for new faiths in religion and mysticism. In October 1928, Croly experienced a paralytic stroke and died two years later at the age of sixty-one, mourned by his old prewar colleagues as a humanitarian and the father of political-cultural nationalism.[17]

Bourne suffered a similar disillusionment with certain Little Renaissance values. Pragmatic liberalism, progress, and idealism became dead faiths for him after 1917. Although the picture of an embittered poverty-stricken Bourne has been overexaggerated, he did grow increasingly pessimistic and radical. The social critic's spirits were occasionally lifted by several good friends, particularly

Rosenfeld, and Esther Cornell, who he was hoping to marry. During 1918 he published book reviews in *The Dial,* worked on an autobiographical novel, and wrote the poignant essay, "The History of a Literary Radical." Bitter about the war and political nationalism, he penned an inflammatory tract against militarism, chauvinism, and conformity entitled, "The State." [18]

Although these works showed that Bourne was still at the height of his creative powers, psychologically he was alternating between moods of hope and despair. Like a homeless child, he moved from one apartment to another in the Village, searching for some meaning to life. For a time he lived in two small rooms on Bank Street and later resided in Rosenfeld's flat. During the cold month of December 1918, when a flu epidemic raged in the city, he was staying in the Eighth Street apartment of his fiancée. Here on December 17 he became ill with pneumonia and died five days later. Oppenheim was immediately summoned, and upon seeing Bourne dead commented that an era had come to an end.[19]

Bourne's *Seven Arts* colleagues shortly began turning his name and life into a legend. Three days after his death Oppenheim wrote Brooks that "our great task is to give Randolph his true place in American life and letters." Desirous of seeing Bourne's uncollected work in print, Oppenheim edited his *Seven Arts* essays for book publication. Bourne was "a great man who had died with a great work unfinished," he eulogized in the forward. Another collection of Bourne's writings, edited by Brooks, appeared the following year, and later, in 1962, Brooks published a long descriptive essay on his friend. Like his colleagues, Frank pictured Bourne in his writing as fighting a lonely heroic battle for cultural and social change. "With him gone," he lamented, "the political and artistic columns of advance . . . are again severed." Perhaps the most important creator of the Bourne legend was Rosenfeld, who wrote an important essay depicting him as a pacifist martyr and the leader of the prewar cult of youth. Bourne's name nonetheless tended to be forgotten by the general reading public as the 1920s progressed until the question of the country's involvement in World War II caused his name to appear frequently in the civil liberties journal *Twice-a-Year.* Despite several interpretive articles and published biographies, Bourne still remains the legendary prewar crusader created by his *Seven Arts* friends.[20]

During the 1920s Bourne's colleagues continued to urge the ideas of cultural unity, organicism, and a usable past in their writings. Only Oppenheim among them branched out into an entirely new direction, turning his attention until his death in 1932 to his new occupation as a practicing Jungian analyst. Despite their loss of idealism due to the war, the remaining *Seven Arts* group still clung to the prewar faith in cultural nationalism. Rosenfeld espoused the idea of national and social regeneration through art in many critical articles on music, painting, and literature. A collection of his early work, *Port of New York* (1924), included sketches of Bourne, Brooks, Stieglitz, and the 291 artists. His impressionistic criticism always took a positive approach to American culture–a point of view he had developed while on *The Seven Arts.*

Despite the iconoclastic nature of Brooks's work during the early 1920s, his crusade for cultural nationalism failed to win favor among the younger cynical writers. Expatriation, a vogue in the twenties, was, according to Brooks, an escapist answer to the problem an artist faced in America. Basically the visionary idealism of *The Seven Arts* writers hardly fit in with the general pessimistic postwar intellectual climate. Although Brooks gained fame as an important writer at this time, a new corps of literary critics, Allen Tate, Kenneth Burke, and the humanists, were beginning to find his sociological criticism ineffectual for analyzing a piece of literature. After recovering from a nervous breakdown in 1926, Brooks dropped the biting social criticism of his former days and became an even more avid cultural nationalist. Instead of bemoaning the lack of a literary tradition at home, Brooks now set out to create one in book after book. Beginning with *The Life of Emerson* (1932) and climaxing with the five volumes of the Makers and Finders series (1936-1952), he celebrated American writers who had contributed to the development of a national culture. He still clung to his belief in organicism by praising literary movements that had sprung out of the native soil of New England and New York. In *The Confident Years: 1885-1915* and in a book on John Sloan, Brooks presented enlightening accounts of the Little Renaissance years. This later writing, though, lacked the incisive analysis of his earlier work. By the time of his death in 1963, Brooks had recorded the usable literary tradition he had found wanting in 1908.

Frank also continued to believe in the ideals of his *Seven Arts* days and to convert several writers to his beliefs. His attack on materialism and provincialism in *Our America* and *The Re-discovery of American Life* (1929) brought him into favor with certain younger writers. He too played a major role in the postwar literary ferment by writing many fine experimental psychoanalytical novels. Equally important, Frank spread the gospel of cultural nationalism to his two friends, Hart Crane and Gorham Munson. Frank, Crane, and Munson formed a close coterie during the 1920s, sharing a prophetic faith in the cultural mission of America. As a young man Munson had enjoyed reading *The Seven Arts* and the writing of Frank. After meeting Frank in 1923, Crane became influenced by his admiration for Whitman and his mythical view of America. In the novel *The Unwelcome Man* (1917), Frank had already interpreted Brooklyn Bridge as a symbol of the country's mechanical civilization and spiritual promise. Although several other influences entered into Crane's epic poem *The Bridge* (1930), including Joseph Stella's paintings and the historical figures in William Carlos Williams's *In the American Grain* (1925), Frank helped initiate the thematic conception of the poem. Thus, *The Seven Arts'* apocalyptic vision of America as a land of cultural promise came to be reexpressed in one of the most important poems of the postwar years.[21]

The former *Seven Arts* staff also played instrumental roles in several postwar magazines. When Scofield Thayer became the new editor of *The Dial* in 1919, he built the journal partly on the model of *The Seven Arts*. Thayer had been a friend and admirer of Bourne and shared his aspirations for American culture. Under Thayer's direction *The Dial* published some of the best American writing of the twenties, including T. S. Eliot's *The Waste Land*. Besides Brooks, other former participants were associated with *The Dial,* including Rosenfeld, who wrote a monthly column of music criticism, and Marianne Moore, who edited the magazine between 1926 and 1929. Brooks, Rosenfeld, and Kreymborg also helped edit *The American Caravan,* a yearbook of contemporary American writing sporadically issued between 1927 and 1936. *The Seven Arts'* message of cultural regeneration and creative freedom reappeared again in the journal *Twice-a-Year,* published between 1938 and 1948. The names of former Little Renaissance writers and artists were frequently found on its pages. Besides Bourne's letters, the magazine published the writing of Rosenfeld and Stieglitz, who was a personal friend of its editor, Dorothy Norman.[22]

The spirit of cultural nationalism was also reflected in the work of Lewis Mumford. As a young man he had been influenced by *The Seven Arts* group and had become friendly with Brooks while the two were on the staff of *The Dial* and *The Freeman.* Beginning in 1926 with *The Golden Day,* a history of American literature, Mumford sought, like Brooks, to record America's literary past. His pioneer books on art and architecture, *Sticks and Stones* (1924) and *The Brown Decades* (1931), discovered a rich tradition in American painting and building.

Mumford's and Brooks's research opened up new fields of interest for scholars. The American Studies movement, which developed during the 1930s and 1940s, carried on the search for a usable past started by Brooks and his colleagues during the Little Renaissance.[23]

Although the cultural nationalists influenced writers such as Crane and Mumford, the prewar generation and their followers stood mostly outside the main literary movements of the next two decades. The climate producing the New York movement had ended in 1917, and the new mood was conducive to only some participants, especially the modernists. This happened even though the Little Renaissance had paved the way for the postwar cultural ferment by destroying the old genteel standards and creating new means of expression. As the years passed the prewar faith in idealistic iconoclasm and cultural nationalism grew steadily more dated and naive. In 1939, Louis Untermeyer wondered what had happened to his generation: "Where are the music-makers, the dreamers of dreams? Where, by what desolate streams, are the movers and shakers, world-losers and world-forsakers?"[24] Some, like Reed and Bourne, were long since dead, but others who were alive no longer stamped succeeding eras as they had in the Little Renaissance.

NOTES

1. Harold Stearns, *America and the Young Intellectuals* (New York: George H. Doran Company, 1921), p. 167.

2. Alfred A. Knopf, *Some Random Recollections* (New York: Typophiles, 1949); Alfred A. Knopf, *Quarter Century* (Norwood, Mass.: Plimpton Press, 1940); Geoffrey T. Hellman, *Alfred A. Knopf, A Profile* (New York: privately printed, 1952); Alfred A. Knopf, "Publishing's Last Fifty Years, a Balance Sheet," *Saturday Review of Literature,* XLVII (November 21, 1964), 21-23 and (November 28, 1964), 17; Hellmut Lehmann-Haupt, *The Book in America* (2nd ed.; New York: Boker, 1952), pp. 338-39; Charles A. Madison, *Book Publishing in America* (New York: McGraw-Hill, 1966), pp. 321-29.

3. Madison, pp. 296-303.

4. Quoted from "Interesting Publishers," *The Seven Arts,* II (October 1917), 808. See Louis Kronenberger, "Gambler in Publishing: Horace Liveright," *Atlantic Monthly,* CCXV (January 1965), 94-104; Madison, pp. 330-38; Lehmann-Haupt, pp. 339-41; Walter Gilmer, *Horace Liveright, Publisher of the Twenties* (New York: David Lewis, 1970).

5. Malcolm Cowley, *Exile's Return, A Literary Saga of the Nineteen-Twenties* (New York: Compass Books, 1965), p. 72.

6. Mabel Dodge Luhan, *Intimate Memoirs,* Vol. III: *Movers and Shakers* (New York: Harcourt, Brace and Company, Inc., 1936), p. 425.

7. Floyd Dell, "Greenwich Village," *The Liberator,* I (May 1918), 41; "The Rise of Greenwich Village" and "The Fall of Greenwich Village," in *Love in Greenwich Village* (New York: George H. Doran Publishing, 1926); *Homecoming* (New York: Farrar & Rinehart, Inc., 1933), p. 281.

8. Floyd Dell, "A Literary Self-Analysis," *Modern Quarterly,* IV (June-September 1937), 148-52; "A Psychoanalytic Confession," *The Liberator,* III (no. 4), 15-19; *The Outline of Marriage* (London: Richards Press, 1927); *Love in the Machine Age* (New York: Farrar & Rinehart, Inc., 1930). Dell's postwar literary views are revealed in "Critic's Magic," *The Bookman,* LXIV (December 1926), 448.

9. See Eastman's denunciation of Lippmann for criticizing the Bolshevik Revolution in "A Demobilized Editor," *The Liberator,* II (May 1919), 7.

10. Floyd Dell, "Color of Life," *The Liberator,* I (December 1918), 44-45; John Reed, "The Russian Peace," *The Masses,* IX (July 1917), 35; Philip S. Foner, ed., *The Bolshevik Revolution, Its Impact on American Radicals, Liberals, and Labor* (New York: International Publishers Company, Inc., 1967), p. 54.

11. Max Eastman, *Heroes I Have Known; Twelve Who Have Lived Great Lives* (New York: Simon & Schuster, Inc., 1942), pp. 232-37; Richard O'Connor and Dale L. Walker, *The Lost Revolutionary, A Biography of John Reed* (New York: Harcourt, Brace & World, 1967), pp. 280-306. This latter work sees Reed as a disillusioned Communist, while a more left-wing interpretation is Granville Hicks, *John Reed, The Making of a Revolutionary* (New York: Benjamin Blom, 1968).

12. Joseph Freeman, *An American Testament, A Narrative of Rebels and Romantics* (London: Victor Gallancz, 1938), pp. 63, 71-72, 107, 459; Max Eastman, *Enjoyment of Living* (New York: Harper, 1948), p. 415.

13. Michael Gold, "Floyd Dell Resigns," *The New Masses,* V (July 1929); V. F. Calverton, *The New Masses* (October 1926), 288 and his *The Liberation of American Literature* (New York: Charles Scribner's Sons, 1932), p. 456.

14. Max Eastman's *Reflections on the Failure of Socialism* (New York: Devin-Adair Co., 1955), pp. 9-20; *The End of Socialism in Russia* (Boston: Little, Brown and Company, 1937); *Stalin's Russia and the Crisis in Socialism* (New York: W. W. Norton & Company, Inc., 1940); *Artists in Uniform* (New York: Alfred A. Knopf, Inc., 1934); *Since Lenin Died* (New York: Boni and Liveright, 1925).

15. Michael Gold, "The *Masses* Tradition," *Masses and Mainstream,* IV (August 1951), 48.

16. Harold E. Stearns, *Liberalism in America; Its Origins, Its Temporary Collapse, Its Future* (New York: Boni and Liveright, 1919); Walter Weyl, *Tired Radicals and Other Papers* (New York: B. W. Huebsch, 1921).

17. Charles Forcey, *The Crossroads of Liberalism; Croly, Weyl, Lippmann, and the Progressive Era, 1900-1925* (New York: Oxford University Press, 1961), pp. 300-16; David Noble, "The *New Republic* and the Idea of Progress, 1914-20," *Mississippi Valley Historical Review,* XXXVIII (December 1951), 402; David Noble, "Herbert Croly and American Progressive Thought," *Western Political Quarterly,* VII (1954), 537-53.

18. Randolph Bourne, "History of a Literary Radical," *Yale Review,* VIII (April 1919), 468-84; Randolph Bourne, "An Autobiographical Chapter," *The Dial,* LXVIII (January 1920), 1-21; "Unfinished Fragment on the State" in Randolph Bourne, *Untimely Papers,* ed. James Oppenheim (New York: B. W. Huebsch, 1919); reprinted in Randolph Bourne, *War and the Intellectuals, Collected Essays, 1915-1919,* ed. Carl Resek (New York: Harper Torchbooks, 1964), pp. 65-104.

19. Van Wyck Brooks, *Fenollosa and His Circle* (New York: E. P. Dutton & Co., Inc., 1962), pp. 312-21; John Adam Moreau, *Randolph Bourne: Legend and Reality* (Washington, D.C.: Public Affairs Press, 1966), pp. 200-3; Nicholas Joost, *Years of Transition, The Dial, 1912-20* (Barre, Mass.: Barre Publishing Company, 1967), pp. 187-89; letter of Agnes de Lima to Alyse Gregory, February 28, 1949, in the Bourne Collection, Columbia University; Louis Filler, *Randolph Bourne* (New York: The Citadel Press, 1966), pp. 126-28.

20. Letter of Oppenheim to Brooks, Christmas Day, 1918, in the Van Wyck Brooks Collection, University of Pennsylvania; James Oppenheim, "Editor's Forward," *Untimely Papers,* p. 6; Brooks, *Fenollosa and His Circle,* pp. 259-321; Waldo David Frank, *Our America* (New York: Boni and Liveright, 1919), p. 200; Paul Rosenfeld, "Randolph Bourne," *The Dial,* LXXV (December 1923), 559.

21. Gorham Munson, "The Fledgling Years, 1916-1924," *Sewanee Review,* XL (Spring 1932), 53; Gorham Munson, *Waldo Frank, A Study* (New York: Boni and Liveright, 1923); Gorham Munson, "Herald of the Twenties: A Tribute to Waldo Frank," *Forum,* III (Fall 1961), 4-15. On the relationship between Frank and Crane, see Robert L. Perry, *The Shared Vision of Waldo Frank and Hart Crane* (Lincoln: University of Nebraska, 1966); John Unterecker, *Voyager, A Life of Hart Crane* (New York: Farrar, Straus & Giroux, Inc., 1969), pp. 153-55, 277-84; Waldo Frank, "Hart Crane," *In the American Jungle* (New York: Farrar & Rinehart, Inc., 1937), pp. 96-108; William Wasserstrom, *The Time of the Dial* (Syracuse, N.Y.: Syracuse University Press, 1963), pp. 45-46.

22. Joost, pp. 99-100, 116, 130-44; Wasserstrom, pp. 1-2, 66-80, 110, 145-46, 155; Alfred Kreymborg, "The Caravan Venture," *Paul Rosenfeld, Voyager in the Arts* (New York: Creative Age Press, 1948), pp. 26-37.

23. Lewis Mumford, "Lyric Wisdom," *Paul Rosenfeld, Voyager in the Arts,* p. 43; *The Van Wyck Brooks, Lewis Mumford Letters, The Record of a Literary Friendship, 1921-1963,* ed. Robert E. Spiller (New York: E. P. Dutton & Co., Inc., 1970).

24. Louis Untermeyer, *From Another World, The Autobiography of Louis Untermeyer* (New York: Harcourt, Brace and Company, Inc., 1939), pp. 78-79.

Conclusion

The Little Renaissance participants were linked together in a common cause to create a new American culture by overthrowing the genteel tradition. They viewed the culture of the nineteenth century as irrelevant and outdated and called for new writing and painting expressing the indigenous aspects of American life. This is why so many artists and writers shared the Little Renaissance spirit of iconoclasm, modernism, and cultural nationalism. Writers as different as Mencken and Dell could write on feminism, while articles on educational reform and the new psychology were found in *The New Republic, The Seven Arts,* and *The Masses.* Besides *The Seven Arts* group, participants as different as Croly, Mencken, Stieglitz, Henri, and George Cram Cook voiced to some degree the philosophy of cultural nationalism.

Although the Little Renaissance members were united behind a common purpose, they often relied on conflicting ideas in their eagerness to overturn the establishment. Some writers and artists put their faith in the emotions and intuitions, while others revered science and pragmatism. Various philosophers, such as Bergson, Nietzsche, Santayana, James, and Dewey, were important influences on the prewar generation. Thus both rationality and intuition were equally valued by the artists and writers.

On one hand a spirit of individualism ran through the era; on the other a desire for community life. Gallery 291 stood for both the group ideal and the importance of the individual creative act. Greenwich Village was a place of individualism and artistic freedom where a community of artists enjoyed the stimulation of salons and coteries. *The Masses* staff fought for libertarianism, while *The Seven Arts'* utopianists preferred the ideal of the cooperative society dedicated to cultural pursuits. Thus, the participants cherished both the values of individual freedom and the community.

The Little Renaissance too had both a radical and conservative tone. The writers and artists were really moralistic rebels. They could argue for social reform in several fields, but these arguments often conveyed a note of righteous indignation. Despite their slanders against the church, they often urged society to follow traditional Christian ethics. The wildness of their bohemianism has been overexaggerated; indeed, their sexual behavior was constrained by moral qualms. Although the Little Renaissance took place in a large city, the writers tended to idealize a life close to nature. The radicals' desire for change was not motivated by anarchy but by the purpose of overturning outdated standards preventing a new American culture. Despite the participation of *The New Republic* staff, the era's politics were generally antiprogressive. Most artists and writers never supported the progressivism of Woodrow Wilson and Theodore Roosevelt. A majority instead espoused some brand of socialism, including Lippmann until he joined *The New Republic* in 1914. The era's spirit of progress and idealism rather than its politics linked the Little Renaissance to the progressive period. The rebels advocated social change that went well beyond liberal reform.

Because of conflicting ideologies, quarrels often occurred between the participants. Politics sometimes created dissension between progressives and radicals, while the Socialist and modernist groups had opposing aesthetic views. *The Masses* published very few experimental poems, while the avant-garde poets and painters generally kept politics out of their work. The Little Renaissance community was divided between those who experimented with the new modern forms and those who did not. Differences between modernists and realists, however, did not prevent the groups from working in unison against the genteel establishment and sharing a need to create a new American culture. The spirit and goals of the rebellion held the loosely connected groups together.

The attack on nineteenth-century genteel painting and literature led to the very type of new national culture the participants were so desirous of establishing. The *Others* group, motivated by an antipathy toward orthodox poetic standards, wrote important ground-breaking modern poems. The little theater movement was highlighted by new playwrights and production methods that contributed to the improvement of the Broadway stage. The Eight painters, breaking with the Academy's jurisdiction, forged a tradition of realism in twentieth-century painting. The Stieglitz group created new painting forms that revolutionized American art. Because established publishing firms rejected avant-garde writing, new companies were established that disseminated the new literature. The period also contained two of the most dramatic events in American cultural history, the Armory Show and the Paterson Strike Pageant. In sum, the participants' innovative writing and painting added up to a rich period of creativity.

The many important little magazines contained some of the best social criticism written in America. *The Masses, The Smart Set, The Seven Arts,* and *The New Republic* were in themselves an important part of the new culture. In their pages the literary-social critics wrote moving tracts on the subjects of youth, education, socialism, psychoanalysis, and feminism. If the modernists' rebellion led to new forms in the arts, the critics' revolt against outdated standards created a body of superb iconoclastic writing arguing for social and cultural change.

The Little Renaissance helped make New York the nation's leading art and literary capital. Although the city was already an important center of the magazine and book publishing trade in 1908, the new publishers contributed to its predominance in this area. Gallery 291 and the Armory Show were crucial events in New York's growth as the headquarters of avant-garde painting. Because of its increasing importance the city attracted critics and writers from all over America. Chicago Renaissance intellectuals eventually came to New York because it offered more opportunity than the Windy City. Compared to the Chicago movement, the New York Little Renaissance, with its modern art, was broader in scope. Because of the Little Renaissance, New York would always remain in the forefront of American culture.

The prewar rebellion also helped pave the way for further developments in American art and literature. Thanks to the social critics the new generation of artists in the 1920s lived in a relatively freer climate. The participants' efforts led to the decline of the genteel tradition despite the fact that antipuritanism became a fad during the 1920s. Actually, the puritan-baiting of this decade had started during the prewar era. *The Seven Arts'* cultural nationalism continued to influence the editorial policies of several magazines, while during the 1930s social protest painters looked back to The Eight for inspiration. Much of the modern poetry, painting, and drama of the 1920s derived from prewar developments. The Little Renaissance movements based on iconoclasm, modernism, and nationalism helped change the entire course of twentieth-century American painting and literature.

Selected Bibliography

I. PRIMARY SOURCES

A. MANUSCRIPT COLLECTIONS

Randolph Bourne Collection, Butler Library, Columbia University, New York City, N.Y.

Van Wyck Brooks Collection, Van Pelt Library, University of Pennsylvania, Philadelphia, Pa.

Waldo Frank Papers, Van Pelt Library, University of Pennsylvania, Philadelphia, Pa.

Walt Kuhn Collection of Armory Show Papers, Archives of American Art, Microfilm Division, New York City, N.Y.

Mabel Dodge Luhan Papers, Beinecke Library, Yale University, New Haven, Conn.

New York Public Library Theatre Collection, Lincoln Center, New York City, N.Y.; contains material on the Provincetown and Washington Square Players.

James Oppenheim Collection, New York Public Library, New York City, N.Y.

John Reed Collection, Houghton Library, Harvard University, Cambridge, Mass.

John Sloan Trust, Delaware Art Center, Wilmington, Delaware.

Alfred Stieglitz Collection, Beinecke Library, Yale University, New Haven, Conn.

Max Weber Collection, Oral History Research Office, Columbia University, New York City, N.Y.

"Gertrude Vanderbilt Whitney." Unpublished material, Whitney Museum of American Art Papers, Library of the Whitney Museum of American Art, New York City, N.Y.

B. PUBLISHED WORKS

1. Autobiographies

Brooks, Van Wyck. *Days of the Phoenix, the Nineteen-Twenties I Remember.* New York: E. P. Dutton & Co., Inc., 1954.

–––. *From the Shadow of the Mountain, My Post-Meridian Years.* New York: E. P. Dutton & Co., Inc., 1961.

–––. *Scenes and Portraits, Memories of Childhood and Youth.* New York: E. P. Dutton & Co., Inc., 1954.

Dell, Floyd. *Homecoming.* New York: Farrar & Rinehart, Inc., 1933.

Eastman, Max. *Enjoyment of Living.* New York: Harper & Brothers, 1948.

–––. *Love and Revolution, My Journey Through an Epoch.* New York: Random House, 1964.

Glaspell, Susan. *The Road to the Temple.* New York: Frederick A. Stokes Company, 1927.

Hackett, Francis. *American Rainbow, Early Reminiscences.* New York: Liveright Publishing Corporation, 1971.

Hapgood, Hutchins. *A Victorian in the Modern World.* New York: Harcourt, Brace and Company, 1939.

Kreymborg, Alfred. *Troubadour, An American Autobiography.* New York: American Century Series, 1957 (first published New York, 1925).

Langner, Lawrence. *The Magic Curtain.* New York: E. P. Dutton & Co., Inc., 1951.

Luhan, Mabel Dodge. *Intimate Memories.* Vol. 3: *Movers and Shakers.* New York: Harcourt, Brace & Co., 1936.

Myers, Jerome. *Artist in Manhattan.* New York: The Macmillan Company, 1940.

Ray, Man. *Self Portrait.* Boston: Little, Brown and Co., 1963.

Reed, John. "Almost Thirty," *The New Republic Anthology,* ed. Graff Conklin. New York: F. W. Dodge Publishing Company, 1936, 57-73.

Sanger, Margaret. *An Autobiography.* New York: W. W. Norton & Company, 1938.

Stearns, Harold Edmund. *The Street I Know.* New York: Lee Furman, Inc., 1935.

Sterne, Maurice. *Shadow and Light, the Life, Friends, and Opinions of Maurice Sterne,* ed. Charlotte Leon Mayerson. New York: Harcourt, Brace and Company, 1965.

Untermeyer, Louis. *From Another World, the Autobiography of Louis Untermeyer.* New York: Harcourt, Brace and Company, 1939.

Vorse, Mary Heaton. *A Footnote to Folly: Reminiscences of Mary Heaton Vorse.* New York: Farrar & Rinehart, Inc., 1935.

Williams, William Carlos. *I Wanted to Write a Poem; The Autobiography of the Works of a Poet,* ed. Edith Head. Boston: Beacon Press, 1958.

–––. *The Autobiography of William Carlos Williams.* New York: New Directions Publishing Corporation, 1967 (first published New York, 1951).

Young, Arthur. *Art Young, His Life and Times,* ed. John N. Beffel. New York: Sheridan House, 1939.

–––. *On My Way: Being the Book of Art Young in Text and Picture.* New York: Sheridan House, 1939.

Zorach, William. *Art Is My Life; the Autobiography of William Zorach.* New York: The World Publishing Company, 1967.

2. Major Nonfiction Works

Brooks, Van Wyck. *America's Coming-of-Age.* New York: B. W. Huebsch, 1914.

–––. *Letters and Leadership.* New York: B. W. Huebsch, 1918.

–––. *The Wine of the Puritans, a Study of Present-Day America.* London: Sisley's Ltd., 1908.

Croly, Herbert David. *The Promise of American Life.* New York: Capricorn Books, 1964 (first published New York, 1909).

Dell, Floyd. *Intellectual Vagabondage: An Apology for the Intelligentsia.* New York: George H. Doran Company, 1926.

Frank, Waldo. *Our America.* New York: Boni and Liveright, 1919.

–––. *The Re-discovery of America.* New York: Charles Scribner's Sons, 1929.

Lippmann, Walter. *A Preface to Politics.* Ann Arbor: Ann Arbor Paperback, 1962 (first published New York, 1914).

–––. *Drift and Mastery, an Attempt to Diagnose the Current Unrest.* Englewood Cliffs, N.J.: Prentice-Hall, Inc., 1961 (first published New York, 1914).

Mencken, H. L. *A Book of Prefaces.* New York: Garden City Publishing Company, 1927 (first published New York, 1917).

–––. *The American Language, a Preliminary Inquiry into the Development of English in the United States.* New York: Alfred A. Knopf, Inc., 1919.

Wright, Willard H. *Misinforming a Nation.* New York: B. W. Huebsch, 1917.

3. Poetry

Evans, Donald. *Sonnets from the Patagonian.* Philadelphia: Nicholas Brown, 1918 (first published New York, 1914).

Giovannitti, Arturo. *Arrows in the Gale.* Riverside, Conn.: Hillacre Bookhouse, 1914.

Hartley, Marsden. *Selected Poems,* ed. Henry W. Wells. New York: The Viking Press, Inc., 1945.

Moore, Marianne. *Collected Poems.* New York: The Macmillan Company, 1961.

Reed, John. *The Day in Bohemia.* New York: privately printed, 1913.

Stevens, Wallace. *Harmonium.* New York: Alfred A. Knopf, Inc., 1953 (first published New York, 1923).

– – –. *The Collected Poems of Wallace Stevens.* New York: Alfred A. Knopf, Inc., 1961.

Weber, Max. *Cubist Poems.* London: Elkin Mathews, 1914.

Williams, William Carlos. *The Complete Collected Poems of William Carlos Williams, 1906-1938* (contains *The Tempers,* 1913 and *Al Que Quiere!, A Book of Poems,* 1917). Norfolk, Conn.: New Directions, 1938.

4. American Painting

a. The Eight Painting Movement

Henri, Robert. "Progress in Our National Art Must Spring from the Development of Individuality of Ideas and Freedom of Expression: A Suggestion for a New Art School," *The Craftsman,* XV (January 1909), 387-401.

– – –. "An Ideal Exhibition Scheme, the Official One a Failure," *Arts and Decoration,* V (December 1914), 49-52, 76.

– – –. "The New York Exhibition of Independent Artists," *The Craftsman,* XVIII (May 1910), 160-72.

– – –. *The Art Spirit.* New York: Keystone Books, 1960 (first published New York, 1923).

– – –. "What About Art in America?," *Arts and Decoration,* XXIV (November 1925), 35-37, 75.

Sloan, John. *Gist of Art, Principles and Practise Expounded in the Classroom and Studio.* New York: American Artists Group, 1939.

– – –. *John Sloan's New York Scene; from the Diaries, Notes, and Correspondence, 1905-1913,* ed. Bruce St. John. New York: Harper & Row Publishers, 1965.

– – –. "The Independent, an Open Door," *The Arts,* XI (April 1927), 187-88.

b. The Stieglitz Group

Hartley, Marsden. *Adventures in the Arts: Informal Chapters on Painters, Vaudeville, and Poets.* New York: Boni and Liveright, 1924.

Marin, John. *Letters of John Marin,* ed. H. J. Seligmann. New York: Pellegrini &
  Cudahy, 1931.
–––. *The Selected Writings of John Marin,* ed. Dorothy Norman. New York:
  Pellegrini & Cudahy, 1949.
Norman, Dorothy. "Alfred Stieglitz: From Writings and Conversations,"
  Twice-a-Year, no. 1 (Fall-Winter 1938), 75-110.
Seligmann, Herbert J. *Alfred Stieglitz Talking, Notes on Some of His Conversations,
  1925-1931.* New Haven: Yale University Library, 1966.
Stieglitz, Alfred. "Ten Stories," *Twice-a-Year,* nos. 5-6 (Fall-Winter 1940;
  Spring-Summer 1941), 135-63.
–––. "Four Happenings," *Twice-a-Year,* nos. 8-9 (1942), 105-36.
–––. "Six Happenings," *Twice-a-Year,* nos. 14-15 (1946-1947), 188-202.

                                c. Armory Show

Armory Show, Fiftieth Anniversary Exhibition, 1913-1963. New York: Henry
  Street Settlement, 1963.
Arts and Decoration (Special Armory Show Number), III (March 1913).
Catalogue to the International Exhibition of Modern Art. New York: Association
  of American Painters and Sculptors, 1913.
Kuhn, Walt. *The Story of the Armory Show.* New York: W. Kuhn, 1938.
Pach, Walter. *Queer Thing, Painting.* New York: Harper & Brothers, 1938.

                                5. Theater

                                a. Plays

Cook, George Cram and Frank Shay, eds. *The Provincetown Plays.* Cincinnati:
  Stewart Kidd Co., 1921.
Dell, Floyd. *King Arthur's Socks and Other Village Plays.* New York: Alfred A.
  Knopf, Inc., 1922.
Glaspell, Susan. *Plays.* New York: Dodd, Mead, & Company, 1931.
O'Neill, Eugene. *The Plays of Eugene O'Neill,* vol. 1. New York: Random House,
  Inc., 1955.
–––. *Ten "Lost" Plays.* New York: Random House, Inc., 1964.
–––. *Lost Plays of Eugene O'Neill.* New York: The Citadel Press, 1973.
The Provincetown Plays. Second Series. New York: F. Shay, 1916.
Washington Square Plays. Garden City, N.Y.: Doubleday, Page & Company,
  1916.

b. Memoirs

Crowley, Alice Lewisohn. *The Neighborhood Playhouse, Leaves from a Theatre Scrapbook.* New York: Theatre Art Books, 1959.

Kemp, Harry. "Out of Provincetown, a Memoir of Eugene O'Neill," *Theatre Magazine,* LI (April 1930), 22-23, 66.

Kenton, Edna. "Provincetown and MacDougal Street," preface to George Cram Cook, *Greek Coins, Poems.* New York: George H. Doran Company, 1925.

Mackay, Constance D'Arcy. *The Little Theatre in the United States.* New York: Henry Holt, 1917.

Vorse, Mary Heaton. "The Provincetown Players," *Time and the Town, a Provincetown Chronicle.* New York: The Dial Press, Inc., 1942.

6. Themes of the Little Renaissance

a. Youth and Education

Bourne, Randolph Silliman. *Youth and Life.* Boston: Houghton Mifflin Company, 1913.

———. *The Gary Schools.* Boston: Houghton Mifflin Company, 1916.

———. *Education and Living.* New York: Century Company, 1917.

Cook, George Cram. "Third American Sex," *The Forum,* L (October 1913), 445-63.

———. "The C. T. U.," *The Forum,* LII (October 1914), 543-61.

Dell, Floyd. *Were You Ever a Child.* New York: Alfred A. Knopf, Inc., 1919.

Naumburg, Margaret. *The Child and the World, Dialogues in Modern Education.* New York: Harcourt, Brace, and Company, 1928.

Pratt, Caroline. *I Learn from Children.* New York: Simon & Schuster, Inc., 1948.

Stearns, Harold E. "The Confessions of a Harvard Man," *The Forum,* L (December 1913), 819-26; LI (January 1914), 69-81.

b. Socialism

Eastman, Max. *Max Eastman's Address to the Jury in the Second Masses Trial in Defense of the Socialist Position and the Right of Free Speech.* New York: Liberator Publishing Company, 1918.

———. *Reflections on the Failure of Socialism.* New York: Devin-Adair Company, 1955.

Goldman, Emma. *Anarchism and Other Essays.* New York: Mother Earth Publishing Company, 1910.

Reed, John. *The War in Eastern Europe.* New York: Charles Scribner's Sons, 1917.

———. *Ten Days That Shook the World.* New York: Vintage Books, 1960 (first published New York, 1919).

———. *Insurgent Mexico.* New York: International Publishers, 1969 (first published New York, 1914).

The Pageant of the Paterson Strike, Performed by the Strikers Themselves (program). New York: Survey Press, 1913.

c. Greenwich Village and New York City

Croly, Herbert. "New York as the American Metropolis," *Architectural Record,* XIII (March, 1903), 193-206.

Dell, Floyd. *Love in Greenwich Village.* New York: George H. Doran Company, 1926.

Hapgood, Hutchins. *Types from City Streets.* New York: Funk & Wagnalls Company, 1910.

———. *The Spirit of the Ghetto, Studies of the Jewish Quarter of New York.* New York: Schocken Books, Inc., 1966 (first published New York, 1902).

d. The New Psychology

Dell, Floyd. "Speaking of Psychoanalysis: The New Boon for Dinner Table Conversationalists," *Vanity Fair,* V (December 1915), 53.

Eastman, Max. "Exploring the Soul and Healing the Body," *Everybody's Magazine,* XXXII (June 1915), 741-50.

———. "Mr. Er-Er-Er- Oh! What's His Name?," *Everybody's Magazine,* XXXIII (July 1915), 95-103.

Frank, Waldo. "Sigmund Freud," *Virginia Quarterly Review,* X (October 1934), 529-34.

Lippmann, Walter. "Freud and the Layman," *The New Republic,* II (April 7, 1915), 9-10.

———. "The Most Dangerous Man in the World," *Everybody's Magazine,* XXVIII (July 1912), 100-1.

e. Feminism

Dell, Floyd. *Women As World Builders: Studies in Modern Feminism.* Chicago: Forbes & Co., 1913.

Eastman, Max. *Is Woman Suffrage Important?* New York: Men's League for Woman Suffrage, 1912.

–––. *Woman Suffrage and Sentiment.* New York: Equal Franchise Society, 1913.

Mencken, H. L. *In Defense of Women.* New York: Garden City Publishing Company, 1922 (first published New York, 1918).

Sanger, Margaret. *My Fight for Birth Control.* New York: Farrar & Rinehart, Inc., 1931.

"Sex O'clock in America," *Current Opinion,* LV (August 1913), 113-14.

C. MAGAZINES

Architectural Record (1901-1903); *Camera Work* (1902-1917); *Columbia Monthly* (1910-1913); *The Dial* (1916-1920); *The Glebe* (1913-1914); *Greenwich Village* (1915); *The Liberator* (1918-1924); *The Masses* (1911-1917); *The Modern School* (1912-1922); *Mother Earth* (1906-1918); *The New Republic* (1914-1917); *Others* (1915-1919); *Revolt* (1916); *Rogue* (1915); *The Seven Arts* (1916-1917); *Slate* (1917); *The Smart Set* (1908-1922); *Twice-a-Year* (1938-1942); *291* (1915-1916).

II. SECONDARY SOURCES

A. PUBLISHED WORKS
1. Studies of American Culture

Aaron, Daniel. *Writers on the Left.* New York: Avon Books, 1965.

Duffey, Bernard L. *The Chicago Renaissance in American Letters, a Critical History.* East Lansing: Michigan State College Press, 1954.

Forcey, Charles. *The Crossroads of Liberalism; Croly, Weyl, Lippmann, and the Progressive Era, 1900-1925.* New York: Oxford University Press, 1967.

Gilbert, James B. *Writers and Partisans; a History of Literary Radicalism in America.* New York: John Wiley and Sons, 1968.

Hilfer, Anthony C. *The Revolt from the Village, 1915-1930.* Chapel Hill: University of North Carolina Press, 1969.

Hoffman, Frederick J. *The Twenties; American Writing in the Postwar Decade.* New York: The Free Press Paperback, 1965.

Kazin, Alfred. *On Native Grounds: An Interpretation of Modern American Prose Literature.* New York: Anchor Books, 1956.

Kramer, Dale. *Chicago Renaissance; the Literary Life in the Midwest, 1900-1930.* New York: Appleton Century Crofts, 1966.

May, Henry F. *The End of American Innocence, a Study of the First Years of Our Time, 1912-1917.* Chicago: Quadrangle Books, Inc., 1964.

Rideout, Walter B. *The Radical Novel in the United States, 1900-1954*. New York: American Century Series, 1966.

Ruland, Richard. *The Rediscovery of American Literature, Premises of Cultural Taste, 1900-1940*. Cambridge: Harvard University Press, 1967.

Tomsich, John. *A Genteel Endeavor, American Culture and Politics in the Gilded Age*. Stanford, Calif.: Stanford University Press, 1971.

2. Studies of Writers

Bittner, William Robert. *The Novels of Waldo Frank*. Philadelphia: University of Pennsylvania Press, 1958.

Bode, Carl. *Mencken*. Carbondale: Southern Illinois University Press, 1969.

Cantor, Milton. *Max Eastman*. New York: Twayne Publishers, Inc., 1970.

Carter, Paul J. *Waldo Frank*. New York: Twayne Publishers, Inc., 1967.

Childs, Marquis and James Reston, eds. *Walter Lippmann and His Times*. New York: Harcourt, Brace and Company, 1959.

Drinnon, Richard. *Rebel in Paradise, a Biography of Emma Goldman*. Chicago: The University of Chicago Press, 1961.

Elias, Robert H. *Theodore Dreiser: Apostle of Nature*. New York: Alfred A. Knopf, Inc., 1949.

Engle, Bernard F. *Marianne Moore*. New York: Twayne Publishers, Inc., 1964.

Filler, Louis. *Randolph Bourne*. New York: Citadel Press, 1966 (first published Washington, D.C., 1943).

Goldberg, Isaac. *The Man Mencken; a Biographical and Critical Survey*. New York: Simon and Schuster, Inc., 1925.

Guimond, James. *The Art of William Carlos Williams, a Discovery and Possession of America*. Urbana: University of Illinois Press, 1960.

Hicks, Granville. *John Reed; the Making of a Revolutionary*. New York: Benjamin Boom, 1968 (first published New York, 1936).

Kellner, Bruce. *Carl Van Vechten and the Irreverent Decades*. Norman: University of Oklahoma Press, 1968.

Manchester, William R. *Disturber of the Peace, the Life of H. L. Mencken*. New York: Harper, 1951.

Mellquist, Jerome and Lucie Wiese, eds. *Paul Rosenfeld, Voyager in the Arts*. New York: Creative Age Press, 1948.

Moreau, John Adam. *Randolph Bourne: Legend and Reality*. Washington, D.C.: Public Affairs Press, 1966.

Munson, Gorham H. *Waldo Frank, a Study*. New York: Boni & Liveright, 1923.

Nolte, William H. *H. L. Mencken, Literary Critic*. Seattle: University of Washington Press, 1966.

O'Connor, Richard and Dale L. Walker. *The Lost Revolutionary, a Biography of John Reed.* New York: Harcourt, Brace & World, 1967.

Paul, Sherman. *Randolph Bourne.* Minneapolis: University of Minnesota Press, 1966.

Swanberg, W. A. *Dreiser.* New York: Bantam Books, 1967.

Vitelli, James R. *Van Wyck Brooks.* New York: Twayne Publishers, Inc., 1969.

Wasserstrom, William. *Van Wyck Brooks.* Minneapolis: University of Minnesota Press, 1968.

–––. *The Legacy of Van Wyck Brooks, a Study of Maladies and Motives.* Carbondale: Southern Illinois University Press, 1971.

Weingast, David Eliot. *Walter Lippmann, a Study of Personal Journalism.* New Brunswick, N.J.: Rutgers University Press, 1949.

Wellborn, Charles. *Twentieth Century Pilgrimage, Walter Lippmann and the Public Philosophy.* Baton Rouge: Louisiana State University Press, 1969.

3. American Painting

a. The Eight and Masses Artists

Christ-Janer, Albert. *Boardman Robinson.* Chicago: University of Chicago Press, 1946.

Glackens, Ira. *William Glackens and the Ashcan Group; the Emergence of Realism in American Art.* New York: Universal Library, 1957.

Goodrich, Lloyd. *John Sloan.* New York: Whitney Museum of American Art, 1952.

Homer, William Innes. *Robert Henri and His Circle.* Ithaca, N.Y.: Cornell University Press, 1969.

Morgan, Charles H. *George Bellows, Painter of America.* New York: Reynal & Company, 1965.

New Masses (Feb. 1, 1944), contains articles on Art Young.

Perlman, Bernard. *The Immortal Eight; American Painting from Eakins to the Armory Show.* New York: Exposition Press, 1962.

Walker, Donald D. "American Art on the Left, 1911-1950," *Western Humanities Review,* VIII (Autumn 1954), 326-46.

b. The Stieglitz Group

Doty, Robert. *Photo-Secession; Photography As a Fine Art.* Rochester, N.Y.: George Eastman House, 1960.

Frank, Waldo, et al., eds. *America and Alfred Stieglitz; a Collective Portrait.* Garden City, N.Y.: Doubleday, Doran & Co., 1934.

Helm, Mackinley. *John Marin.* New York: Pellegrini & Cudahy, 1948.

McCausland, Elizabeth. *Marsden Hartley.* Minneapolis: University of Minnesota Press, 1952.

Norman, Dorothy, ed. *Stieglitz Memorial Portfolio, 1864-1946.* New York: Twice-a-Year Press, 1947.

Reich, Sheldon. "John Marin: Paintings of New York, 1912," *American Art Journal,* I (Spring 1969), 43-52.

Rich, Daniel Calton. *Georgia O'Keeffe.* Chicago: Art Institute of Chicago, 1943.

Wight, Frederick S. *Arthur G. Dove.* Berkeley: University of California Press, 1958.

c. Armory Show

Brown, Milton W. *The Story of the Armory Show.* New York: New York Graphic Society, 1963.

Reid, B. L. *The Man from New York, John Quinn and His Friends.* New York: Oxford University Press, 1968.

Schapiro, Meyer. "Rebellion in Art," *America in Crisis,* ed. Daniel Aaron. New York: Alfred A. Knopf, Inc., 1952, pp. 203-42.

4. Theater

Alexander, Doris. *The Tempering of Eugene O'Neill.* New York: Harcourt, Brace & World, Inc., 1962.

Clark, Barrett H. *Eugene O'Neill.* New York: Dover Publications, Inc., 1947.

Deutsch, Helen and Stella Hanau. *The Provincetown; a Story of the Theatre.* New York: Farrar & Rinehart, Inc., 1931.

Gagey, Edmund M. *Revolution in American Drama.* New York: Columbia University Press, 1947.

Gelb, Arthur and Barbara. *O'Neill.* New York: Harper & Brothers, 1962.

Sheaffer, Louis. *O'Neill, Son and Playwright.* Boston: Little, Brown, and Company, 1968.

Waterman, Arthur E. *Susan Glaspell.* New York: Twayne Publishers, Inc., 1966.

5. Themes of the Little Renaissance

a. Youth and Education

Beck, Robert H. "Progressive Education and American Progressivism: Caroline Pratt," *Teachers College Record,* LX (November 1958), 129-37.

———. "Progressive Education and American Progressivism: Margaret Naumburg," *Teachers College Record,* LX (January 1959), 198-208.

Cremin, Lawrence A. *The Transformation of the School, Progressivism in American Education, 1876-1957*. New York: Vintage Books, 1961.
Jones, Howard Mumford. *The Bright Medusa*. Urbana: University of Illinois Press, 1952.

b. Socialism

Bell, Daniel. *Marxian Socialism in the United States*. Princeton, N.J.: Princeton University Press, 1967.
Draper, Theodore. *The Roots of American Communism*. New York: Viking Compass, 1963.
Egbert, D. D. and Stow Persons, eds. *Socialism and American Life*. 2 vols. Princeton, N.J.: Princeton University Press, 1952.
Renshaw, Patrick. *The Wobblies, the Story of Syndicalism in the United States*. New York: Doubleday Anchor, 1958.
Shannon, David A. *The Socialist Party of America*. Chicago: Quadrangle Books, Inc., 1967.
Weinstein, James. *The Decline of Socialism in America, 1912-1925*. New York: Monthly Review Press, 1967.

c. Greenwich Village

Churchill, Allen. *The Improper Bohemians; a Recreation of Greenwich Village in Its Heyday*. New York: E. P. Dutton & Co., Inc., 1959.
DeLaney, Edmund T. *New York's Greenwich Village*. Barre, Mass.: Barre Publishers, 1968.
Grand Pierre, Charles. *Rambling Through Greenwich Village*. New York: Greenwich Village Weekly News, 1935.
– – –. *The Legend of Free Love in Greenwich Village, a Badly Misinterpreted Phase of the Fascinating History of Its Bohemia*. New York: Greenwich Village News, 1937.
Parry, Albert. *Garrets and Pretenders; a History of Bohemianism in America*. New York: Dover Publications, Inc., 1958 (first published New York, 1933).
Ware, Caroline F. *Greenwich Village 1920-1930, a Comment on American Civilization in the Post-War Years*. New York: Harper Colophon Books, 1965 (first published New York, 1935).

d. The New Psychology

Burnham, John C. *Psychoanalysis and American Medicine, 1894-1918; Medicine, Science, and Culture*. New York: International Universities Press, Inc., 1967 *(Psychological Issues, V, no. 4, monograph 20)*.

Hale, Nathan G. *Freud and the Americans, the Beginnings of Psychoanalysis in the United States, 1876-1917.* New York: Oxford University Press, 1971.

Hoffman, Frederick J. *Freudianism and the Literary Mind.* Baton Rouge: Louisiana University Press, 1945.

Matthews, F. H. "The Americanization of Sigmund Freud: Adaptations of Psychoanalysis before 1917," *Journal of American Studies,* I (April 1967), 39-62.

e. Feminism

McGovern, James R. "The American Woman's Pre-World War I Freedom in Manners and Morals," *Journal of American History,* LV (September 1968), 315-33.

O'Neill, William L. *Divorce in the Progressive Era.* New Haven: Yale University Press, 1967.

–––. *Everyone Was Brave, the Rise and Fall of Feminism in America.* Chicago: Quadrangle Books, 1969.

Sochen, June. *The New Woman in Greenwich Village, 1910-1920.* New York: Quadrangle Books, Inc., 1972.

6. Magazines

Dolmetsch, Carl Richard. *The Smart Set, a History and Anthology.* New York: The Dial Press, Inc., 1966.

Hoffman, Frederick, et al. *The Little Magazine; a History and a Bibliography.* Princeton: Princeton University Press, 1946.

Joost, Nicholas. *Scofield Thayer and The Dial.* Carbondale: Southern Illinois University Press, 1964.

–––. *Years of Transition: The Dial, 1912-1920.* Barre, Mass.: Barre Publishing Co., 1967.

Mott, Frank Luther. *A History of American Magazines.* Vol. V: *Sketches of Twenty-One Magazines.* Cambridge: Belknap Press, 1968.

Wasserstrom, William. *The Time of the Dial.* Syracuse, N.Y.: Syracuse University Press, 1963.

B. UNPUBLISHED WORKS

Burnham, John C. "Psychoanalysis in American Civilization before 1918." Ph.D. dissertation, Stanford University, 1958.

Dusoir, Ilse. "The History of the *Seven Arts.*" Master's thesis, New York University, 1940.

Healy, Doty. "A History of the Whitney Museum of American Art, 1930-1954." Ph.D. dissertation, New York University, 1960.

Jennings, John H. "A History of the New Theatre, New York, 1909-1911." Ph.D. dissertation, Stanford University, 1953.

Kloucek, Jerome W. "Waldo Frank, the Ground of His Mind and Art." Ph.D. dissertation, Northwestern University, 1958.

Levy, David W. "The Life and Thought of Herbert Croly, 1869-1914." Ph.D. dissertation, University of Wisconsin, 1967.

Richwine, Keith Norton. "The Liberal Club: Bohemia and the Resurgence in Greenwich Village." Ph.D. dissertation, University of Pennsylvania, 1968.

Sacks, Claire. "The *Seven Arts* Critics; a Study of Cultural Nationalism in America, 1910-1930." Ph.D. dissertation, University of Wisconsin, 1956.

Tanselle, George Thomas. "Faun at the Barricades: The Life and Work of Floyd Dell." Ph.D. dissertation, Northwestern University, 1959.

Test, George Austin. "The Vital Connection: A Study of the *New Republic* as a Literary Journal, 1914-1922." Ph.D. dissertation, University of Pennsylvania, 1960.

Wertheim, Arthur F. "Floyd Dell: A Study of His Ideas." Master's thesis, New York University, 1967.

———. " 'The Fiddles are Tuning': The Little Renaissance in New York City, 1908-1917." Ph.D. dissertation, New York University, 1970. Contains complete bibliographical references used in the published study.

Index

Page references to illustrations are indicated by italic numerals